Medieval Academy Reprints for Teaching 32

Medieval Academy Reprints for Teaching

Marie de France

FABLES

Edited and translated by Harriet Spiegel

Published by University of Toronto Press
Toronto Buffalo London
in association with the Medieval Academy of America

© Medieval Academy of America 1994
Printed in Canada
ISBN 0-8020-7636-X

∞

Printed on acid-free paper

First published in 1987 in the Toronto Medieval Texts and
Translations series by University of Toronto Press. This edition
is reprinted by arrangement with University of Toronto Press.

Canadian Cataloguing in Publication Data

Marie, de France, 12th cent.
  Fables

  (Medieval Academy reprints for teaching ; 32)
  Fables in Old French with English translations on opposite pages.
  ISBN 0-8020-7636-X

  1. Fables, French – Translations into English.
  2. Marie, de France, 12th cent. – Translations into
  English.   1. Spiegel, Harriet, 1949–   II. Medieval
  Academy of America.   III. Title.   IV. Series.

  PQ1494.F3E5 1994   841'.1   C94-932249-0E

The illustrations have been taken from the following manuscripts: the
illustration on page 69 is from BN fr 24428; all others are from BN fr
2173. Harley 978, which provides the base text for this edition, is
unillustrated. The fragments of text included with the illustrations,
taken from mss of continental provenance, lack the Anglo-Norman
scribal feature of Harley 978.

Publication of the original edition was made possible by a grant from
the Canadian Federation for the Humanities, using funds provided by
the Social Sciences and Humanities Research Council of Canada.

Contents

Acknowledgments

In many ways, from a heightened awareness of the dangers of treacherous hedgehogs to an occasional impulse to burst out in rhymed couplets, my life has been enriched by Marie and her fables. I consider it a rare privilege to have been able to work on a project I have enjoyed so much. I also consider myself privileged while working on these fables to have been able to count on the knowledge and wisdom of many friends. Professor Judith Rothschild introduced me to Marie and pointed me to the *Fables*. My medieval colleagues at Tufts, Jane Bernstein, Madeline Caviness, Elizabeth T. Howe, Steven P. Marrone, Charles G. Nelson, Vincent Pollina, Peter Reid, and Anne Van Buren, have been the best of critics, advisors, and friends; as have Professors C. David Benson, James Dean, and Christine M. Rose.

Many libraries, particularly the British Library, the Bibliothèque Nationale, the Bibliothèque de l'Arsenal, the Bodleian Library, the Cambridge University Library, and York Minster Library, have been gracious and generous in giving me ready access to manuscripts of Marie's *Fables*.

The University of Toronto Press has been helpful and encouraging, and has carefully and kindly seen the project through its many stages – even retrieving the manuscript from a premature obscurity deep in Canadian Customs. I owe special thanks to my outside readers – their comments and suggestions have been particularly useful and appropriate – and to Jean Wilson, my copy editor, Brian Merrilees, the Series editor, and Prudence Tracy, the Press editor.

I am grateful to the Canadian Federation for the Humanities for their financial support in the publication of this work. I must also mention financial assistance from Tufts University through a Faculty Research Award and a Mellon Grant Research Semester.

My deepest gratitude is to my husband, Benjamin Beard Hoover, who has rescued me time and again with just the right word. This book is for Ben, with love.

I know that Marie wanted to be remembered by her *Fables*. I hope that she is not displeased with this tribute to her spirit.

INTRODUCTION

Introduction

Marie de France has been praised as 'perhaps the greatest woman author of the Middle Ages and certainly the creator of the finest medieval short fiction before Boccaccio and Chaucer.'[1] That claim might be expanded to read that she is one of the great writers of the Middle Ages and one of the greatest of all women writers. She is not a new discovery, but she was virtually forgotten until the early nineteenth century.[2] Since then, her reputation has rested primarily on her *Lais*, short stories in verse of love and adventure. But the *Fables*, a longer work, was probably the more popular one in the Middle Ages; twenty-three manuscripts of the *Fables* survive from the thirteenth to the fifteenth centuries, compared to only five manuscripts of the *Lais*. The relative neglect of the *Fables* for the past hundred years may be explained in part by the modern history of the fable itself, which is now seen primarily as a form of children's literature (and an unattractively moralistic one at that), and in part by a misunderstanding of Marie's claim that her work is a translation. In fact it is a lively and charming, wry and witty verse rendering of tales, some in the Aesopic tradition and some of which hers is the first recorded version. These fables are historically important as the earliest extant collection in the vernacular of western Europe. They are identifiably Marie's, marked by wit and sympathy, a biting social commentary, and a point of view that can be seen as distinctly feminine. These are not fables for children.

AUTHOR AND DATE

Marie, the author of these fables, remains elusive, for little more is known about her than what she herself announces in the Epilogue: 'Marie ai nun, si sui de France' – Marie is my name and I am from (or of) France (l 4). That she needed to designate herself 'de France' suggests that she was living in Norman England, a supposition strengthened by the English provenance of the oldest manuscripts and their Anglo-Norman orthography. It is too bad that we know little more than this about Marie – as she herself would be the first to agree – for she clearly wanted to be known and remembered by her writings. She states this desire directly in the three works generally recognized as hers. In the *Espurgatoire Seint Patriz*, a verse translation of a Latin saint's life, Marie states, 'Jo, Marie, ai mis en memoire / le livre de l'Espurgatoire' – I, Marie, have recorded, in order to be remembered, the book of Purgatory.[3] In the Lais of Guigemar, she identifies herself as 'Marie, ki en sun tens pas ne s'oblie' – Marie, who in her time should not be forgotten.[4] And she makes her strongest claim for recognition, after identifying herself by name, in the Epilogue to her *Fables*:

Put cel estre que clerc plusur
Prendreient sur eus mun labur.
Ne voil que nul sur li le die!
E il fet que fol ki sei ublie! (ll 5–8)

And it may hap that many a clerk
Will claim as his what is my work.
But such pronouncements I want not!
It's folly to become forgot!

While Marie reveals no additional specific autobiographical information, she does offer two other names that scholars have used in an unsuccessful attempt to find an historical Marie. The less informative name clue appears in the *Fables*, which are dedicated to a Count William, 'the doughtiest in any realm' (Epilogue, l 10). Naturally, however, there is no shortage of Williams one hundred years after the Norman Conquest, each more valiant than the other. The other name clue is in the *Lais*, dedicated to a 'noble reis.' This king is believed to be Henry II of England, great-grandson of William the Conqueror, who ruled from 1154 to 1189. He was unusually well educated for a king; his most lasting accomplishment was the establishment of the English common law. His queen, Eleanor of Aquitaine, although alienated from him after 1170, was famous in her own right as a patron of learning and the arts. One could easily imagine Marie's fables being read at Henry's court, and perhaps first to the women.

If the *Fables*, the *Lais*, and the *Espurgatoire* are works by the same Marie, then establishing their dates and sequence of composition could tell us something about Marie and her career. The only specifically datable reference is in the *Espurgatoire*, which mentions a Saint Malachais, thereby establishing a date for the *Espurgatoire* after 1189, the year of his canonization.[5] A contemporary poet, Denis Piramus, refers to a 'dame Marie' as the author of the *Lais*.[6] If the generally accepted date for Piramus's work, 1170–80, is correct, then the *Lais* would have been composed some time before that. Unfortunately, the dating of Piramus's work is also open to question. Many scholars, basing their conclusions on studies of contemporary poems, notably Wace's *Brut* (c 1155), *Piramus and Tisbé* (1155–60), and the *Eneas* (c 1160), believe that the *Lais* were composed around 1155–60.[7] We have then a plausible, though fairly long, period of creative activity, from about 1155 to some time after 1189. Common sense (but unfortunately no historical evidence) suggests that Marie wrote the *Fables* within that time span, after the *Lais* and before the *Espurgatoire*, roughly between 1160 and 1190. If this sequence is accepted, it may be that Marie, true to 'human nature,' began with youthful questions of love and romance, of fidelity and conflicting loyalties – the *Lais*; then moved in her middle years to skilfully rendered entertainment directed toward contemporary social and political concerns – the *Fables*; and finally turned her attention to sober and religious matters – the *Espurgatoire*.

Beyond these speculative observations, we learn most about Marie from her own works. She was well educated, probably knew English, and certainly knew Latin as well as her native French. She was well versed in classical literature, as the Ovidian influence in the *Lais* and the classical sources of many of her fables indicate, and she was familiar with contemporary French literature as well. She was a woman of courtly connections; her poems are clearly directed to that audience. Yet since no records have been found indicating that she was married or owned property, she probably had taken vows and lived in a convent, as was customary for unmarried women of rank. Marie was an artist proud of her work and jealous of her reputation, making clear her desire to be remembered by name. As a writer and learned person, she felt a keen sense of responsibility to communicate what she knew, as she states in the prologues to the *Lais* and the *Fables*. In the *Lais* we see a writer concerned not so much with the conventions of courtly love as with the psychological motivation of individual characters. Marie shows her concern for human misfortune, unhappy and restricting marriages, trapped heroes and heroines, and seems to have a special sympathy for the females in her stories. Similarly, in the *Fables* Marie reveals her compassion for the less fortunate characters, and frequently points to the urgent need for a system of justice that treats everyone fairly. Marie had a particular interest in the political and economic conditions of her day. Many of her fables describe these conditions directly; others convey an attitude of irony, scepticism, even pessimism about the world, particularly in the often condensed and cryptic morals to the fables. Wry and humorous, compassionate and realistic, Marie remains, above all, a versatile and gifted poet.

MARIE DE FRANCE AND THE FABLE TRADITION

As 'fable' is a broad term, it will be helpful to establish what Marie herself may have meant by it, using her practice as evidence. Some of her fables are the familiar ones of Aesop; about half, however, are not. Contrary to general expectation, hers are not all beast fables (indeed this is true of the Aesopic fables as well); one-third include human characters. In many ways Marie's fables are a varied lot, but they do have several features in common. All are short narratives, clearly fictitious; no historical people or events figure in them. All are directed toward an instructive message, presented in a brief story that generally disguises the moral seriousness with an assumed naïve simplicity. And finally the lesson is underscored by the epimythium, the often ironic or sharp moral that follows each fable.

In her Prologue, Marie establishes her connection with the ancient fabulists, tracing her work back to Aesop, who (she says) translated his Latin version from the Greek original. Along with her contemporaries, she was mistaken, of course, about the Greek Aesop, who remains for us a shadowy figure, but a teller (probably illiterate), not a writer (or translator!) of fables. And the actual progression from Aesop (sixth-century BC) is more complicated than a medieval writer could have known. Marie had good reason to connect herself with the classical fable tradition, however, for these fables were important and popular in medieval Europe, as models for rhetoric as well as lessons for life. Medieval Europe knew the classical fables through the two main branches of the Aesopic tradition, the first-century Latin iambic verses of Phaedrus and the second-century Greek verses of Babrius. Babrius' version was put into Latin elegiac verses by Avianus in the fourth century; this came to be known as the *Avionnet*. From the *Avionnet* were drawn the school texts widely used by young students, studied in the *trivium* as part of the rhetoric; over one hundred of these manuals survive. As for Phaedrus, while his name was apparently not known to medieval Europe, his fables were well known, popularized through a fourth-century prose collection called *Romulus*. A great many medieval Latin derivations of *Romulus* survive, both in verse and in prose.[8] One branch of the *Romulus* became the source of popular French verse translations, later than Marie's and not directly connected with hers, known as *Isopets*.[9] Another branch is the one of interest here. It includes three prose manuscripts called the *Romulus Nilantii*.[10] The first forty of Marie's 103 fables correspond closely in sequence and generally in content with the *Romulus Nilantii*. Her first forty fables therefore seem to be based on a direct source, one that is part of the classical fable tradition, although a specific manuscript that Marie may have used has not been identified.

Finding a source or sources for the remaining sixty-three fables has proved more problematic. Karl Warnke, in his important but preliminary study of the sources of Marie's fables, cites as sources or analogues an impressive array of literary traditions; he notes parallels to her fables in *Bidpai*, the *Panchatantra*, Poggius, Abstemius, Odo, *Le Roman de la Rose*, *Le Roman de Renard*, and folk traditions of Germany, Italy, Arabia, the Hebrew, Serbia, Lesbos, Russia – and more.[11] As this list demonstrates, some of Marie's fables are associated with a learned and written tradition, others with a folk and oral tradition. Such, indeed, is the elusive nature of the medieval fable; some are part of the rhetorical curriculum, others seem more closely related to fabliaux, popular narratives intended more for entertainment than edification.[12] In some cases, in fact, Marie seems to have put into fable form oral narratives that were not originally fables; this may account for an occasionally obscure connection between a tale and its moral application. The sense we have of a unified collection, in spite of the apparent diversity of sources, is a tribute to Marie's skill as a fabulist and to her strong poetic personality.

MARIE'S CONTRIBUTION

Since only the first forty of Marie's fables derive from the *Romulus* collection, and since the remaining sixty-three appear together nowhere before Marie's collection (so far as is known), it is at least worth considering that Marie herself could have gathered and recorded these fables for the first time. Although no one has yet suggested this possibility, one of Marie's contributions may well have been that of compiling the earliest extant collection of fables in the vernacular of western Europe.

Lacking proof, this suggestion can best be argued by negative evidence and common sense. First we must address Marie's claim, in the Prologue and Epilogue, that she has translated and put into rhyme the English text of 'li reis Alfrez.' But was there such a manuscript? Could there have been one? There is no surviving manuscript of any Old English fables, nor indeed any reference to one. As to 'King Alfred,' Marie de France, living in England, may have intended only to establish her connection with native English literary tradition through Alfred the Great, famed for his translations and his patronage of literature.[13]

History makes it unlikely that these fables of such diverse origin could have been collected by an English man – or woman – much earlier than Marie's time.[14] The first two crusades, which may account for some of those fables of eastern origin, had few native English participants. Normans, however, not only marched in the crusades but traveled widely in southern Europe and established settlements there. In Sicily, for example, they would have had access to Greek, Spanish, Roman, German, and Arabic cultures, all of which are represented in Marie's collection. And finally, one should remain sceptical about the possibility of an English source for this collection, for none of these fables seems to be of English origin.

Not only is it possible that a Norman compiled these fables, it is certainly worth considering that Marie herself could have done so. The two other works generally attributed to her bear witness to her skill in the two literary activities involved in creating this collection. If some of the fables were drawn from a Latin source, Marie might well have done so, for she translated and put into verse the Latin *Espurgatoire*. If some of the fables were received orally, again Marie might have recorded them herself and put them into verse, as she appears to have done with the Breton *Lais*. At any rate, it is improbable that Marie derived her entire collection from a single text, be it English or Latin.[15]

Marie's claim that she *translated* these fables has been accepted by modern scholars quite literally, and has been used all too frequently to dismiss them. An example is the recent, excellent study of the *Lais* by Paula Clifford where the *Fables* are identified simply as 'a translation' while the *Espurgatoire* is allowed the more dignified status of 'a moralizing poem ... based on a Latin *Tractatus*.'[16] Emanuel Mickel begins his chapter on the *Fables* in the same vein: 'Sometime in the second half of the twelfth century, Marie de France translated a collection of fables...'[17] However, by the end of the chapter, his tone has changed, as he compares the *Fables* to the *Lais* and comments, 'It is not difficult to see in Marie the author of both texts.'[18] It is interesting that both M. Dominica Legge and U.T.

Holmes use the elusive phrase 'professed to be translating' in discussing Marie's *Fables*, thus implying their doubts about her translation claim while withholding any positive judgment as to her originality.[19]

The truth is that post-Romantic assumptions about originality are inappropriate when applied to the fabulist, whose work is adapting and transforming existing tales. La Fontaine himself, universally recognized as the father of the modern fable, claims no more than this in his preface, stating that he has translated and put into verse a selection from a fixed store of fables handed down from the ancients. And as we have seen, Marie thought that even Aesop was a translator.

Such a claim, especially by a medieval author, must be understood for what it was. Crediting one's superiors and predecessors as the source of one's work was commonplace in the Middle Ages. Translation itself was a loosely defined concept. Today we have no trouble seeing other medieval claims to translation as conventional gestures of modesty, as tributes to authority, or as a means of disclaiming responsibility for features that some might find objectionable. Chaucer's claim to have translated his *Troilus and Criseyde* from Lollius has not put into question the work's originality, nor has the discovery of an actual source, Boccaccio's *Filostrato*. And of course the fable, by its very nature, pays tribute to its classical origins.

As part of her translation claim, Marie says that she has put her English source into verse. Such a statement seems almost formulaic for the fabulist; indeed Phaedrus and Babrius, the great classical fabulists, claim exactly this, identifying their contributions as essentially versification. Yet most of us would consider such a re-creation in verse as an 'original work,' even if translation were not involved. Marie's verse form, the octosyllabic rhymed couplet of the period, differs radically in feeling and impact, in tone, from a prose version or one in another verse form. The short, snappy lines, the often witty rhymes which come fast one after another, the epigrammatic morals and other pithy remarks, even the fact that many of these cleverly constructed lines are uttered by animals, add to the wit (and the bite) of these fables. Surely these qualities associated with the versification must be acknowledged as Marie's contribution.

Marie did more than put these fables into verse; she made them her own. Most basically, she medievalizes her classical fables; hers are manifestly a product of the twelfth century, providing commentary on contemporary life, particularly on feudal social structure and questions of justice – the obligation of a ruler to be aware of his people's needs and to respond to them, and the people's awareness of what constitutes a beneficent kingship and their obligations of loyalty to a good ruler.[20] The Normans brought to England a strong concern for judicial reform and equity, and Marie shared this concern. In 'The Dog and the Ewe' (Fable 4) Marie speaks sharply to the rich who use the court system to victimize the poor, and who thereby reap financial reward. In 'The Peasant and His Jackdaw' (Fable 56) Marie warns specifically against the possibility and dangers of legal corruption through bribery.

She seems particularly concerned with the importance of the mutual obligations of the ruler and the ruled, a concern often emphasized in the pointed morals she brings to traditional stories. Marie presents many examples of the dangers of an ignorant populace: the frogs who abuse their log king (Fable 18), the doves who ill-advisedly choose the hawk as king (Fable 19), and the animal community which ignorantly selects the wolf as king (Fable 29). Yet these fables are not only critical but instructive. People should be well informed and able to give their allegiance wisely. The birds who select the eagle to be their king do so only after learning about the cuckoo's dirty nature and rejecting that choice. The birds discover what the qualities of a good king are, and are then able wisely to choose the eagle (Fable 46). This solution seems typical of Marie. She does not suggest, of course, that human rulers should be democratically chosen. Indeed the eagle is the 'right' king, the one decreed by Nature.[21] Yet Marie values every component of society. Not only should the eagle be king, everyone should understand and believe in the justice of this order.

Marie gives immediacy and importance to all her characters, no matter how lowly, and thus individualizes them in spite of the fact that the various animals are given their stock traits. Thus Marie brings a special drama to the concerns of her own time. Her characters spar with one another in spirited, realistic dialogue; the action is strongly visualized and the setting vividly suggested by a few words. Her beasts are all too human yet intensely felt as animals; the lady mouse of Fable 3, full of small domestic pride, sitting on her stoop and combing out her whiskers with her feet, is entirely Marie's contribution. Marie also brings a new sensitivity to these fables and a strong sympathy for the poor and powerless characters. Our lady mouse, for example, does not die, as she (actually he) does in the Latin versions, but is able to peep out a cry that saves her life.

Indeed, Marie sometimes adds a special concern for the female characters in her fables, most notably when these fables present situations of particular concern to women. To 'The Wolf and the Sow' (Fable 21)

Marie adds a direct appeal to all women in childbirth to shun the company of men. Marie's account of 'The Pregnant Hound' (Fable 6) presents details of the birth, weaning of the pups, and then their tearing through the house and wreaking havoc, details not in the traditional Latin versions. Her account of 'The Fox and the Bear' (Fable 70) presents a startling picture of a bear tricked, trapped, and raped by a fox. Marie's concern for the helpless bear is in sharp contrast to analogues of this episode, such as the roughly contemporary Latin *Ysengrimus*, which, while making clear that the wolf is being raped, delights in Reynard's playful antics and then concludes, 'The book tells how she enjoyed these tricks.'[22] Similarly, a parallel version in *Le Roman de Renard* presents the female bear, Hersent, actually inviting the fox Renard's advances, enticing him with 'Acolez moi, si me baissiez!' (Hug me and kiss me!) and then welcoming him between her thighs.[23] Marie's bear is very different; she did not want it and did not like it.

Even to those inherited stories presenting women as the source of man's ruin, woman as the agent of the Devil (Fables 44 and 45), Marie changes the perspective slightly, wryly presenting these women as clever tricksters playing a good joke on their silly husbands.[24]

Perhaps the clearest indication of Marie's interest in females is her treatment of the traditionally male gods. It is striking indeed that all the gods of animals (usually Jove or Jupiter and definitely male in the Latin versions) become female in Marie's fables, called variously *la deuesse* (the Goddess), *la destinee* (Destiny), *la sepande* (Wisdom), and *la crïere* (the Creator) – but always distinctly female.[25] However, when the fable includes human beings, Marie conservatively and safely sticks with the masculine *Dieu*. Marie does more than personify these gods as female, she also modifies their nature. In 'The Sun Who Wished to Wed' (Fable 6), for example, the Latin Jupiter (*Romulus Nilantii* I.8) does nothing; he gives absolutely no response to the crowd's appeal for protection. Marie's goddess, however, responds directly with the specific promise that she will not allow the Sun's power to grow and with an assurance of her protection.[26]

However we assess Marie's contribution as compiler, translator, and versifier, it is clear that she has, above all, made these fables – even the most 'traditional' – her own by her poetic artistry and personal voice.

EARLIER EDITIONS OF THE FABLES

No manuscript of the *Fables* survives from Marie's time; the twenty-three extant manuscripts, all dating from the thirteenth to the fifteenth centuries, are at least one or two transcription generations after Marie's work. The first printed edition of Marie's *Fables* was published in 1820, edited by Jean-Baptiste-Bonaventure de Roquefort.[27] This is a pleasant but unscholarly edition, with no systematic use of the manuscripts or account of editorial procedure. In 1898 Karl Warnke published his important critical edition of the *Fables*.[28] He based his presentation on a detailed study and classification of all the manuscripts; his main conclusions about the interrelation of manuscripts, as Ewert and Johnston note, 'are hardly open to question.'[29] However, Warnke followed nineteenth-century editorial practices in regularizing his Anglo-Norman text, basing conjectural emendations on what he presumed the original manuscript to have been and often adopting from the various manuscripts what he considered the 'best' readings. In 1926 Warnke published a selection of these fables and modified somewhat his editorial procedure, making fewer emendations.[30] During this same period, A. Marshall Elliott of Johns Hopkins University was preparing an edition based on a manuscript at York (ms Y). Unfortunately, he died before the completion of his work.[31] In 1942 a collection of Marie's fables, edited by A. Ewert and R.C. Johnston, was published.[32] Ewert and Johnston used Harley 978 (ms A) as their base text and made few emendations, those being primarily to regularize the meter and to eliminate certain scribal features. They include, however, only a selection: forty-seven of Marie's fables. This present volume then is the first complete edition of Marie's *Fables* based on a single manuscript.[33]

Surprisingly, there is no modern French version of Marie's *Fables*.[34] There are two complete modern prose translations, one in German by Hans Gumbrecht[35] and one in English by Mary Lou Martin,[36] both based on Warnke's 1898 text. Two samplings of verse translation have appeared recently. Norman Shapiro includes eleven of Marie's fables in his *Fables from Old French*; his versions are jolly but loose (he says he 'enjoys a comfortable latitude') and he does not mention what he used for his French text.[37] Jeannette Beer's translation of thirty of the shorter fables into unrhymed free verse, based on Harley 978, appears in a lavishly illustrated book not quite intended for children; she makes major adjustments, particularly in Marie's morals, which she finds 'too wordy, or, even, self-contradictory.'[38] The present edition is the first complete verse translation of Marie's *Fables* into any modern language, and the first complete translation to be based on the single best manuscript.

THE TEXT

The twenty-three manuscripts, as identified by Warnke, which contain the fables are as follows:

A BL Harley 978, ff 40a–67b; mid-thirteenth century
B BL Vesp. B.XIV, ff 19a–32b; thirteenth century
C BL Harley 4333, ff 73–96; thirteenth century
D Bodl. Douce 132, ff 35–61b; thirteenth or fourteenth century
E Camb. E.e.6.11, ff 39–83; first half of thirteenth century
F BN fr. 12603, ff 279c–301b; thirteenth or fourteenth century
G BN fr. 4939, ff 123–44; fifteenth or sixteenth century
H Arsenal 3142, ff 256–71; end of thirteenth century
I BN fr. 24310, ff 55–92; fifteenth century
K BN fr. 25545, ff 29a–45d; fourteenth century
L BN fr. 25406, ff 31a–49b; thirteenth or fourteenth century
M BN fr. 1822, ff 198a–217b; thirteenth century
N BN fr. 1593, ff 74a–98d; thirteenth century
O BN fr. 1446, ff 88d–108c: thirteenth or beginning of fourteenth century
P BN fr. 2168, ff 159a–186b; thirteenth century
Q BN fr. 2173, ff 58a–93b; thirteenth century
R BN fr. 14971, ff 1–41; fourteenth century
S BN fr. 19152, ff 15a–24d; thirteenth or fourteenth century
T BN fr. 24428, ff 89a–114d; thirteenth century
V BN fr. 25405, ff 55c–81c; fourteenth century
W Brussels BR 10296, ff 206c–230d; fifteenth century
Y York Minster XVI, K. 12, Pt I, ff 1–21d; early thirteenth century
Z Vatican Ottob. 3064, ff 235–42; fourteenth or fifteenth century

A table of concordances to these manuscripts is found on page 279.

In classifying the manuscripts, Warnke established three groups: α (ADMY), β (BEGINQTZ), and γ (CFHKLOPRSVW). There is general agreement that the first of these, Group α, seems to be of superior authority.

Although ms Y is the oldest extant, ms A is considered the best and is the one used here. It is complete, is relatively free of scribal errors, and is the only collection of Marie's fables bound in the same codex with her lais. Harley 978 is a small, handsome codex, notable also for its inclusion of 'The Cuckoo-Song' (Summer is icumen in). The fables begin with the announcement, 'Ci cumence le ysope.' The individual fables are untitled; each begins with a coloured initial, alternating red and blue. A coloured paragraph sign, also alternating red and blue, announces the beginning of each moral.

The present edition reproduces as closely as possible the text of ms A. Modern punctuation has been supplied; i and j, u and v have been silently adjusted to conform with conventional usage. Only those scribal errors which obscure the meaning have been corrected; emendations have been made only on the few occasions when the manuscript reading was incoherent. Although Marie's octosyllabic line and couplet rhymes are predominantly regular, no adjustment of meter or rhyme has been made for the occasional irregular line. Corrections within the text are indicated by parentheses for suppressed letters or words and square brackets for added letters or words. When possible, emendations are drawn from other manuscripts, particularly from the closest ones, D, M, and Y, with the source and original reading noted. On the few occasions when, for the sake of a coherent reading, supplemental lines from another manuscript are introduced into the text, the lines are supplied directly from the other, without editorial adjustments, and are enclosed in square brackets. The source and the original reading are cited in the textual notes. All other emendations are cited in the textual notes.

Because ms A does not give titles to the fables, titles have been provided by the editor, either those given in other manuscripts or, for familiar fables, familiar titles. The numbering of the fables differs slightly from other editions. Warnke treats what is here Number 66 as an appendage to Number 65 and numbers it 65b, while this edition treats the latter as a separate fable (see note to fable 66). After Number 65, therefore, the numbering in this edition differs by one from Warnke's edition.

Though this is primarily an edition of the text of ms A, I have included a selection of variant readings in the notes. Variants from other manuscripts of Marie's fables are provided when they either clarify the given text or provide a major difference in meaning. Variants of more than a single word or phrase have been taken directly from manuscript. Other variants are, for the most part, based on Warnke's full edition. For variant readings found in more than one manuscript orthographic differences are not noted; when a variant is cited, all manuscripts with the same word are cited as well, whether or not identically spelled. I have also included in the notes some comparisons with versions other than Marie's when they are helpful either in clarifying Marie's fable or in highlighting her originality. Comparisons are made only with other early texts: primarily the *Romulus Nilantii* for the first forty, and for the fables not in the *Romulus Nilantii*, with other Latin versions, particularly a collection later than Marie's but related to hers, found in manuscripts in London, Brussels, and Göttingen, and labeled LBG by Warnke.[39]

THE TRANSLATION

The translation is intended to be read as a parallel text; it follows the original closely, generally line by line, occasionally couplet by couplet. Because the form of the fable may well be as much a part of the 'meaning' as the literal text, the translation attempts to present Marie's verse in an equivalent English form. Fortunately, such a verse form did not need to be 'created' for this translation, as English verse fables since the seventeenth century have adopted a standard verse form – iambic tetrameter rhymed couplets. Translations, such as Bernard Mandeville's in 1704 of La Fontaine and Christopher Smart's in 1768 of Phaedrus, adopt this form as the appropriate one for English verse. John Gay, England's finest original fable writer, used this form, as did Cotton, Swift, Cowper, Wilkie, Langhorne, and others. The form remains a favourite for current versions of Aesop's fables, though most of them are intended for children. Even today the form is apt, for it conveys the lighthearted yet pithy wit and wisdom of the fable and invites reading aloud. Fortuitously, this is the closest English form to Marie's, as both are in fact rhymed octosyllabic couplets.

Rendering a literally accurate translation in an exacting verse form required some negotiation, notably in rhyme and meter. Rhyme is not easy in English. In French, words of like gender or tense can rhyme, but not in English. Marie's best rhymes are those that underscore a connection or contrast; those that punctuate the fable with a kind of wit. This translation, similarly, attempts to use rhyme for wit and emphasis. Sometimes near rhymes have been necessary; but, sparingly used, it is hoped that they contribute to the improvisational, the oral spirit of these fables.

The English metrical line posed another challenge, for English verse, accentual rather than syllabic, presents an additional metric requirement not applicable to the French. It was hard to keep to the iambic tetrameter line and resist the lure of dactylic or anapestic 'limerick' rhythms. For example, 'A fox will meet his nemesis / However smart he claims he is' (#98, ll 39–40), could well have been 'The fox will thus often be stopped / No matter how clever his talk,' and we are into limerick. Indeed, the iambic tetrameter rhymed couplet, with its short lines and rhyme words close on the heels of one another, will irresistibly drift toward doggerel. The tetrameter is by nature a difficult line in English. The pentameter, perhaps because of its additional length, perhaps because five is an indivisible number, holding a line together as a unit or calling for variation in the placement of the medial caesura, resists the two-and-two sing-song of the tetrameter. But the apparent simplicity of tetrameter seems more appropriate to the fable and its apparent naïveté, its chirping profundities.

For these reasons, therefore, the translation adheres rather strictly to the four-stress iambic pattern, but not so strictly as to depart from the rhythms of natural speech. The major liberties that have been taken are those conventional in English verse, accepted even by strict eighteenth-century practitioners of the couplet: namely, 1/ an occasional inverted foot, especially at the beginning of a line; 2/ an occasional clipped initial syllable, especially at the beginning of a fable or the beginning of the epimythium, thus underscoring the feeling of the poem by creating a natural break or pause; and 3/ an occasional feminine rhyme adding an extra, unstressed, syllable.

Translation is an act not only of versification but of interpretation. One question that proved particularly challenging and revealing in translating Marie's fables was that of gender. Specifically, if a word is *grammatically* feminine in French, should it be translated as *significantly* feminine in English? This issue is not generally a problem in translating from French to English, for usually something either does have biological gender (man, woman) or it does not (table, watermelon). But the fables are about animals, and animals have grammatical gender in French that may or may not indicate biological gender. In the translations, when Marie's text is consistent, the gender is generally considered intentional and has been translated literally.

NOTES

1 *The Lais of Marie de France*, translated and introduced by Robert Hanning and Joan Ferrante (New York: E.P. Dutton 1978) 1
2 The first modern edition of Marie's *Lais*, edited by Jean-Baptiste-Bonaventure de Roquefort, was published in 1819: *Poésies de Marie de France, poète anglo-normand du XIIIe siècle* (Paris: Didot) 1. The *Fables* and the *Espurgatoire* were first published in the second volume of this work in 1820. For an annotated account of texts and studies of Marie's work, see Glyn S. Burgess, *Marie de*

France: An Analytical Bibliography (London: Grant and Cutler 1977). A second volume is forthcoming.

3 *L'Espurgatoire Seint Patriz of Marie de France*, edited by Thomas Atkinson Jenkins (Philadelphia: Alfred J. Ferris 1894) ll 2297–8

4 Marie de France, *Lais*, edited by Alfred Ewert (Oxford: Basil Blackwell 1944) ll 3–4

5 Ewert, *Lais* viii

6 *La Vie Seint Edmund le Rei, poème anglo-normand du XIIe siècle de Denis Piramus*, edited by Hilding Kjellman (Göteborg: Elander 1935) ll 35–40

7 Ezio Levi, 'Sulla cronologia delle opere di Maria di Francia,' *Nuovi Studi Medievali* I (1923) 41–72. Margaret Pelan, *L'Influence du Brut de Wace sur les romanciers français de son temps* (Paris: Droz 1931) 104–24. Ernest Hoepffner, 'Pour la chronologie des *Lais* de Marie de France,' *Romania* 59 (1933) 351–70; 60 (1934) 36–66. Hoepffner, 'Thomas d'Angleterre et Marie de France,' *Studi Medievali* NS 7 (1934) 8–23. R.N. Illingworth, 'La chronologie des *Lais* de Marie de France,' *Romania* 87 (1966) 433–75. Paula Clifford, *Marie de France: Lais* (London: Grant and Cutler 1982) 10–11

8 The name comes from its purported author, Romulus, who claims in the prologue to have translated the fables from Greek to Latin for his son Tiberinus (Tiberius). For discussion of the identification and classification of these fables, see Leopold Hervieux, *Les Fabulistes latins, depuis le siècle d'Auguste jusqu'à la fin du moyen âge* 2nd edition (Paris: Firmin-Didot 1893) I, 293–314. Romulus collections can be found in Hervieux II, 195–761; Hermann Oesterley, *Romulus: die Paraphrasen des Phaedrus und die Aesopische Fabel im Mittelalter* (Berlin: Weidmann 1870); George Thiele, *Der Lateinische Äsop des Romulus und die Prosa-Fassungen des Phädrus* (Heidelberg: C. Winter 1910).

9 Julia Bastin, ed, *Recueil général des Isopets* 2 vols (Paris: Champion 1929–30)

10 The name comes from the first editor of one of these mss in 1709. The fables are in Hervieux II, 653–755.

11 Karl Warnke, *Die Quellen des Esope der Marie de France* (Halle: Niemeyer 1900)

12 For an excellent, succinct discussion of the close relationship between fable and fabliau, see Omer Jodogne, *Le Fabliau*, in *Typologie des sources du moyen âge occidental* fasc 13 (Turnhout: Brepols 1975).

13 She may also have intended a discreet compliment to Henry II, who could claim descent (through his grandmother, Matilda of Scotland) from the ancient line of English kings, including Alfred the Great.

14 Hélène Chefneux used the animals in the decorative border of the Bayeux Tapestry, attempting to prove the existence of a single source for Marie's fables. These animals are apparently unrelated to the main narrative of the Norman invasion of England ('Les Fables dans la Tapisserie de Bayeux,'

Romania 60 [1934] 1–35, 153–94. See also Sir Frank Stenton et al, *The Bayeux Tapestry* [New York: Phaidon 1957] esp. 27–8, 164–74); Léon Herrmann, 'Apologues et anecdotes dans la tapisserie de Bayeux,' *Romania* 65 [1939] 376–82; Hermann, 'Les fables antiques de la broderie de Bayeux' [Brussels: *Latomus, Revue d'études latines* 69, 1964]; David M. Wilson, *The Bayeux Tapestry* [New York: Knopf 1985]). Chefneux believed that some of these animals were pictorial representations of some of Marie's fables, or more specifically, of Marie's literary source. However, a basic assumption of her argument (and Herrmann's) is not tenable: that those who designed the embroidery must have had a literary source in mind, a single written text. It seems much more likely that these animals, as well as the hundreds of others in this border, terrestrial and mythological, were drawn from a store of traditional designs and folk literature. However speculatively identified, none of the illustrations presents features that are convincingly unique to Marie's version.

15 In an effort to substantiate Marie's claim of an English original, Karl Warnke argued for the existence of a *Middle* English source now lost. As there is no external evidence for this, Warnke based his thesis on meagre linguistic evidence in Marie's text. The argument is complicated, and, based as it is primarily on only four words, the conclusions must be considered highly speculative. Warnke identified three words, *wibet* (wasp), *widecoc* (woodcock), and *welke* (whelk), which he claimed could have come only from a Middle English source and said that, because Marie did not translate them, she did not recognize them or know what they meant. This assumes that Marie could not have made inquiries in her host country or that she would not have substituted other animals rather than produce nonsense. It seems far more plausible that Marie, living in England, could have known these three animals by these words and so used them rather than the equivalent French terms. Might it not be the later Continental scribes who were not familiar with these words? Warnke made a similar argument for the fourth word, *la sepande* (the creator). He claimed that Marie received this word from a Middle English source without understanding that it was grammatically masculine. Yet Marie renders as feminine all her gods of animals; to fail to appreciate this is to misread Marie. Karl Warnke, *Die Fabeln der Marie de France, mit Benutzung des von Ed. Mall hinterlassenen Materials* (Halle: Niemeyer, Bibliotheca Normannica VI, 1898) xliv–xlviii

16 Clifford, *Marie de France: Lais* 10

17 Emanuel J. Mickel, jr, *Marie de France* (New York: Twayne 1974) 34

18 Mickel, *Marie de France* 40

19 M. Dominica Legge, *Anglo-Norman Literature and Its Background* (Oxford: Oxford University Press 1963) 107; U.T. Holmes, *History of Old French Literature* (Chapel Hill, NC: Robert Linker 1937) 210

19 Introduction

20 For a discussion of Marie's *Fables* as a product of the twelfth century, see E.A. Francis, 'Marie de France et son temps,' *Romania* 72 (1951) 78–99; and Erich Köhler, *Ideal und Wirklichkeit in der Höfischen Epik*, 2nd ed (Tübingen: Max Niemeyer 1970), translated by Eliane Kaufholz as *L'aventure chevaleresque: Idéal et réalité dans le roman courtois* (Paris: Gallimard 1974) 29–32. For a discussion of the medieval quality of the morals, see Arnold Clayton Henderson, 'Medieval Beasts and Modern Cages: The Making of Meaning in Fables and Bestiaries,' *PMLA* 97 (January 1982) 40–9.

21 Similarly, Marie adapts Fable 29 to emphasize the rightness of a social order with the lion as 'Nature's' king. The Latin versions present a lion as a wicked king; Marie makes the wicked king a wolf.

22 Gauisam scriptura refert his lusibus illam. *Ysengrimus* v, 181.17, ed. Ernst Voigt (Halle: Buchhandlung des Waisenhauses 1884). This comment concludes a direct presentation of the rape of the wolf and Reynard's mocking banter. The rape scene is included in the majority of Ysengrimus manuscripts, but not in Voigt's ms A, which omits the sexual encounter entirely. See Voigt, xvi and 305–6.

23 *Le Roman de Renart*, edited by Mario Roques (Paris: Champion 1955) vii[a], 5787. 'Hersant a la cuisse haucie / A qui plaissoit mout son ator' vii[a], 5792–3

24 Of course, there are some fables that Marie does not change, even some, such as 'The Peasant and the Snake' (Fable 73), presenting the traditional view of the unreliable and ill-advising woman, albeit far more clever than her husband.

25 The only fable with a female god in Marie's version which in its classical version also has a female god is 'The Peacock' (Fable 31); the god is Juno. See Phaedrus iii, 18; and *Rom. Nil.* iii, 2.

26 A manuscript illustration to this fable (BN ms fr. 2173, f 59v) presents not only the deity but also the audience as female.

27 *Poésies de Marie de France* ii

28 Warnke, *Die Fabeln*

29 Alfred Ewert and Ronald C. Johnston, *Marie de France: Fables* (Oxford: Blackwell 1942) xiii

30 *Aus dem Esope der Marie de France: Eine Auswahl von dreissig Stücken* 1st ed (Halle: Niemeyer, Sammlung romanische Übungstexte ix, 1926); 2nd ed (Tübingen: Niemeyer 1962)

31 George C. Keidel, *Old French Fables: The Interrupted Work of the Late Professor Elliott* (Baltimore 1919)

32 *Fables* (Oxford: Blackwell 1942)

33 An unpublished dissertation, based on a fresh examination of all the manuscripts, presents a critical edition of the Prologue, Epilogue, and ten of

Marie's fables (Karen K. Jambeck, 'Les Fables de Marie de France: Edition critique de fables choisies,' University of Connecticut 1980).

34 There are two eighteenth-century French translations of some of Marie's fables. Pierre-Jean-Baptiste Legrand d'Aussy includes forty-three in *Fabliaux ou contes du XIIe et du XIIIe siècles* (Paris 1779) IV, 169–248. The first ten lines of the Prologue and five fables are included in Marc-Antoine-René de Voyer d'Argenson, marquis de Paulmy, *Mélanges tirés d'une grande bibliothèque* (Paris: Moutard 1779–88) IV (1781).

35 Hans Ulrich Gumbrecht, *Marie de France, Äsop* (Munich: Wilhelm Fink 1973)

36 *The Fables of Marie de France* (Birmingham, AL: Summa 1984)

37 Norman R. Shapiro, *Fables from Old French: Aesop's Beasts and Bumpkins* (Middletown, CT: Wesleyan University Press 1982) ix

38 *Medieval Fables: Marie de France* (New York: Dodd, Mead, and Co 1983)

39 Warnke, *Die Fabeln* xlviii–lx. Hervieux II, 564–649. In his first edition, Hervieux placed these fables anterior to Marie, as a possible source. In his second edition, responding to Gaston Paris, 'Compte rendu: Hervieux, *Les Fabulistes latins*' (*Journal des Savants*, 1884, 670–86; 1885, 37–51), Hervieux revised his assessment.

THE FABLES

Prologue
1 Del cok e de la gemme
2 Del lu e de l'aignel
3 De la suriz e de la reine
4 Del chien e de la berbiz
5 Del chien e del furmage
6 Del soleil ki volt femme prendre
7 Del lu e de la grue
8 De la lisse ki ot chaëlé
9 De la suriz de vile e de la suriz de boiz
10 Del gupil e de l'egle
11a Del leün, del bugle, e del lu
11b Del leün, de la chevre, e de la berbiz
12 De l'egle e de la corneille
13 Del corbel e del gupil
14 Del leün malade
15 De l'asne ki volt jüer a sun seignur
16 Del leün e de la suriz
17 De l'arunde e del lin
18 Des reines ki demanderent rei
19 Des colums e de l'ostur
20 Del larun e del chien
21 Del lu e de la troie
22 Des lievres e des reines
23 De la chalve suriz
24 Del cerf a une ewe
25 De la femme ki fist pendre sun mari
26 Del lu e del chien
27 De l'humme, de sun ventre, e de ses membres
28 Del singe e del gupil
29 Del lu ki fu reis
30 Del lu e del berker
31 Del poün
32 De l'aignelet e de la chevre
33 De bucher e des berbiz
34 Del singe ki se fist reis
35 De l'asne e del leün
36 Del leün malade e del gupil
37 Del leün e del vilein
38 De la pulce e del chameil

39 Del hulchet e de la furmie
40 De la corneille e de la berbiz
41 Del riche humme e de dui serf
42 Del mire, del riche humme, e de sa fille
43 Del vilein e de l'escarbot
44 Del vilein ki vit un autre od sa femme
45 Del vilein ki vit sa femme od sun dru
46 Del oiseaus e del cuccu
47 Del vilein e de sun cheval
48 Del larun e de la sorcere
49 Del fevre e de la cuinee
50 Del lu e del mutun
51 De la singesse e de sun enfant
52 Del dragun e del vilein
53 Del reclus e del vilein
54 Del vilein ki ura aver un cheval
55 Del vilein ki pria pur sa femme e ses enfanz
56 Del vilein e de sa caue
57 Del vilein e del folet
58 Del gupil e de la lune
59 Del lu e del corbel
60 Del cok e del gupil
61 Del gupil e del colum
62 De l'egle, de l'ostur, e des colums
63 Del cheval e de la haie
64 Del riche humme, del cheval, e del buc
65 Del lu e de l'escarbot
66 Del gris lu
67 De l'ostur e del ruissinol
68 Del corbel ki s'aürne des pennes al poün
69 Del leün e del gupil
70 Del gupil e de l'urse
71 Del leün malade, del cerf, e del gupil
72 Del lu e del heriçun
73 Del vilein e de la serpent
74 Del mulez ki quist femme
75 De l'escarbot
76 Del sengler e de l'asne
77 Del teissun e des pors
78 Del lu e del heriçun

Prologue

Cil ki seivent de lettruüre,
Devreient bien mettre cure
Es bons livres e escriz
4 E as [es]samples e as diz
Ke li philosophe troverent
E escristrent e remembrerent.
Par moralité escriveient
8 Les bons proverbes qu'il oieient,
Que cil amender se peüssent
Ki lur entente en bien eüssent.
Ceo firent li ancïen pere.
12 Romulus, ki fu emperere,
A sun fiz escrit, si manda,
E par essample li mustra,
Cum il se deüst cuntreguater
16 Que hum nel p[e]üst enginner.
Esop[es] escrist a sun mestre,
Que bien cunust lui e sun estre,
Unes fables ke ot trovees,
20 De griu en latin translatees.
Merveille en eurent li plusur
Qu'il mist sun sen en tel labur;
Mes n'i ad fable de folie
24 U il n'en ait philosophie
Es [es]samples ki sunt aprés,

Prologue

Those persons, all, who are well-read,
Should study and pay careful heed
To fine accounts in worthy tomes,
4 To models and to axioms:
That which philosophers did find
And wrote about and kept in mind.
The sayings which they heard, they wrote,
8 So that the morals we would note;
Thus those who wish to mend their ways
Can think about what wisdom says.
The ancient fathers did just this.
12 The emperor, named Romulus,
Wrote to his son, enunciating,
And through examples demonstrating,
How it behooved him to take care
16 That no one trick him unaware.
Thus Aesop to his master wrote;
He knew his manner and his thought;
From Greek to Latin were transposed
20 Those fables found and those composed.
To many it was curious
That he'd apply his wisdom thus;
Yet there's no fable so inane
24 That folks cannot some knowledge gain
From lessons that come subsequent

U des cuntes est tut li fes.
A mei, ki dei la rime faire,
28 N'avenist nïent a retraire
Plusurs paroles que i sunt;
Mes nepuruc cil me sumunt,
Ki flurs est de chevalerie,
32 D'enseignement, de curteisie.
E quant tel hume me ad requise,
Ne voil lesser en nule guise
Que n'i mette travail e peine;
36 Ki que m'en tienge pur vileine,
De fere mut pur sa preere.
Si comencerai la premere
Des fables ke Esopus escrist,
40 Que a sun mestre manda e dist.

1 Del cok e de la gemme

Del cok cunte ke munta
Sur un femer e si grata;
Sulum nature se purchaçot
4 Sa viande cum il meuz sot.
Une chere gemme trova,
Clere la vit; si l'esgarda.
'Jeo quidai,' fet il, 'purchacer
8 Ma viande sur cest femer.
Ore ai ici gemme trovee –
Ja n'i ert pur mei honuree!
Si un riche hume vus trovast,
12 Bien sai ke de or vus aürnast,
Si acreüst vostre beauté

To make each tale significant.
To me, who must these verses write,
28 It seemed improper to repeat
Some of the words that you'll find here.
Thus he commissioned me, however –
That one, the flower of chivalry,
32 Gentility and courtesy.
And when I'm asked by such a man,
I can do nothing other than
Labour with pained exactitude;
36 Though some may think that I am crude
In doing what he asked me for.
I'll start off with the first, therefore,
Of fables Aesop formulated
40 Which, for his master, he related.

1 The Cock and the Gem

About a cock this tale is found
Who climbed a dungheap, scratched around
In nature's way, as he best could,
4 Searching for a scrap of food.
Discovering a precious stone,
He studied how it brightly shone.
'I thought,' he said, 'I might procure
8 A little food in this manure.
Instead, this precious stone I see –
Fat lot of honour you'll do me!
A rich man finding you, I'm sure,
12 Would have you set in gold most pure;
And thus your beauty he'd augment

Par l'or, que mut ad grant clarté!
Quant ma volenté n'ai de lei,
16 Ja nul honur n'averas de mei!'
   Autresi est de meinte gent
Si tut [ne] veit a lur talent.
Cum del kok e de la gemme,
20 Veü l'avums de humme e de femme:
Bien e honur mut poi prisent;
Le pis pernent, le meuz despisent.

2 Del lu e de l'aignel

Ci dit del lu e de l'aignel
Ki beveient a un clincel.
Li lus en la surse beveit
4 E li aignels aval esteit.
Irïement parla li lus,
Que mut esteit cuntrarïus,
Par maltalent parla a lui,
8 'Tu me fes,' dist il, 'grant ennui!'
Li aignel ad respundu,
'Sire, de quei?' – 'Dun ne veiz tu?
Tu m'as cest ewe si trublee,
12 N'en puis beivre ma saülee.
Arere m'en irai, ceo crei,
Cum jeo vienc ça, murant de sei.'
Li aignelez dunc li respunt,
16 'Sire, ja bevez vus amunt.

With gold – so very radiant!
Since I have no desire for thee,
16 No honour will you have from me!'
   Many people are like this
When something does not suit their wish.
What for the cock and gem is true
20 We've seen with men and women too:
They neither good nor honour prize;
The worst they seize; the best, despise.

2 The Wolf and the Lamb

This tells of wolf and lamb who drank
Together once along a bank.
The wolf right at the spring was staying
4 While lambkin down the stream was straying.
The wolf then spoke up nastily,
For argumentative was he,
Saying to lamb, with great disdain,
8 'You give me such a royal pain!'
The lamb made this reply to him,
'Pray sir, what's wrong?' – 'Are your eyes dim!
You've so stirred up the water here,
12 I cannot drink my fill, I fear.
I do believe I should be first,
Because I've come here dying of thirst.'
The little lamb then said to him,
16 'But sir, 'twas you who drank upstream.

De vus me vient ceo que ai beü.'
'Quei!' fet li lus, 'maudiz me tu?'
Cil li ad dit, 'N'en ai voleir!'
20 Li lus respunt, 'Jeo en sai le veir.
Cest memes me fist tun pere
A ceste surse, u od lui ere –
Ore ad sis meis, si cum jeo crei.'
24 'Que retez vus ceo,' fet il, 'a mei?
Ne fu pas nez dunc, si cum jeo quit.'
'E ke pur ceo?' li lus ad dit;
'Ja me fez tu ore cuntrere –
28 E chose que ne deussez fere.'
Dunc prist li lus l'aignel petit,
As denz l'estrangle, si l'ocit.
Issi funt li riche seignur,
32 Li vescunte e li jugeür,
De ceus qu'il unt en lur justise:
Faus acheisuns par coveitise
Treovent asez pur eus confundre;
36 Suvent les funt a pleit somundre.
La char lur tolent e la pel,
Si cum li lus fist a l'aignel.

3 De la suriz e de la reine

Sulum la lettre des escriz,
Vus musterai de une suriz
Que par purchaz e par engin
4 Aveit message a un mulin.
Par essample cunter vus voil
Que un jur s'asist de sur le suil;
Ses gernunez apparailla
8 E de ses piez les pluscha.

My water comes from you, you see.'
'What!' snapped the wolf. 'You dare curse me?'
'Sir, I had no intention to!'
20 The wolf replied, 'I know what's true.
Your father treated me just so
Here at this spring some time ago –
It's now six months since we were here.'
24 'So why blame me for that affair?
I wasn't even born, I guess.'
'So what?' the wolf responded next;
'You really are perverse today –
28 You're not supposed to act this way.'
The wolf then grabbed the lamb so small,
Chomped through his neck, extinguished all.
    And this is what our great lords do,
32 The viscounts and the judges too,
With all the people whom they rule:
False charge they make from greed so cruel.
To cause confusion they consort
36 And often summon folk to court.
They strip them clean of flesh and skin,
As the wolf did to the lambkin.

3 The Mouse and the Frog

Now following the written text,
About a mouse I'll tell you next
Who by her cleverness and skill
4 Had made her household at a mill.
I'll show you, through this tale, her way:
The mouse sat on her stoop one day;
She smoothed her whiskers, made them neat,
8 And combed them out with tiny feet.

Devant lui passa une reine –
Si cume aventure la meine.
Demanda li, en sa reisun,
12 Si ele ert dame de la meisun
Dunt ele se feseit issi mestre,
Si li acuntast de sun estre.
La suriz li respunt, 'Amie,
16 Pieça k'en oi la seignurie.
Bien est en ma subjectïun
Quant es pertuz tut envirun.
Puis herberger e jur e nuit
20 Jüer e fere mun deduit.
Ore remanez anuit od mei!
Jeo vus musterai, par dreite fei,
Sur la mole mut a eise –
24 N'i averez rien que vus despleise.
Asez averez ferine e greins
Del blé que remeint as vileins.'
La reine vient par sa prïere;
28 Amdeus s'asïent sur la piere.
Mut troverent a manger,
Sanz cuntredit e sanz danger.
La suriz par amur demande
32 A la reine de sa viande:
Quei l'en semble, verité l'en die.
'N'en mentirai,' fet ele, 'mie.
Mut par esteit bien apparaillé,
36 Si en ewe eüst esté muillé.
En mi cel pré en un wascel
Fussums ore, que mut est bel –
La est la meie mansïun.
40 Bele amie, kar i alum!
Tant i averez joie e deduit,
Jamés n'avriez talent, ceo quit,
De repeirer a cest mulin.'
44 Tant li premet par sun engin
E la blandist par sa parole,
Que la creï, si fist ke fole.
Ensemble od li s'en est alee.
48 Le prez fu plein de rusee;

And now a frog came up to her –
As if by chance she did appear.
The frog, in mouse-talk, asked the mouse
12 If she were lady of this house
Where she'd assumed the mastery,
And how she lived from day to day.
The mouse then answered her, 'My dear,
16 Some time I've been landlady here.
And all is under my control
When I'm protected by my hole.
Here I have shelter day and night
20 To play and follow my delight.
Why don't you spend the night with me!
I'll show you, most assuredly,
The mill and its amenities –
24 There's nothing here that will not please.
Here ample grain and wheat you'll find
In what the peasants leave behind.'
To this request the frog came round;
28 Upon the stone they both sat down.
And there they found much nourishment,
No peril and no argument.
Most lovingly the mouse then asked
32 The frog concerning her repast:
How was it, in all honesty?
'I will not lie to you,' said she,
'Though you've prepared a splendid meal,
36 Some water now would help, I feel.
Oh, how I wish we could go romp
Across the field to that fine swamp –
It's there that I have made my home.
40 Dear friend, let's go there now – do come!
There you'll have such delight, such bliss
That I believe you'll have no wish
Ever to come back to this mill.'
44 Such promises and crafty skill
And flattery went to her head.
She trusted frog – but was misled.
So off together went the two.
48 The meadow was awash with dew;

La suriz fu issi muillee,
Que ele quida bien estre nëe[e].
Arere voleit returner,
52   Kar ne poeit avant aler.
Mes la reine l'ad apelee,
Que a force l'en ad amenee;
Tant par amur, tant par preere,
56   Tant qu'il vienent a une rivere.
Dunc ne pot la suriz avant.
A la reine dist en plurant:
'Ci ne puis jeo pas passer –
60   Kar jeo ne soi unkes noër!'
'Pren,' fet la reine, 'cest filet,
Sil lïez ferm a tun garet,
E jeo l'atacherai al mien –
64   La rivere passum bien.'
La suriz s'est del fil lïee,
A la reine s'est atachee;
El gué se mettent, si s'en vunt.
68   Quant eles vindrent al parfunt,
Si la volt la reine neier,
Od li cumence a plunger.
La suriz pipe en aut e crie,
72   Que quida tut estre perie.
Un escufle i vient roant,
Vit la suriz, ki veit pipant.
Les eles clot, aval descent;
76   Li e la reine ensemble prent –
Amdui furent al fil pendant.
La reine fu corsu e grant;
Li escufles par cuveitise
80   La suriz lait, la reine ad prise.
Mangïe l'ad e devoree,
E la suriz est deliveree.
    Si est des veizïez feluns:
84   Ja n'averunt si bons compainuns,
Tant facent a eus grant honur,
Si rien lur deit custer del lur,
Que durement ne seient liez,
88   Si par eus seient enginniez.

And thus the mouse got wet all 'round
And thought for certain she'd be drowned.
She must return now, go back home,
52 She knew she could no farther roam.
But then once more the frog addressed her;
Against the mouse's will, she pressed her.
She urged her onward, praised her so,
56 Until the mouse had reached the flow.
The mouse now saw no point in trying.
She tried to speak, though she was crying:
'I'm sure I cannot get across –
60 For I can't swim! I'm at a loss!'
'Now take and tie this little thread
Around your knees,' the frog then said,
'And I'll attach it thus to mine –
64 We'll cross the river then just fine.'
So with this plan the mouse complied,
With string both frog and mouse were tied;
And thus attached they made their start.
68 But when they reached the deepest part,
The frog intended mouse to drown,
And so she started plunging down.
The mouse let out a peeping cry,
72 She was convinced that she would die.
High overhead there soared a kite
Who heard her peeps and saw her plight.
He closed his wings, flew down to get her,
76 And grabbed the frog and mouse together –
For to each other they'd been tied.
The frog was plump and stout and wide;
The kite ignored the mouse, for greed
80 Told him the frog was better feed.
The kite devoured the frog quite fast,
And thus the mouse was free at last.
With cunning villains this is clear:
84 They never will have friends so dear
That they, in honour of their friend,
Could bear a single penny spend.
Without compunction, they are glad
88 If they can trick their good comrade.

Mes il ravient asez sovent
Que de memes le turment,
Que as autres quident purchacer,
92 Avient lur cors a periller.

4 Del chien e de la berbiz

Ci cunte de un chien menteür,
De male guisches e tricheür,
Que une berbiz enpleida.
4 Devant justise la mena,
Si li ad un pain demandé,
Qi'il li aveit, ceo dit, (a)presté.
La berbiz tut le renea –
8 E dit que nul ne li (a)presta!
Li juges al chien demanda
Si nul testimoine en a.
Il li respunt qu'il en ad deus,
12 Ceo est li scufles e li lus.
Cil furent avant amené.
Par serment unt afermé
Que ceo fu veirs que li chiens dist.
16 Savez pur quei chescun le fist?
Qu'il en atendeient partie,
Si la berbiz perdist la vie.
Li jugere dunc demanda
20 A la berbiz qu'il apela.
Pur quei il ot le pain neié
Que li chiens li aveit baillé,

And yet it happens every day:
Those folk who torment in this way
And think that others they'll ensnare, will
92 Find that they place themselves in peril.

4 The Dog and the Ewe

This story's of a dog's deceit,
An evil, cunning dog, a cheat.
He sued a ewe – he held a grudge –
4 And brought the ewe before a judge.
He sought from her a loaf of bread
Which he had lent her, so he said.
The ewe denied it resolutely –
8 He'd lent her nothing, absolutely!
The judge then asked the dog if he
Had witnesses to back his plea.
The dog replied that he could cite
12 Two witnesses: the wolf and kite.
To prove his case, he brought in both.
Each swore and stated under oath
That all the dog had said was true.
16 Why did they act this way, those two?
Each one was waiting for his share,
If death should be her sentence there.
At this the judge then asked the ewe,
20 The one he sent his summons to,
'Why do you still deny the bread,
That which the dog has lent,' he said.

Menti en ot pur poi de pris –
24 Ore li rendist, einz qu'il fust pis!
La cheitive n'ot dunt rendre:
Dunc li covient sa leine vendre.
Yvern esteit, de freit fu morte.
28 Li chiens i vient, sa leine en porte,
E li escufles d'autre part,
E puis li lus, trop est li tart
Que la chars fust entre eus destreite,
32 Kar de viande eurent suffreite.
Ne la berbiz plus ne vesqui;
Sis sires del tut la perdi.
      Par ceste essample nus veut mustrer:
36 E de meint hume le puis prover,
Ki par mentir e par tricher
Funt les povres suvent pleider.
Faus tesmoines sovent traient,
40 De l'aveir as povres les (a)paient.
Ne lur chaut que li las devienge,
Mes que chescun sa part tienge.

5 Del chien e del furmage

Par une feiz, ceo nus recunt,
Passot un chien desur un punt;
Un furmage en sa buche tient.
4 Quant enmi le puncel vient,
En l'ewe vit l'umbre del furmage.
Purpensa sei en sun curage
Que aveir les voleit amduis.
8 Ileoc fu il trop coveitus!
En l'ewe saut, la buche overi,
E li furmages li cheï!
E umbre vit, e umbre fu,
12 E sun furmage aveit perdu.
      Pur ceo se deivent chastïer
Cil di trop sulent coveiter.
Ki plus coveite que sun dreit,
16 Par sei memes se recreit;

'Why lie about such petty stuff –
24 Return it, or the going's rough!'
  The poor thing couldn't, she had naught:
  She had to sell her woollen coat.
  She froze to death in winter's grip.
28 The dog was there, her fleece to strip.
  The kite came for his share of fleece;
  The wolf was anxious for his piece.
  They could not wait her flesh to eat,
32 For they'd been hankering after meat.
  No life was left to that poor ewe;
  Her lord entirely lost her, too.
    This example serves to tell
36 What's true for many men as well:
  By lies and trickery, in short,
  They force the poor to go to court.
  False witnesses they'll often bring
40 And pay them with the poor folks' things.
  What's left the poor? The rich don't care,
  As long as they all get their share.

5 The Dog and the Cheese

  It happened long ago, they say:
  A dog, crossing a bridge one day,
  Was clasping with his teeth some cheese.
4 Half way across the bridge, he sees
  His cheese's shadow in the stream.
  Deep in his heart he has this dream:
  He'd like that second morsel, too.
8 Now there's a greedy dog for you!
  He jumps right in, opens his mouth,
  And as he does, the cheese falls out!
  Shadow it is, shadow he sees,
12 And that is how he lost his cheese.
    So therefore people should take heed
  Who are misguided by their greed.
  Those who desire more than is just
16 Will be undone by their own lust.

Kar ceo qu'il ad pert sovent,
E de autrui n'a il nent.

6 **Del soleil ki volt femme prendre**

Par essample fet ci entendre
Que li soleil volt femme prendre.
A tute creature le dist,
4 E que chescun se purveïst.
Les creatures s'asemblerent;
A la Destinee en alerent,
Si li mustrerent del soleil,
8 Que de femme prendre quert conseil.
La Destinee lur cumande
Que veir li dient de la demande,
E ceo que avis lur en esteit.
12 Cele parla ke meuz saveit:
'Quant le soleil,' fet ele, 'est hauz,
El tens d'esté, est il si chauz
Qu'il ne lest rien fructifier;
16 Tere e herbe fet sechïer.
E s'il ad esforcement –
E cumpaine a sun talent –
Nule riens nel purra suffrir,
20 Desuz li vivre ne garir.'
La Destinee respundi:
'Veir avez dit. Leissum le issi,
Cum il ad esté, grant tens a,

They'll lose whatever they had before,
And get from others nothing more.

6 The Sun Who Wished to Wed

Apply this story to your life:
The sun once wished to take a wife.
He told all creatures his intent:
4 Each should prepare for the event.
The animal community
Then met and went to Destiny.
The sun, they told her, would be wise
8 To seek advice in choosing wives.
Destiny asked them to attest
The truth concerning sun's request:
What did they think of this affair?
12 Thus spoke the wisest of them there:
'The summer sun's so hot,' she said,
That when the sun's high overhead,
No trees can blossom or bear fruit;
16 The earth is parched, no plants take root.
If reinforcement he acquires,
A partner sharing his desires,
We'll not be able to survive,
20 For under them no life could thrive.'
Said Destiny, 'It seems to me
You speak the truth. We'll let it be
As it has been since long ago.

24 Kar ja par mei n'esforcera!'
   Issi chastie les plusurs
  Qui sur eus unt les maus seignurs,
  Que pas nes deivent esforcïer
28 N'a plus fort de eus acumpainer
  Par lur sen ne par lur aveir,
  Mes desturber a lur poeir.
  Cum plus est fort, pis lur fet:
32 Tuz jurs lur est en mal aguet.

7 Del lu e de la grue

  Issi avint que un lus runga
  Un os, que al col li vola;
  E quant el col li fu entrez,
4 Mut durement en fu grevez.
  Tutes les bestes asembla,
  E les oiseus a sei manda.
  Puis ad fet a tuz demander
8 Si nul se seit mediciner.
  Entre eus en unt lur cunseil pris;
  Chescun en dist le suen avis.
  Fors la grue – ceo dïent bien –
12 N'i ad nul de eus que en sache rien.
  Le col ad lung e le bek gros;
  Ele en purreit bien entreire l'os.
  Li lus li pramist grant loër
16 Pur ceo ke lui vousist aider.
  La grue lance le bek avant
  Dedenz la gule al malfesant.

24 I won't allow his strength to grow!'
   Thus everyone should cautioned be
   When under evil sovereignty:
   Their lord must not grow mightier
28 Nor join with one superior
   To them in intellect or riches.
   They must do all they can to thwart this.
   Stronger the lord, the worse their fate:
32 His ambush always lies in wait.

7 The Wolf and the Crane

   A wolf once gulped, in times remote,
   A bone which stuck fast in his throat;
   And when he found the bone remained,
4 He was distressed and sorely pained.
   Assembling every beast and bird,
   He called them to him with a word.
   He asked them all if there was one
8 Who was well versed in medicine.
   Each in the group then had his say,
   And each replied in the same way:
   None knew a cure for his distress –
12 Except the crane – who answered yes.
   Her neck was long, her beak was great;
   With these, the bone she'd extricate.
   The wolf promised a grand reward
16 If he were cured, his health restored.
   The crane, with lance-like beak then sought
   The bone deep in his wicked throat.

L'os en ad treit. Puis li requist
20 Que sa pramesse li rendist.
Li lus li dist par maltalent,
E aferma par serement –
Que li semblot e verité fu
24 Que bon lüer aveit eü!
Quant sa teste en sa buche mist,
Qu'il ne l'estrangla e escist.
'Tu es,' fet il, 'fole pruvee,
28 Quant de mei es vive eschapee,
Que tu requers autre lüer!
(Que) de ta char ai grant desirer,
Mei, ki sui lus, tieng jeo pur fol –
32 Que od mes denz ne trenchai tun col.'
    Autresi est del mal seignur:
Si povres hum li fet honur
E puis demant sun guerdun,
36 Ja n'en avera si maugré nun!
Pur ceo qu'il seit en sa baillie,
Mercïer li dit de sa vie.

8 De la lisse ki ot chaëlé

De une lisse voil ore cunter,
Que preste esteit de chaëler;
Mes ne sot u estre peüst
4 Ne u ses chaël aver deüst.
A un autre lisse requist
Que en sun ostelet la suffrist,
Tant ke ele eüst chaëlé –
8 Mut l'en savereit, ceo dist, bon gré!
Tant l'ad requise e preié,
Que cele od lui l'ad herbergé.
Puis, quant ele ot eü chaëls,
12 E espeldriz furent e bels,
Cele a ki l'ostel esteit
Par eus sovent damage aveit.
De sa meisun les ruve eissir,
16 Nes veut mes plus cunsentir.

She pulled it out. The bone extracted,
20 She asked for the reward contracted.
The wolf replied with spirit wroth,
Asserting with a cursing oath –
What's on her mind has come to pass;
24 Already her reward she has!
When she into my throat was poking,
I might have cut her off by choking.
'You have been proved a fool,' he said;
28 You owe me thanks that you're not dead.
Now more reward you dare require!
Your flesh provoked a great desire,
And I, the wolf, am fool instead –
32 Losing my chance to bite off your head.'
    With wicked lords it is this way:
A poor man his respects will pay
And then he'll ask for his reward.
36 He'll never get that from his lord!
Yet unto him the poor must give
Thanks that their lord has let them live.

8 **The Pregnant Hound**

Now listen to this tale I've found
About a very pregnant hound.
Although she knew her time was up,
4 She didn't have a place to pup.
And so she asked another bitch
If she would share her homey niche
Only until the pups arrive –
8 A thousand thanks! Long may she thrive!
She prayed, she begged, in such a way,
The other soon said she could stay.
Then when the pups were born to her,
12 And weaned and beautiful they were,
The owner of the habitation
Now found her home near devastation.
She told the dogs 'twas time they went,
16 But they in no way would consent.

L'autre se prist a dementer
E dit que ele ne seit u aler.
Yver esteit, pur la freidur
20 Murrat la fors a grant dolur.
Dunc li requist par charité
Que ele l'erberge desque a l'esté.
Cele ot de li mut grant pité,
24 Si li ad issi otrïé.
Quant le bel tens vit revenir,
Dunc les en ruve fors eissir.
L'autre comence a jurer,
28 Se jamés l'en oeit parler,
Que si chaël le detrareient
E ors a l'us la butereient.
La force ert lur e la vigur,
32 Fors l'en unt mise a deshonur.
    Ceste essample purrez saveir
E par meint produmme veeir
Que par bunté de sun curage,
36 Est dechacié de heritage.
Ki felun humme od li acuilt,
Ne s'en part mie quant il le veut.

i dist d'une suriz vilainne
E ki a une vile prochaine

9 De la suriz de vile e de la suriz de bois

Ci dit de une suriz vilaine,
Que a une vile proceine
Voleit aler pur deporter.

Said mother dog, with tears of woe,
She had no other place to go.
And outside, winter's icy breath
20 Would freeze them all – a wretched death.
She asked her now for charity:
Just until summer, let her stay.
With tender pity for her guest,
24 The other granted her request.
But when she saw the days improve,
She wished that they'd be on the move.
The mother cursed at her, and swore
28 That if she talked thus any more,
The pups would tear her flesh from bone
And hurl her out of house and home.
With might and main they ruled the place,
32 And forced her out in great disgrace.
    This model serves to guide us then
And shows what comes to worthy men
Who for their hearts' benevolence,
36 Are chased from their inheritance.
Should you a wicked man receive,
When once you've had it, he'll not leave.

9 The City Mouse and the Country Mouse

A certain city mouse, they say,
Went to a nearby town one day
Wishing to find what fun she could.

4   Par mi un bois l'estut passer.
    Dedenz le bois li anuita.
    Une hulette ileoc trova,
    Que une suriz de bois ot fete,
8   Sa viande i ot atrete.
    La suriz de vile demande
    Si ele ot iluec point de viande.
    Cele respunt, 'Jeo en ai asez!
12 Venez avant e sil veez!
    Si plus eüssez de cumpainie,
    Si en serïez vus bien servie!'
    Quant ele ot piece iluec esté,
16 A sa cumpaine ad parlé;
    Dist que od li est sun estre mauveis –
    E que ele ne volt demurer meis.
    Od li vienge, si avera
20 Riches sales, ke li durra,
    Beles despenses, beaus celers,
    E bons beivres e bons mangers.
    Cele la crei; od li s'en va.
24 En riches sales la mena.
    Si li ad mustré ses solers,
    Ses despenses, ses celers,
    Plenté de farine e de miel.
28 Cele quida bien estre el ciel.
    Mes ore viendrent li buteler,
    Que entrer durent el celer.
    Si tost cum il ovrirent l'us,
32 La suriz s'en fuit es pertus.
    La boscage fu esbaïe,
    Que lur estre ne saveit mie.
    Quant cil eissirent del celer,
36 Les suriz revindrent manger.
    Cele fu murne e en dolur,
    Ki ot eü de mort poür.
    Sa cumpaine la regarda,
40 Par grant duçur li demanda:
    'Quel semblant fet ma duce amie?'
    'Jeo sui,' fet ele, 'maubaillie
    Pur la poür que jeo ai eüe;

4 Her journey took her through a wood.
  Deep in the wood, as it grew dark,
  A little hole she chanced to mark,
  One which a country mouse had made
8 And there a store of food conveyed.
  The city mouse asked if she could
  Please have from her a bite of food.
  The country mouse said, 'I've a lot!
12 Come in and see what food I've got!
  And if you'd brought some friends with you,
  They all would be well-treated, too!'
  The city mouse a while had stayed,
16 When to her country friend she said
  That life out here was far from good –
  She wished to go and thought she would.
  Now if her friend would choose to come,
20 She'd show her many a fancy room,
  And splendid pantries, cellars fine,
  Excellent drinks, and meals divine.
  She trusted her; they went together.
24 The city mouse to rich rooms led her.
  And here she showed the country mouse
  The pantries, cellars, all her house –
  Of flour and honey great supplies;
28 'Twas heaven to the other's eyes.
  But suddenly the butlers enter,
  They needed something in the cellar.
  The instant that they opened the door,
32 Back to the mouse's hole she tore.
  The country mouse was in a daze,
  For she knew nothing of their ways.
  But soon the butlers left, and then
36 The mice returned to eat again.
  Saddened, the country mouse despaired.
  She'd almost died, she'd been so scared.
  City mouse, watching her companion,
40 Now questioned her with great compassion:
  'My friend, why do you look so sad?'
  She answered, 'My condition's bad.
  For I've just had a dreadful shock;

44 Mut me repent que te ai cr[e]üe!
Tu me cuntoues tut tun bien,
Mes de tun mal ne deïstes rien.
Ore as tu poür de la gent,
48 De chaz, de oiseus – tut ensement –
E des engins que hum fet pur tei.
Meuz amereie al bois par mei,
A seürté e sanz destresce,
52 Que en tes solers od tristesce.
    Ceste fable dit pur respit:
Chescun aimt meuz le suen petit
Que il ad en pes e sanz dutance,
56 Que autri richesce od mesestance.

10 Del gupil e de l'egle

De un gupil cunt la manere,
Que ert eissuz de sa tesniere;
Od ses enfanz devant jua.
4 Un egles vient, l'un enporta.
Li gupilz vet aprés criant
Qu'il li rendist sun enfant.
Mes il nel volt mie escuter,
8 Si l'en cuvient a returner.
Un tisun prist de feu ardant,
E secche buche vet cuillant;
Entur le chesne le meteit,

44 I'm sorry I believed your talk!
   You told me many pleasing tales
   But left out all the bad details.
   Yet now I see how much you fear
48 Men, cats, birds – all around us here –
   And traps men set to snap. I own
   That I prefer my woods, alone,
   In safety and without distress,
52 To grand rooms and unhappiness.'
     This fable teaches us a lesson:
   Each one prefers his small possession,
   Which he enjoys in tranquil pleasure,
56 To anxious woes of others' treasure.

10 **The Fox and the Eagle**

   A fox is what this tale's about
   Who, from his foxhole ventured out
   To his front yard, with cubs to play.
4 An eagle came, swooped one away.
   The fox, as he pursued them, cried
   For eagle to return his child.
   But eagle showed him no concern,
8 And fox must to his hole return.
   Then picking up a burning brand,
   And with dry kindling close at hand,
   Around an oak a fire he laid,

12 U li aigles sun ni aveit.
   Li egles vit le fu espris;
   Al gupil prie e dit, 'Amis,
   Estein le feu! Pren tun chaël!
16 Ja serunt ars tut mi oisel!'
     Par ceste essample entendum nus
   Que si est del riche orguillus:
   Ja del povre n'avera merci
20 Pur sa pleinte, ne pur sun cri.
   Mes si cil se pust dunc venger,
   Sil verreit l'um tost suppleer.

11A Del leün, del bugle, e del lu

   Jadis esteit custume e leis
   Que li leüns deust estre reis
   Sur tutes bestes ki sunt
4 E ke conversent en cest munt.
   Del bugle ot fet sun senescal,
   Que pruz le tient e leal.
   Al lu bailla sa provosté.
8 Tut treis sunt en bois alé.
   Un cerf trevent, sil chacerent;
   Quant pris l'eurent, si l'escorcerent.
   Li lus al bugle demanda
12 Coment le cerf departira.
   'Ceo est,' fet il, 'en mun seignur,
   Que nus devum porter honur.'
   Li leüns ad dit e juré
16 Que tut ert suen pur verité.
   La primere part avereit
   Pur ceo que reis ert e dreiz esteit.
   [E l'altre part pur le guain.

12 The tree where eagle's nest was made.
   The eagle saw the fire was lit;
   He begged the fox, 'Extinguish it! –
   My friend, take back your cub!' he urged.
16 'The fire will burn my little birds!'
      This story has a lesson which
   Tells of a man haughty and rich:
   He shows the poor no charity
20 No matter what their cry or plea.
   But if the poor can wreak vengeance,
   The rich will bow in deference.

11A The Lion, the Buffalo, and the Wolf

   It once was law and customary
   For lion to be king of every
   Creature that existed, and
4 Of all that dwelt upon the land.
   Buffalo, seneschal made he
   For worthiness and loyalty.
   The lion made the wolf his provost.
8 All three went off into the forest.
   They came upon and chased a deer.
   They captured it and flayed it there.
   The wolf then asked the buffalo
12 How portioning the deer should go.
   'That's up to my seignior,' said he.
   'We owe him honour, certainly.'
   The lion swore, affirming this:
16 All of the deer was truly his.
   The first of these parts ought to be
   For him who was king rightfully.
   [The next part was his profit due

20 Pur ceo quil ert le terz cumpain.]
   L'autre partie avera, ceo dist,
   Raisun esteit, kar il l'ocist;
   E ki la quarte part prendreit,
24 Ses enemis morteus serreit.
   Dunc n'i osa nul atucher;
   Tut lur estut le cerf lesser.

11B Del leün, de la chevre, e de la berbiz

   Un autre fez ot li leüns
28 En bois od lui plus cumpainuns:
   La chevre e la berbiz i fu.
   Un cerf unt pris e retenu.
   En quatre part le voleient partir.
32 Li leüns dit, 'Jeo le voil saisir.
   La greinur part deit estre meie,
   Kar jeo sui reis, la curt l'otreie.
   [L'altre avrai, kar jeo i curui,
36 E la tierce, kar plus fort sui.]
   Le surplus ai si divisee
   Que nul ne l'avera sanz mellee.
   Tuit li cumpainun, quant l'oïrent,
40 Tut li laisserent, si fuïrent.
     Autresi est, ne dutez mie,
   Si povres hum prent cumpainie
   A plus fort hume qu'il ne seit,
44 Ja del guain n'avera espleit.
   Li riches volt aver l'onur,
   U li povres perdra s'amur.
   E si nul guain deivent partir,
48 Li riches vout tut retenir.

20 As the third member of their crew.]
He said the next part was his share
By right because he killed the deer.
If any took the fourth, he'd be
24 The lion's mortal enemy.
None dared to touch; for it was clear
They must leave lion all the deer.

11B The Lion, the Sheep, and the Goat

Another time, the lion went
28 Into the woods with other friends,
Specifically, the sheep and goat.
A deer they hunted out and caught.
Into four parts they wished it split.
32 Said lion, 'I'll take all of it.
The biggest part should be for me
Because I'm king, by court decree.
[The next part's mine: I chased the deer;
36 The third as well: I'm strongest here.]
The rest I have apportioned right:
It goes to none without a fight.'
When they heard what the lion said,
40 His friends left all the deer and fled.
    Doubt not that here a truth is penned:
Whenever a poor man makes a friend
Of one more powerful than he,
44 He'll never any profit see.
The rich man values glory most,
And doesn't care if love is lost.
If there is gain to be divided,
48 The rich man keeps all, that's decided.

12 De l'egle e de la corneille

Ci dit que uns egles vient volant
Juste la mer, peissun querant.
Une welke truva entiere,
4 Mes ne sot en quel manere
Peüst la scale depescer.
Quant a sun ni volt repeirer,
Une corneille l'(en) encuntra;
8 Si dit que bien li enseignera
Cum la scale purra overir,
Si ele al peissun p[e]üst partir.
Puis li rova amunt voler,
12 Tant haut cum plus purreit munter.
Quant il sera munté la sus,
Si lest la welke cheïr jus
Sur dure tere u sur rocher:
16 Si la purra bien depescer.
Li egles ad mut grant desirer
De la welke qu'il tient manger.
Haut la porte, cheïr la leit;
20 La corneille fu en agueit.
Avant ala, del bek feri,
Si que la scale un poi overi.
Le peissunet dedenz manga;
24 L'escale lest, si s'en ala,
Einz que li egles i fust venuz,
Ne qu'il se fust aparceüz.
Le pertuset ot fet petit,

12 The Eagle and the Crow

This tells how eagle flying went
Along the sea, on fishing bent.
He found a whelk entire, but now
4 He couldn't figure out just how
To open up the shell; and so
Back to his nest he thought he'd go.
Just then a crow came up to say
8 That she could well explain a way
For him to open up the shell
If she could have a share as well.
The crow advised him to climb high,
12 Until he could no higher fly.
Then when he'd flown and reached the summit,
He should allow the whelk to plummet
Onto hard ground or on a rock:
16 And thus the shell he'd easily break.
The eagle fervently desired
To eat the whelk which he'd acquired.
He bore it high, he let it go;
20 Lying in wait for it was crow.
She ran right up, her beak struck it,
And opened the shell a tiny bit.
She ate the morsel found inside;
24 She left the shell, away she hied
Before the eagle had returned
And of her strategy had learned.
The little hole was very small,

28 Que li egles pas nel vit.
    Par ceste fable del peissun,
  Nus mustre essample del felun,
  Que par agueit e par engin
32 Mescunseille sun bon veisin;
  Tele chose li cunseille a fere,
  Dunt cil ne peot a nul chief trere.
  E quant il unkes sunt meuz asemble,
36 Par traïsun li tout e emble
  L'aveir que cil ad purchacié
  Par grant travail e guainié.

13 Del corbel e del gupil

  Issi avient, e bien pot estre,
  Que par devant une fenestre
  Que en une despense fu,
4 Vola un corf, si ad veü
  Furmages que dedenz esteient
  E (de) sure une cleie giseient.
  Un en ad pris, od tut s'en va.
8 Un gupil vient, qui l'encuntra.
  Del furmage ot grant desirer
  Qu'il en peüst sa part manger.
  Par engin vodra essaier
12 Si le corp purra enginner.

28 So eagle saw it not at all.
　　Thus in this fable of a fish
　　We're shown a man most villainous.
　　He uses tricks and cunning lies
32 To give his neighbour bad advice,
　　Counselling him to do a deed
　　That cannot possibly succeed.
　　And even when they get on well,
36 This man deceitfully will steal
　　All of the goods the other got
　　Who laboured hard for what he bought.

13 The Crow and the Fox

　　It came to pass (and could be so)
　　That once in front of a window
　　Which in a pantry chanced to be,
4 A crow happened to fly by and see
　　That there, within, some cheeses lay
　　All spread out on a wicker tray.
　　He took a whole one; off he flew.
8 Along came fox, walked up to crow.
　　Fox very much desired the cheese;
　　He felt he had to eat a piece.
　　He thought he'd set a trap and see
12 If he could trick crow cunningly.

'A, Deu sire!' fet li gupilz,
'Tant par est cist oisel gentilz!
El mund nen ad tel oisel!
16 Unc de mes oilz ne vi si bel!
Fust teus ses chanz cum est ses cors,
Il vaudreit meuz que nul fin ors!'
Li corps se oï si bien loër;
20 Que en tut le mund n'ot sun per.
Purpensé s'est qu'il chantera;
Ja pur chanter los ne perdra.
Le bek overi, si chanta,
24 E li furmages li eschapa.
A la tere l'estut cheïr,
E li gupil le vet seisir.
Puis n'ot il cure de sun chant;
28 Del furmage ot sun talant.
   Ceo est essample des orguillus
Ki de grant pris sunt desirus:
Par losenger, par mentir,
32 Les puet hum bien a gré servir.
Le lur despendent folement
Pur faus losenge de la gent.

un lion conte lieſcriſ
 Qui ſirs eſtoit ⁊ enueilliꝰ

14 Del leün malade

De un leün cunte li escriz,
Ki fu defreiz e enveilliz.

The fox cried out, 'Oh God! Oh Sir!
Ah, what a noble bird is here!
I've never seen in all this world
16 A sight as lovely as this bird!
Would that his songs were just as fair,
Beyond pure gold he would compare!'
All this grand praise the crow could hear:
20 How through the world he had no peer.
His voice he thought in song he'd raise;
His singing never lost him praise.
And so crow sang, his mouth agape;
24 And thus he let the cheese escape.
No sooner did it hit the ground,
Than fox, he seized it in a bound.
He had no interest in the song;
28 The cheese he'd wanted all along.
   A lesson's here about the proud
Who wish with fame to be endowed:
If you should flatter them and lie,
32 You'll find they readily comply.
They'll spend their all quite foolishly
When they receive false flattery.

14 The Ailing Lion

Lion's the subject of this tale
Who aged had become and frail.

Malades jut mut lungement,
4 Del relever n'i ot nent.
Tutes les bestes s'asemblerent;
Pur lui veer, a curt alerent.
Li plusur sunt pur lui dolent,
8 E as esquanz n'i chaut nent,
E teus i a i vunt pur dun
A la devise del leün,
E saver voleient li plusur
12 Si en lui ad mes nul retur.
Li bucs de ses cornes la but(ut)e.
E li asnes, que pas nel dute,
Od le pié le fiert sur le piz.
16 De l'autre part vient li gupilz,
As denz le mort par les oreilles.
Dit li leüns, 'Jeo vei merveilles!
Bien me sovient que en mun eé,
20 Quant jefnes fu e en sancté,
Que autres bestes me dutouent
Cume seignur e honurouent.
Quant j'ere liez, haitiez esteient;
24 Quant ere irez, mut se cremeient.
Ore me veient afieblïé,
Defulé me unt e avilé.
Mut me semble greinur vilté
28 De ces ki furent mi privé –
A ki jeo fis honur e bien,
Ki n'en remembrent nule rien –
Que des autres, que jeo mesfis.
32 Li nunpuissant ad poi amis.'
    Par memes ceste reisun
Pernum essample del leün.
Ki unc chiece en nunpoeir,
36 Si piert sa force e sun saveir.
Mut le tienent en grant vilté,
Nis les plusurs qui l'unt amé.

Quite ill he lay for many a day
4 And could not get up, come what may.
The beasts assembled, every sort;
To see the lion, they went to court.
Most of the beasts began to mourn,
8 But some of them showed no concern.
Some came to see what they'd receive:
What gifts the lion by will would leave.
Most of them wanted to discover
12 If he might possibly recover.
The goat used horns the lion to butt.
And then the ass, who feared him not,
With hoof struck lion on the chest.
16 Fox, from another side, came next,
And with sharp teeth he bit each ear.
Said lion, 'What wonders I see here!
Oh, I remember well the time
20 When I was healthy, in my prime,
That other animals felt fear
And honoured me as their seignior.
When I was glad, they felt delight;
24 When I was angry, it was fright.
Now that I'm feeble, as they see,
They trample and defile me.
It seems to me a worse offence
28 From those who've been my bosom friends –
Whom I have honoured, treated well,
And yet who nothing now recall –
Than from those beasts whom I did wrong.
32 He has few friends who is not strong.'
    This account should serve therefore
To teach, by lion's tale, this lore:
That he who sinks to impotence,
36 Who's lost strength and intelligence,
Will be regarded with great scorn,
Even by those whose love was sworn.

15 De l'asne ki volt jüer a sun seignur

De un riche hume cunte li escrit,
Que aveit un chenet petit.
Suventefeiz a lui jua,
4 E un sun asnes l'esguarda.
En sun curage entendi bien
Que tuit l'autre aiment le chien
Pur le seignur quil cherisseit
8 E ki od lui se deduieit.
Suz sun mantel le fist muscier,
Sil fist les autres surabaier.
Mut s'est li asnes purpensez
12 Que meuz del chien vaut asez
E de bunté e de grandur.
Meuz savereit a sun seignur
Jüer que li chenez petitz;
16 E meuz sereit oï ses criz.
Meuz savereit il sur li saillir.
Meuz le savereit des piez ferir.
Pur fol se tient que a lui ne veit,
20 Ne que od sa voiz ne crie e breit,
Cum fet li chiens sur le seignur.
Issi avient ke par un jur
Se alot li sires deduiant;
24 E od le chenet va juant.

15 The Ass Who Wanted to Play with His Master

There was a rich man, as I've read,
Who kept a small dog as a pet.
He frolicked with him constantly;
4 This, the man's donkey chanced to see.
The ass knew, deep within his breast,
The dog was loved by all the rest
Because he was his master's treasure
8 And often served to give him pleasure.
The man would hide him in his cloak
And make the dog outbark the pack.
The ass was quite convinced, indeed,
12 That his own value did exceed
The pup's, his size and virtue, too.
Far better than the pup, he knew
How with his master he should play;
16 'Twas easier to hear his bray.
He better knew how to leap up
And paw the man than did the pup.
And what a fool he thought he was
20 Not to bray out and cry hee-haws,
As dog to master, the same way.
And so it happened that one day
The man went out to have some sport;
24 The dog came with him to cavort.

Ne pot li asnes plus suffrir:
Vers le seignur prist a venir.
Sur lui cumença a rechaner,
28 Que tut le fet espoënter.
Des piez le fiert, sur lui sailli,
Si que a la tere l'abati.
Pur un petit ne l'a crevé,
32 Si li sires nen eüst crïé,
'Haro! Haro! Aidez mei!'
Si humme i saillent a desrei;
Chescun od mace u od bastun.
36 L'asne fierent tut envirun –
(A grant martire e a dolur
Porent rescure lur seignur.)
De si que l'asne unt tant batu,
40 Qu'il le leissent tut estendu.
A grant peine vient a sa stable.
Saver poüm par ceste fable
La manere de ceste gent –
44 Mut l'en peot veer sovent:
Que tant se veulent eshaucer
E en tel liu aparagier –
Que ne avient pas a lur corsage,
48 Ensurketut a lur parage.
A meint en est si avenu
Cum a l'asne ki fu batu.

16 Del leün e de la suriz

De un leün dit ki se dormeit
En un boscage u il esteit.
Entur lui se vunt deduiant

The ass, who could not bear this more,
Made his approach toward the seignior.
Now such a bray the ass let out,
28 He frightened everyone about.
   With feet he struck, and with a bound,
   He knocked the master to the ground.
   The master might well have been killed
32 If in distress he had not shrilled,
   'Oh help! Oh help! Oh rescue me!'
   His men rushed up in disarray.
   Each of them had a club or mace,
36 And thoroughly they beat the ass –
   (After great torture and much grief,
   They finally gave their lord relief.)
   The donkey was so beaten that
40 At last they left him stretched out flat.
   He went in anguish to his stable.
      We can learn clearly from this fable
   The way this kind of man will be –
44 We've all observed them frequently:
   Those who to raise themselves aspire
   And who a higher place desire –
   One that's not fitting to their girth
48 And most of all, not to their birth.
   The same result will come to pass
   For many, like the beaten ass.

16 The Lion and the Mouse

It's said a lion was asleep
Where he lived in a forest deep.
Some little mice 'round where he lay

4 Li suriz petiz en juant.
L'une curut – ne s'en garda –
Sur le leün, si l'esveilla.
Li leün fu mut curucez.
8 La suriz prist; tant fu irez,
De li voleit fere justise.
Ele escundist que en nule guise
A escïent ne l'aveit feit.
12 E li leüns atant le leit.
Petit d'onur, ceo dit, avereit
De li s'il la ocieit.
Gueres de tens ne demurra,
16 Que un humme, ceo dit, apparailla
Une fosse cavee dedenz.
La nuit fu pris li leün enz.
Grant poür a ke hum ne l'ocie;
20 Dedenz la fosse breit e crie.
La suriz vient al cri tut dreit,
Mes ne saveit ki ceo esteit.
Que ja el bois aveit esveillé,
24 Quant ele le vit si enginné,
Demanda li qu'il ad la quis.
Cil respunt qu'il esteit pris,
Ocis sereit a grant dolur.
28 Dit la suriz, 'N'eiez poür!
Ore vus rendrai le guerdun
Que a mei feïstes le pardun,
Quant od mes piez vus oi merché.
32 Gratez la tere de vostre pé
Tant que afermer vus i pussez.
E puis amunt bien sachiez;
Que si pussez ça hors eissir.
36 E jeo ferai od mei venir
Autres suriz pur mei aider
As cordes, que ci sunt, (de)trencher,
E as resels, ki sunt tenduz;
40 Ne serez mie si retenuz.'
L'enseignement a la suriz
Fist li leüns, qu'il fu gariz.
De la fosse est eschapez:

4 Came to amuse themselves and play.
   One of them ran – not taking care –
   Over the lion and woke him there.
   The lion now was furious.
8 He grabbed the mouse; so wroth he was,
   He wished to bring the mouse to court.
   She pleaded that she'd surely not
   Acted at all deliberately.
12 And soon the lion set her free.
   There's little honour anyhow,
   He said, if he should kill her now.
   Then just a short time after that,
16 A man, it is reported, had
   Prepared a deep, wide open pit.
   That night the lion fell into it.
   Within the pit, quite terrified
20 That he'd be killed, he roared and cried.
   Hearing this, mouse came hastily,
   Though she knew not who it might be.
   Then when she saw by trap o'ertaken
24 The one whom in the woods she'd wakened,
   She asked him what it was he sought.
   He answered her that he was caught
   And grieved he might be killed in there.
28 The mouse responded, 'Have no fear!
   I'll now return to you the guerdon
   That you once gave me by your pardon
   When over you my feet did bound.
32 Now with your paw scratch at the ground
   Until your foothold is quite stable.
   Then you should climb as best you're able
   Till up out of the pit you'll be.
36 And I'll arrange to bring with me
   More mice who will their help provide
   To cut the ropes with which you're tied,
   And nets as well, about you strained;
40 You'll thus no longer be contained.'
   Then this advice which the mouse gave him
   The lion followed, and it saved him.
   Thus he escaped out of the pit:

44 La li valut humilitez.
 Par ceste essample nus assume
 Que essample prengent li riche hume
 Ki sur les povres unt grant poër.
48 S'il lur mesfunt par nunsaver,
 Qu'il en eient bone merci.
 Avenir peot tut autresi:
 Que cil li avera grant mester
52 E meuz li savera cunseiller
 A sun busuin, s'il est suppris,
 Que li meudres de ses amis.

17 De l'arunde e del lin

 Par veil essample en escrit trois
 Quant hume sema primes linois
 E volst de lin le pru aveir.
4 L'arunde fu de grant saveir;
 Bien se aparceut ke par le lin
 Sereient oiseus mis a lur fin:
 Del lin pot hum la reiz lacier,
8 Dunt hum les pot ruz damager.
 Tuz les oiseus fist asembler,
 Si lur voleit cunseil duner;
 Qu'il alassent le lin manger,
12 Que il ne peüst fructifïer.
 Li plusur nel vodrent fere;
 Al seignur alerent retrere,
 Le cunseil lur aveit doné.
16 Quant l'arundel l'ot escuté –
 Cum il l'aveient encusee –
 De ses parenz fist asemblee
 Od les meillurs de la lignee,
20 Si s'est al vilein appeisee.
 En sa meisun suffri sun ni,
 La furent si oisel nurri.
 Ele duna a sun lin peis –
24 Ja par nul de eus nel perdra meis.
 Cil fist del lin engins plusurs;

44 Humility brought benefit.
   And so this model serves to show
   A lesson wealthy men should know
   Who over poor folks have much power.
48 If these should wrong them, unaware,
   The rich should show them charity,
   For unto them the same might be:
   The rich may need the poor man who
52 Can better tell him what to do
   When he's by sudden need hard pressed,
   Than can his friends, even the best.

17 The Swallow and the Linseed

This fable tells of long ago
   When man did first the linseed sow,
   Hoping for flax from his endeavour.
 4 The swallow was especially clever,
   For she could fully comprehend
   How flax might bring birds to their end:
   With flax a man could weave a net,
 8 Then injure many birds with it.
   Therefore she gathered all the birds
   And gave these cautionary words:
   She said the linseed they should eat,
12 So that it would not germinate.
   Most had no wish to heed her lore
   And so returned to the seignior
   To bring him word of her advice.
16 But when the swallow heard of this –
   How they had made such imputations –
   She gathered some of her relations,
   And with the best of her clan present,
20 She went to pacify the peasant.
   He let her nest in his own place,
   And there her baby birds she raised.
   She left his crops of flax alone –
24 And thus to swallows he'd lose none.
   With flax he fashioned many a snare;

Dunc prist oisels granz e menurs.
N'eüssent pas del mal eü,
28 S'il eüssent dunc cunseil creü.
   Ceste semblance est asez veire:
Quant fous ne veut le sage creire,
Ki bon cunseil li seit duner
32 E de sun mal le volt oster,
Si damage l'en deit venir –
Dunc est trop tart del repentir.

18 Des reines ki demanderent rei

Jadis avient que en un estanc,
Entur les rives e el fanc,
Ot de reines granz cumpainies,
4 Que de lung tens i sunt nurries.
La desdeignerent arester;
A la tere vodreient aler.
A lur Destinee crïerent –
8 Suventefeiz li demanderent –
Que rei lur deüst enveier;
Kar d'autre rien ne eurent mester.
Quant meintefeiz eurent prïé
12 La Destinee ad enveié
Enmi cel ewe un trunc dur
Dunt eles eurent grant poür.
Cele que pres del trunc estut
16 E vit ke pas ne se remut,
Ses cumpaines ad rapelees,
Si sunt ensemble al trunc alees.
Primes le salüent cume rei,
20 E chescune li pramet fei.
Tutes le tienent pur seignur,
Si li portent grant honur.
Mes quant le trunc ne se remut,
24 Celes virent que en pes estut,
Enmi cel ewe jut en pes.
Sur li munterent tut a un fes.
Lur vileinie sur li firent,

Birds large and small he captured there.
Such ills they would not have received,
28 Had they in good advice believed.
 This picture's truth we recognize:
A fool who won't believe the wise
Who could advise him what to do
32 And rescue him from error, too,
Deserves the painful consequence –
Now it's too late for penitence.

18 The Frogs Who Asked for a King

Once, in a pond, it came to pass,
Around the banks and the morass,
There lived great frog confederations
4 Who had been there for generations.
They hated staying in the pond
And wished to move to solid ground.
So they cried out to Destiny –
8 Repeatedly they made their plea –
That she might send to them a king;
They needed not another thing.
When many times the frogs had prayed,
12 Then Destiny to them conveyed
Right in the pond, a sturdy log
Which caused great fear in every frog.
The frog close by the log observed,
16 Since it had come, it had not stirred.
He to his friends a summons croaked;
The log together they approached.
They greeted it as their king royal,
20 And each one promised to be loyal.
The frogs all thought of it as lord,
Thus was it honoured and adored.
But when the log stayed motionless,
24 They saw that it was fixed in place,
Lying so still there in the water.
They climbed upon it all together.
Such dirty deeds performed each frog

28 El funz de l'ewe l'abatirent.
   A la Destinee revunt:
   Rei demandent, car nul ne unt;
   Mauveis fu cil qu'el lur duna.
32 La Destinee lur enveia
   Une coluvre grande e fort,
   Que tuz les dovore e treit a mort.
   Tutes furent en grant turment.
36 Dunc crïerent plus egrement
   A la Destinee merci
   Que lur ostast cel enemi.
   La Destinee lur respundi,
40 'Nenil, nenil! Jeo vus suffri
   Tuz voz volentez a feire.
   Seignur eüstes de bon eire.
   Vileinement le hunisistes;
44 Tel l'aiez cum le quesistes!'
     Issi avient, plusurs le funt
   De bon seignur, quant il l'unt:
   Tuz jurs le veulent defuler;
48 Ne li seivent honur garder.
   S'il nes tient aukes en destreit,
   Ne frunt pur lui tort ne dreit.
   A tel se pernent, quis destruit;
52 De lur aveir meine sun bruit.
   Lores regretent lur bon seignur,
   A ki il firent la deshonur.

19 Des colums e de l'ostur

   Colums demanderent seignur.
   A rei choisirent un ostur,
   Pur ceo que meins mal lur fesist
4 E vers autres les guarantist.
   Mes quant il ot la seignurie,
   E tuz furent en sa baillie,
   N'i ot un sul k'il aprismast,
8 Qu'il ne ocesist e devorast.
   Pur ceo parla un des colums,

28 That to the depths they sank the log.
   They then to Destiny went back
   And begged a king; they felt the lack:
   The one she'd given them was bad.
32 So Destiny then sent that crowd
   An adder powerful and great –
   Death to the frogs he seized and ate.
   Those left were all in great distress.
36 They cried out with much bitterness
   For mercy now from Destiny
   To rid them of their enemy.
   Responding, Destiny avowed,
40 'Oh no! Oh no! You've been allowed
   All of the things which you desired.
   A lord good-natured you acquired.
   You shamed churlishly that seignior,
44 And now you have what you asked for!'
      This is what many folks have done
   To a good lord (should they have one):
   They always want to stamp their lord;
48 His honour they don't know to guard.
   If they're not kept in stressful plight,
   They'll do him neither wrong nor right.
   To him they cling who them destroys;
52 With what they have, he makes his noise.
   Then for their good seignior they long
   To whom they have done shameful wrong.

19 The Doves and the Hawk

   The doves asked for a sovereign.
   They chose a hawk to be their king,
   So that to less harm he'd subject them
4 And against others might protect them.
   But when he got the sovereignty,
   And over all had mastery,
   Then not one could approach him whom
8 He would not kill and then consume.
   Therefore one dove these thoughts expressed

Si apela ses cumpainuns:
'Grant folie,' fet il, 'fesimes,
12 Quant l'ostur a rei choisimes,
Que nus ocist de jur en jur.
Meuz nus fust que sanz seignur
Fuissums tut tens que aver cestui.
16 Einz nus guardum bien de lui,
Ne dutum fors sun aguait.
Puis que l'umes a nus atrait,
A il tut fet apertement
20 Ceo qu'il fist einz celeiement.'
    Cest essample dit as plusurs,
Que choisissent les maus seignurs.
De grant folie s'entremet,
24 Ki en subjectïun se met
A cruel hume u a felun:
Il n'en avera si hunte nun.

20 **Del larun e del chien**

De un larun cunte ki ala
Berbiz embler, qu'il espia
Dedenz la faude a un vilein.
4 Ensemble od lui porta un pein.
Al chien voleit le pain bailler,
Que la faude deveit guaiter.
Li chiens li dit, 'Amis, pur quei
8 Prendrai jeo cest pain de tei?
Jeo nel te puis reguerduner,
Ne a tun eos le pain guarder.'
Li lere dist, 'Jeo n'en quer rien.
12 Mangez le pein e sil retien!'
Li chiens respunt, 'N'en voil nïent!
Jeo sai tres bien a escïent
Que ma buche veus estuper
16 Que jeo ne puisse mot suner,
Si emblerez nos berbiz
Quant li berkers est endormiz.
Trahi avereie mun seignur,

As his companions he addressed:
'We did a very foolish thing
12 When we doves chose the hawk as king
Who murders us now day by day.
We would be better off for aye
Without a lord, than with him here.
16 We watched out for him earlier
And had no fears except ambush.
But ever since he's come to us,
He has done all things openly
20 That he before did secretly.'
    This lesson speaks to everyone
Who's picked an evil sovereign.
That man indeed acts like a fool
24 Who puts himself under the rule
Of one who's cruel and villainous:
Nothing but shame will come from this.

20 **The Thief and the Dog**

This story's of a thief who tried
To steal some sheep which he had spied
Inside the fold of a farmstead.
4 He brought with him a loaf of bread.
He meant to give this to the dog
Whose job it was to guard the flock.
The dog addressed him, 'Friend,' he said,
8 'Why should I take your loaf of bread?
I can't repay and must refuse.
So keep the bread for your own use.'
'I ask for nothing,' said the thief.
12 'Do take the bread; eat it yourself!'
'I will have none!' the dog returned.
'For I can see, yes I've discerned
That you intend my mouth to stuff
16 So that I can't let out a woof,
And then you'd rob us of our sheep
Because the shepherd is asleep.
My master thus I would betray

20 Que m'ad nurri desque a cest jur.
   Malement avereit empleié –
   Qu'il m'ad nurri e afeité –
   Si par ma garde avereit perdu
24 Ceo dunt il m'ad lung tens peü.
   E tu memes m'en harreies
   E pur treïtre me tendreis.
   Ne voil tun pain issi guainer!'
28 E dunc comencet abaier.
     Par essample nus mustri ci:
   Chescun franc hume face einsi.
   Si nuls l'en veut doner lüer
32 Ne par pramesse losenger
   Que sun seignur deive traïr,
   Nel veile mie cunsentir;
   Atendre en deit cel guerdun,
36 Cum le chien fist del larun.

21 Del lu e de la troie

   Jadis avient que un lus erra
   Par un chemin, si encuntra
   Une troie que preinz esteit.
4 Vers li ala a grant espleit,
   E dist que pes li vot duner,
   Ore se hastast de purceler –
   Car ses purceus voleit aveir.
8 Cele respunt par grant saveir:
   'Sire, cument me hastereie?
   Tant cum si pres de mei vus veie,

20 Who's cared for me until this day.
   And he'd be used most wickedly –
   This man who raised and cared for me –
   If he lost all, while in my keep,
24 When he's fed me to guard his sheep.
   Me, even you yourself would hate, for
   You would consider me a traitor.
   I will not earn my bread that way!'
28 With this, the dog began to bay.
    In this example, we see here
   A model of fine character.
   If one would buy his services
32 Or flatter with false promises
   In hope that he'll his lord betray,
   He will refuse emphatically.
   The same reward he would receive
36 As dog knew he would get from thief.

21 The Wolf and the Sow

   Once long ago a wolf strolled down
   A path and chanced to come upon
   A sow who was with piglets big.
4 He hastily approached the pig.
   He'd give her peace, he told the sow,
   If quickly she'd bear piglets now –
   Her piglet babes he wished to have.
8 With wisdom, this response she gave:
   'My lord, how can you hurry me?
   When you, so close to me I see,

Ne me puis pas deliverer;
12 Tel hunte ai de vus esgarder.
Ne savez mie que ceo munte?
Tutes femeles unt grant hunte,
Si mains madles les deit tucher
16 A tel busuin ne aprismer!'
Idunc s'en va li lus mucier,
Ki les purcels voleit manger.
E la troie s'en est alee
20 Que par engin s'est delivree.
    Ceste essample deivent oïr
Tutes femmes e retenir:
Que pur sulement mentir
24 Ne laissent lur enfanz perir!

22 Des lievres e des reines

Ci dit que lievres s'asemblerent
A parlement, si esgarderent
Que en autre tere s'en ireient
4 Hors de la grave u il esteient;
Kar trop furent en dolur:
De humes, de chiens eurent poür.
Si nel voleient mes suffrir,
8 Pur ceo s'en veulent fors eissir.
Li sage lievre lur diseient

I cannot bear my young outright;
12 I'm so ashamed when in your sight.
Do you not sense the implication?
All women suffer degradation
If male hands should dare to touch
16 At such a time, or even approach!'
With this the wolf hid in retreat
Who'd sought the baby pigs to eat.
The mother pig could now proceed
20 Who through her cleverness was freed.
  All women ought to hear this tale
And should remember it as well:
Merely to avoid a lie,
24 They should not let their children die!

22 The Hares and the Frogs

It's said the hares once came together
In council to consider whether
They should to other regions roam
4 Out from the grove that was their home;
For life was too distressful here:
Of dogs and men they lived in fear.
Such woes they could not tolerate,
8 And so they wished to emigrate.
The wise hares then spoke to the rest:

Que folie ert ceo que quereient
A eissir de lur cunissance –
12 U furent nurrie des enfance.
Li autre ne l'en vodrent creire;
Tuz ensemble tiendrent lur eire.
A une mare en sunt venu.
16 Gardent el tai, si unt veü
U reines erent asemblees.
Del poür de eus sunt esfrees;
Dedenz l'ewe se vunt plunger,
20 Desque veient aprismer.
Uns lievres les ad rapelez.
'Seignurs,' fet il, 'kar esgardez!
Par les reines que nus veüms,
24 Que poür unt, nus purpensums
Que nus alum querant folie,
Que nostre grave avum guerpie
Pur estre aillurs asseürez.
28 Jamés tere ne troverez,
U l'um ne dute aucune rien.
Ralum nus en! Si ferum bien!'
A tant li lievre returnerent;
32 En lur cuntree s'en alerent.
    Pur ceo se deivent purpenser –
Cil ki se veulent remüer
E lur ancïen liu guerpir –
36 Que lur en put aprés venir.
Jamés regne ne troverunt
Ne en cele tere ne vendrunt
Que tut tens seient sanz poür,
40 U sanz travail u sanz dolur.

23 De la chalve suriz

De un lïun cunte que assembla
Tutes les bestes e manda
Ki aloënt sur quatre piez;
4 E li egles ad purchaciez
Tuz les oisels que eles unt

They would be seeking foolishness
To leave behind all that they knew –
12 The place where they'd been nurtured, too.
Not heeding what they had to say,
Soon all the hares were on their way.
Their travels took them to a pond.
16 Looking in the mud, they found
Some frogs who had assembled there.
These frogs were overwhelmed with fear;
Into the water they would dive
20 As soon as they saw hares arrive.
One hare then called out to the lot,
'Seigniors! Come look at what we've got!
We've seen the frightened frogs; likewise
24 We should on our part realize
That after foolishness we strove
When we abandoned our home grove,
Thinking that we would safer be.
28 For such a land you'll never see
Where one has not a thing to fear.
Let's go back home! That's best, it's clear!'
With that, the hares all turned around
32 And went back to their native ground.
    All this, those people ought to weigh –
Those folk who wish to move away,
Abandoning their ancient home –
36 They'd best take heed of what could come.
No kingdom will they ever find
Anywhere known to humankind
Where everyone lives free of fear,
40 Where toil and sorrow disappear.

23 The Bat

Once lion did a meeting call
Assembling every animal,
All that on four feet walked about;
4 And eagle sent a summons out
To all the birds with wings to fly

E que volent en l'eir lamunt;
Bataille deivent od li tenir.
8 Quant ensemble durent venir,
La chalve suriz les vit,
En sun queor ad pensé e dit
Que mut redutout cel afaire –
12 Ne sot as quels se dut traire.
Od ceus volt estre que veinterunt
E ki la greinur force averunt.
Sur un haut fust s'en est muntee
16 Pur esgarder cele assemblee.
Ceo li fu vis sun escïent
Que li lïuns aveit plus gent
E qu'il ert de greinur justise:
20 Od les autres suriz s'est mise.
Li egles fu amunt volez
Od les oiseus qu'il ot mandez.
Tant en i ot, tant en viendrent,
24 Que les bestes pur fous se tiendrent.
Quant la chave suriz les veit,
Mut li pesa que od eus n'esteit;
Des bestes est dunc departie.
28 Ses piez musça (si fist folie).
Mes quant les eles entreovri,
Par devant tuz les descovri:
Dunc est sa felunie overte,
32 E sa traïsun tut descuverte.
De si as bestes la hüerent.
A lur Crïere se clamerent –
De la chalve suriz se pleignent;
36 Mut la hunissent e blasteignent
E mustrent li sa felunie,
E cum ele ad sa fei mentie.
Lur Crïere lur ad juré
40 Que ele en fra lur volenté,
E que mut bien les vengera.
Puis la maudist e si jura
Que jamés en liu ne venist
44 Que oisels ne beste la veïst.
Tute clarté li ad tolue,

Who travel high up in the sky;
For they would battle one another.
8 And as these two groups came together,
The scene was witnessed by the bat.
The voices in his heart said that
He was quite terrified with fear –
12 Unsure with which side to adhere.
With those who'd win he wished to be,
Who'd fight with greater potency.
And so he climbed up a tall tree
16 To give the crowd full scrutiny.
And this is what he figured out:
The lion had more troops, he thought,
His kingdom greater, he surmised.
20 Therefore, bat joined the other mice.
The eagle flew high in the air
With all the birds he'd summoned there.
By now there were so many birds,
24 The animals felt quite absurd.
The bat saw them and felt remorse
That he'd not joined the eagle's force.
And so he left the animal pack
28 And hid his feet (a foolish act!)
For when his wings were opened wide,
His feet by everyone were spied:
Exposed thus was his treachery;
32 Revealed was his disloyalty.
The animals then raised a shout.
To their Creator they cried out –
They all accused the bat, he was
36 Contemptible and odious.
They told her of his villainy,
How he had used his wings to lie.
Then their Creator said she'd do
40 Exactly what they wished her to.
He'd get his retribution now.
She cursed the bat and made this vow:
No matter where the bat might be,
44 He'd never bird nor creature see.
His eyesight then she took away:

Ja puis ne seit de jur veüe.
Aprés la ruva issi hunir:
48 Sa plume oster, lui descovrir.
   Autresi est del traïtur
Que meseire ves sun seignur,
A ki il deit honur porter
52 E lëauté e fei garder.
Si sis sires ad de li mestier,
As autres se veut dunc ajuster,
A sun busuin li veut faillir
56 E od autres se veut tenir.
Si sis sires vient el desus,
Ne peot lesser sun mauveis us.
Dunc vodrit a lui returner;
60 De tutes pars veut meserrer.
Si honur en pert e sun aveir,
E repruver en unt si heir.
A tuz jurs en est si huniz,
64 Cum fu dunc la chalve suriz
Que ne deit mes par jur voler,
Ne il ne deit en curt parler.

24 Del cerf a une ewe

Issi avient que un cerf beveit
A une ewe, kar sei aveit.
Guarda dedenz, ses cornes vit.

He'd never know the light of day.
For shame, this sentence she imposed:
48 He lose his plumes and be exposed.
  That traitor's case is similar
Who wrongly acts toward his seignior.
He should give honour to his lord
52 And should be loyal, keep his word.
And when his master is in need,
He should join others and bring aid.
Yet he'll not heed emergency:
56 He'll turn to other company.
But if his lord comes out on top,
His bad behaviour will not stop.
For now he wishes to come back;
60 Thus he goes wrong with every tack.
He loses honour and possessions,
Rebuked are later generations.
Forever he will suffer shame.
64 Our story of the bat's the same:
He cannot ever fly by day
And can't at court have any say.

24 The Stag at the Spring

To quench his thirst, a stag once took
A drink of water at a brook.
He saw his horns mirrored below,

4 A sei memes ad dunc dit
Que nule beste le cuntrevaleit,
Ne si beles cornes n'aveit.
Tant entendi a sei loër,
8 E a ses cornes esgarder,
Qu'il vit chiens venir curant
E lur mestre aprés cornant,
Aprés lui vienent, sil quereient –
12 Pur ceo que prendre le voleient –
El bois se met tut esmaiet.
Par ses cornes est atachiet,
En un buissun est retenuz!
16 Dunc sunt li chien a lui venuz.
Quant il les vit si aprismer,
Si se cumence a desreiner:
'Veirs est,' fet il, 'que vileins dit
20 Par essample e par respit:
Li plusur veulent ceo loër
Qu'il devreient suvent blamer,
E blamer ceo qu'il devreient
24 Forment loër, s'il saveient.'

25 De la femme ki fist pendre sun mari

De un humme cunte li escriz
Que mort esteit e enfuïz.
Sa femme demeine grant dolur
4 Sur sa tumbe e nuit e jur.
Pres de ileoc aveit un larun,
Que ert (des)pendu pur mesprisun.
Un chevaler le despendi,
8 Sun(t) parent ert, si l'enfuï.
Par la cuntree fu crïé,
Que le larun aveit osté,
Sun jugement memes avreit:
12 S'il ert ateint, pendu sereit.
Dunc ne sot cunseil trover
Cum il se puisse deliverer;
Kar sceü ert de mute gent
16 Qu'il le teneit pur sun parent.

4 And to himself asserted so:
  No creature was so valuable
  And none had horns so beautiful.
  So deep was he in his self-praise,
8 Giving his horns his steady gaze,
  That when he saw some dogs come bounding,
  Their master too, his horn resounding,
  Chasing the stag, hot on his scent,
12 (To capture him was their intent) –
  He headed for the woods quite scared.
  There by his antlers he was snared,
  His horns entangled in a bush!
16 The dogs kept coming in a rush.
  And as he saw the dogs approach,
  The stag spoke out in self-reproach:
  'It's true what peasants tell,' said he,
20 'In paradigm and homily.
  Most people are inclined to praise
  What really they should criticize,
  And criticize instead what's to
24 Be strongly praised, if they but knew.'

25 The Widow Who Hanged Her Husband

  The book tells how this all occurred.
  A man had died and was interred.
  His wife mourned him most woefully
4 Over his grave both night and day.
  A thief was close by at the time
  Who had been hanged there for his crime.
  A knight who was this villain's kin
8 Cut down the thief and buried him.
  It was proclaimed through every town
  That he who'd taken the thief down
  Would now receive the same sentence:
12 If caught, be hanged in consequence.
  The knight knew not who'd help him shape
  A plan whereby he could escape.
  For most folks knew this fact: in brief –
16 He was related to the thief.

Al cimiterie vet tut dreit
U la prudefemme esteit,
Que sun seignur ot tant pluré.
20 Cuintement ad a li parlé:
Dit li que ele se cunfortast.
Mut sereit lez, se ele l'amast.
La prudefemme l'esgarda;
24 Grant joie fist, si li otria
Que ele fera sa volenté.
Li chevaler li ad cunté
Que mut li ert mesavenu
28 Del larun qu'il ot despendu.
Si ele ne li seit cunseil doner,
Hors del païs l'estut aler.
La prudefemme li respundi,
32 'Desfuium mun barun d'ici;
Puis sil pendum la u cil fu:
Si n'ert jamés aparceü.
Deliverer deit hum par le mort
36 Le vif dunt l'em ad cunfort.'
Par iceste signefiance
Peot hum entendre queil creance
Deivent aveir li morz es vifs;
40 Tant est li mund faus e jolifs.

26 **Del lu e del chien**

Un lu e un chien s'encuntrerent
Par mi un bois u il alerent.
Li lus ad le chien esgardé,
4 E puis si l'ad areisuné:
'Frere,' fet il, 'mut estes beaus!
E mut est luisant tis peaus!'
Li chiens respunt, 'Ceo est veritez;
8 Jeo manguz bien, si ai asez,
E süef gis puis tut le jur;
Devant les piez mun seignur
Puis chescun jur runger les os,
12 Dunt jeo me faz gras e gros.
Si vus volez od mei venir
E vus li voliez obeïr –

He went straight to the burial ground
And there that worthy woman found
Who wept so much for her seignior.
20 Then cunningly he spoke to her.
He said that comfort now was near.
Love him, and she would soon find cheer.
The worthy woman looked him through;
24 She felt great joy, and vowed to do
Whatever he might wish or want.
And so the knight gave this account:
He told how ill-turned was his life
28 Since he had taken down the thief.
If she knew not what he must do,
Out of the country he must go.
Here's the reply the woman gave:
32 'Let's dig my husband from his grave;
We'll hang him where the thief has been:
The difference never will be seen.
One ought to use the dead to free
36 The living, who can comfort be.'
    And thus we learn this story's thrust:
A man had better know what trust
The dead in living folks should place:
40 The world's so false and frivolous.

26 The Wolf and the Dog

A wolf and dog met on the way
While passing through the woods one day.
The wolf looked closely at the dog,
4 And then began this dialogue:
'Brother,' he said, 'you look so fine!
And oh, such fur! How it does shine!'
The dog replied, 'That's very true;
8 I eat quite well, a great deal, too.
Each day I make my cozy seat
While resting at my master's feet
Where daily I gnaw bones, and that
12 Is what makes me so big and fat.
If you would like to come with me,
If to obey him you'll agree –

Si cum jeo faz – asez averez
16 Plus viande que ne vodrez.'
'Si ferai, veirs!' li lus respunt.
Dunc s'acumpainent, si s'en vunt.
Einz que a vile feussent venu,
20 Garda li lus, si ad veü
Cum le chien porta sun coler;
Sa chaëne le vit traïner.
'Frere,' fet il, 'merveilles vei
24 Entur tun col – mes ne sai quei.'
Li chiens respunt, 'C'est ma chaëne,
Dunt humme me lie la semaine.
Kar suventefeiz mordereie
28 A plusurs riens mesfereie,
Que mes sires veut garantir;
Si me fet lïer [e] retenir.
La nuit vois entur la meisun,
32 Que n'i aprisment li larun.'
'Quei!' fet li lus, 'est il íssi
Que aler ne poëz fors par li!
Tu remeindras, jeo m'en irai;
36 Ja chaëne ne choiserai!
Meuz voil estre lus a delivre
Que en cheine richement vivre,
Quant uncore pois estre a chois.
40 Va a la vile, jeo vois al bois!'
Par la chaëne est departie
Lur amur e lur cumpainie.

27 De l'humme, de sun ventre, e de ses membres

De un humme voil ci cunter,
E par essample remembrer.

And act like me – you'll have from this
16 More food than you could ever wish.'
'I'll do that! Sure!' the wolf replied.
Together off they went, allied.
Before they'd at the town arrived,
20 The wolf looked at the dog and eyed
The way the dog a collar wore
And how a dragging chain he bore.
'Brother,' he said, 'how odd is that
24 Thing 'round your neck – I know not what.'
'That's my chain-leash,' the dog replied,
'With which all through the week I'm tied;
For his possessions I would chew on,
28 And many items I would ruin.
My master wants them all protected,
And that's why I'm tied and restricted.
At night, around the house I peer
32 And make sure that no thieves draw near.'
'What!' cried the wolf. 'By this you mean
You can't go out except with him!
Well, you can stay! I won't remain.
36 I'll never choose to wear a chain!
I'd rather live as a wolf, free,
Than on a chain in luxury.
I still can make a choice, and so
40 You fare to town; to woods I'll go.'
A chain thus brought the termination
Of friendship and fraternization.

27 A Man, His Stomach, and His Members

A story of a man is here:
The lesson it conveys is clear.

De ses meins cunte e de sez piez
4 E de sun chief – k'ert iriez
Vers sun ventre qu'il porta,
Pur lur guaainz qu'il gasta.
Dunc ne volstrent mes travailler,
8 Li tolirent li manger.
Mes quant li ventre jeüna,
Hastivement afeblia
Meins e piez qu'il ne poeient
12 Si travailler cum il suleient.
Quant grant febleté sentirent,
Manger e beivre al ventre offrirent.
Mes trop l'eurent fet juner,
16 Si qu'il ne poeit rien guster.
Li ventres reverti a nïent
E meins e piez tut ensement.
  Par ceste essample peot hum veer
20 E chescun franc humme le deit saver:
Nul ne peot aver honur
Ki hunte fet a sun seignur;
Ne li sire tute ensement,
24 Pur qu'il voille hunir sa gent.
Si l'un a l'autre est failliz,
Ambur en erent maubailliz.

28 Del singe e del gupil

De un singe dit que demanda
A un gupil qu'il encuntra,
De sa kue li prestast,

Of hands and feet I will relate
4 And of his head – all were irate
About the stomach he maintained;
He wasted on it all they gained.
Their labour they resolved to quit
8 And thus withhold all food from it.
But when the stomach was deprived,
The hands and feet no longer thrived.
So feeble now, they could not do
12 The work they were accustomed to.
When its infirmity they sensed,
They offered drink and sustenance.
But for too long they'd forced its fast,
16 It could not handle a repast.
The stomach's breakdown was complete,
And withered too were hands and feet.
   This example serves to show
20 What every gentleman should know:
No man can ever honour claim,
Whose actions bring his master shame;
Nor does a lord deserve esteem
24 Who wishes to disgrace his men.
When to another you're untrue,
Trouble results for both of you.

28 The Ape and the Fox

An ape once asked, the story goes,
A fox he chanced to come across,
If fox part of his tail would lend –

4 Si lui plust – u en dunast.
 Avis li fu que trop le ot grant,
 E tuz sunt sanz kue si enfant.
 Li gupil demande quei ceo deit
8 Que sa cue li requereit.
 Le singe dist, 'Ceo m'est avis –
 Ne vus en ert nïent de pis,
 Si m'en voliez un poi duner;
12 Que ele vus nuist pur tost aler.'
 Dist le gupil, 'Ne vus en chaut!
 Cest requeste poi vus vaut.
 Ja de ma cue, que est granz,
16 Ne aleverez vos enfanz
 N'en autre regne(d), n'entre gent;
 Jeo vus di bien apertement,
 Més que ele fust de tel afaire
20 Que jeo ne la pussse a mei traire!'
  Ceste essample pur ceo vus di
 De l'aveir humme est autresi:
 Si il ad plus ke li n'estut,
24 Ne volt suffrir (kar il ne peot)
 Qu'autre en ait eisse ne honur;
 Meuz le volt perdre de jur en jur.

29 **Del lu ki fu reis**

D'un lëon dit que volt aler
En autre tere converser.
Tutes les bestes assembla

4 Or give him – should he condescend.
  He thought the fox had too much tail
  While his ape babes had none at all.
  What made him think, the fox inquired,
8 That his tail was in fact required.
  The ape replied, 'That's my affair –
  But you'll be none the worse for wear
  If a small piece you would concede,
12 Since it restricts your running speed.'
  Said fox, 'That's not your business!
  And your request is meaningless.
  My tail, which is so grand, will not
16 Ever better your children's lot –
  Raise them to higher kind or station;
  I tell you true the situation.
  I'll use my tail, now have no doubt,
20 Only where I can pull it out!'
    Through this example, I've shown you
  What men with their possessions do:
  If one has more than need or want,
24 He won't allow (indeed, he can't)
  Another to be helped thereby;
  He'd rather waste it day by day.

29 The Wolf King

It's said that once a lion planned
To go live in another land.
Then all the beasts held a convention.

4 E tut sun estre li mustra
E qu'il deüssent rei choisir:
Kar ne quidot mes revenir.
N'i ot beste ke li ne preiast
8 Que un autre leün lur baillast.
Il lur respunt qu'il ne l'a:
Ne nurri nul – kar il ne osa.
De eus memes deivent garder
12 Ki meuz les puisse guverner.
Dunc aveient le lu choisi,
Kar il n'i ot nul si hardi
Que osast prendre si lui nun –
16 Tant le tienent a felun –
E a plusurs aveit premis
Que mut les amereit tutdis.
Al lïun vunt, si li unt dit
20 Qu'il aveient le lu eslit.
Il lur respunt: N'en dutent mie,
Que cuinte beste unt choisie,
Prest e ignel e enpernant,
24 Si de curage e de talant
Esteit si francs cum il devereit.
Mes de une chose se cremeit –
Qu'il ne preisist a cunseiller
28 Le gupil que tant sot tricher;
Amdui sunt felun e engrés.
Si del lu veulent aver pes,
Si le facent sur sainz jurer
32 Qu'il ne deie beste adeser
Ne que jamés a sun vivant
Ne mangast char, tant ne quant.
Li lus ad volenters juré
36 Plus qu'il li unt demandé.
Mes quant il fu asseürez
E li leün s'en fu alez,
Grant talent a de char manger.
40 Par engin vodra purchacer
Que les bestes otrïerunt
Sa volenté jugerunt.
Dunc ad un cheverol apelé.

4 He told them all of his intention,
   And that they should select a king:
   He thought he'd not be back again.
   The beasts requested, every one,
8 That he provide another lion.
   He answered that he had no heir:
   He had not raised one – did not dare.
   Among themselves must be their quest
12 To find the one who'd govern best.
   And thus it was they chose the wolf,
   For no one else was bold enough
   To dare take anyone but him
16 (Though all thought wolf a villain grim).
   Yet he assured them all, and swore
   He'd love them best forevermore.
   They went to lion next and stated
20 That wolf had now been designated.
   He said to doubt not in the least
   That they had picked a clever beast,
   Extremely fast and versatile,
24 Provided that his heart and will
   Were as they ought to be: sincere.
   But one thing caused the lion fear –
   That wolf for counsellor would pick
28 The fox who knew well how to trick;
   Both are insidious and base.
   If from the wolf they wanted peace,
   On holy relics he must swear
32 That he'd touch no beast anywhere
   And that forever he would not
   Eat any meat, no matter what.
   The wolf most willingly then swore
36 To more than they had asked him for.
   But when he had been bound by oath,
   And when the lion had set out,
   Such craving wolf had for some meat,
40 That he made plans to use deceit
   To get the beasts all to agree
   And give him leave accordingly.
   The wolf then summoned a roe deer,

44 En cunseil li ad demandé
Que par amur veir li desist
De sa aleine si ele puïst.
Cil li respun que si pueit
48 Que a peine suffrir le poeit.
Li lus se fist mut curuciez.
Pur ses hummes ad enveiez,
A tuz ensemble demanda
52 Quel jugement chescun fra
De celi ki dit a sun seignur
Hunte, leidesce, e deshonur.
Cil li dïent qu'il deit murir.
56 Li lus vet le cheverol seizir;
Sil l'ad ocis par lur esgart,
Puis si manga la meillur part.
Pur sa felunie coverir,
60 En fet autres departir.
Aprés icele saülee
Une autre beste ad apelee.
Tut autretel li demanda
64 De sa aleine – quei li sembla?
La dolente volt meuz mentir
Que pur verité mort suffrir.
Dit li que plus süef odur
68 Ne senti mes, ne meillur.
Li lus ad concilie asemblé;
A ses baruns ad demandé
Que il deit fere par jugement
72 De celui que li triche e ment.
Tuz jugent que ele seit ocise.
Dunc ad li lus la beste prise.
Si l'ad ocise e depecïe,
76 E devant eus tuz ileoc mangïe.
Gueres aprés ne demurra
Que li lus vit e esgarda
Un singe gras e bien peü.
80 De lui ad grant talent eü!
Manger le volst e devorer.
Un jur li ala a demander
De sa aleine – si ele ert puiant

44 And secretly he questioned her
If for his love the truth she'd tell
About wolf's breath: How did it smell?
She said it smelled so terrible
48 It was almost unbearable.
The wolf was very angry then.
He sent a summons to his men.
He questioned all those who had come:
52 What kind of sentence they'd give one
Who spoke such things to his lord's face,
Such words of shame, slur, and disgrace.
This one should die, they all attested.
56 The wolf then had the deer arrested.
While they all watched, he killed the deer
And ate the better part of her.
His crime to cover – he proclaimed
60 He'd portion to them what remained.
After his hunger pains had ceased,
He called for yet another beast.
He questioned her in the same way –
64 How smelled his breath – what would she say?
The poor thing would much rather lie
Than for truth's sake suffer and die.
So she replied she knew no scent
68 So fragrant and so excellent.
The wolf summoned his cabinet;
He asked his barons, when they met,
What punishment he should decree
72 To one who'd lied deceitfully.
All judged that she must die. When caught,
She thus before the wolf was brought.
He killed her, tore her limb from limb,
76 And ate her up in front of them.
After a little time passed by,
The wolf, observing, chanced to spy
A monkey fat and quite well fed –
80 How he that monkey coveted!
To eat, devour him, he desired.
One day wolf went to him, inquired
About his breath – now did it stink

84 U si ele esteit süef ulant?
   Le singe fu mut veizïez:
   Ne voleit mie estre jugez.
   Ele ne saveit, itant li dist.
88 Ne sot li lus qu'il en fesist;
   Kar il nel poeit treire a mort,
   S'il ne li vousist fere tort.
   En sun lit malade se feint.
92 A tutes bestes si se pleint,
   Qu'il ne pot mie (t)respasser,
   Quil l'alouent revisiter.
   Cil li firent mires venir
96 Pur saver s'il peüst gaarir.
   Li mire sunt tut esguaré.
   N'unt rien veü, ne trové,
   Qu'il eüst mal que li neüst,
100 Si mangers a talent eüst!
   'Jeo ne ai,' fet il, 'nul desirer
   Fors de char de singe manger.
   Mes jeo ne voil beste adeser –
104 Mun serment m'estut garder –
   Si jeo n'eüsse tele reisun
   Que l'otriassent mi barun.'
   Dunc li loënt cummunement
108 Qu'il le face seürement.
   Cuntre sun cors de mal guarir
   Ne püent il nul guarantir.
   Quant il oi k'em li loa,
112 Le singe prist, sil manga.
   Puis eurent tut lur jugement:
   Ne tient vers eus nul serment.
     Pur ceo mustre li sage bien
116 Que hum ne deüst pur nule rien
   Felun hume fere seignur,
   Ne trere le a nul honur.
   Ja ne gardera lëauté
120 Plus a l'estrange que al privé.
   Si se demeine envers sa gent,
   Cum fist li lus del serment.

84 Or smell quite sweet – what did he think?
The monkey was extremely sly:
He'd be no way condemned to die.
Thus he replied, he did not know.
88 Now wolf did not know what to do.
The monkey could not be condemned
Because he did no harm intend.
Wolf went to bed; illness he feigned.
92 To all the beasts he then complained;
He thought he never would get well.
They came in turn to pay a call.
They sent out for some doctors then
96 To know if he'd be well again.
The doctors all were at a loss.
None saw a thing, nor found a cause,
No injury which brought this mood.
100 If only he'd desire some food!
'I have,' he said, 'no other wish
Except to eat some monkey flesh.
Of course, to touch a beast I'm loath! –
104 I must, you know, keep my sworn oath –
Unless I can well justify it;
My barons then could ratify it.'
They met together, gave this view,
108 That that is just what he must do.
Against his heart's desire, no cure –
Their remedies could not be sure.
When he heard what they advocated,
112 He seized the monkey and he ate it.
On all in turn was sentence passed:
His oath to none of them was fast.
   Thus by the wise man we are taught
116 That we, no matter what, must not
A wicked man e'er make seignior,
Nor show to such a one honour.
His loyalty's as much pretence
120 With strangers as with his close friends.
And toward his people he will act
As did the wolf, with his sworn pact.

30 Del lu e del berker

D'un veneür nus cunte ici,
Que un lu aveit acuilli.
Par mi un champ fuï li lus,
4 U un berker seeit tut suls.
Par sa franchise li requist
Qu'il le muscast, e si desist
Al veneür, quil ensiweit,
8 Que al bois esteit alé tut dreit.
Li pastre dist que si fera;
Desuz sa faude le musça.
Li venere vient criant,
12 D'ures en autres demandant
Si'il aveit le lu veü.
Il li respunt, ne seit u fu;
Od sa mein li vet enseignant
16 Que al bois le deit aler querant.
Endementers qu'il li enseignot,
Vers le lu tuz jurs gardot,
Ne pot ses oilz pas remüer;
20 Mes nepurquant l'en fist aler.
Quant il le vit bien esluiné,
Si dist al lu, qu'il ot muscé,
'Ne me sez tu ore bon gré –
24 Que jeo te ai issi deliveré.'
Li lus respundi cuintement,
'Ta lange, tes meins vereiment
Dei jeo,' fet il, 'bon gré saveir.
28 Mes une rien te di pur veir –
S'il alast a ma volenté,
Ti oil sereient ja crevé!
Ta lange, tes meins me garirent;
32 Ti oil pur poi me descovrirent.'

30 **The Wolf and the Shepherd**

I'll tell you of a hunter who
Did long ago a wolf pursue.
Into a clearing ran the wolf;
4 A shepherd sat there by himself.
The wolf asked him, for courtesy
Would he please hide him and then say
To the hunter who pursued
8 That he'd gone straight into the wood.
The shepherd said he'd do as bidden;
Within his fold the wolf was hidden.
The hunter entered shouting then,
12 Asking the man, time and again,
If he had seen the wolf. He said,
'I don't know where the wolf has fled,'
And with his hands he indicated
16 The woods should be investigated.
But while he pointed out the way,
He watched the wolf continually.
He could not take his eyes from wolf,
20 And yet he sent the other off.
Then when he saw he'd left the field.
He said to wolf, whom he'd concealed,
'Now don't you owe great thanks to me –
24 For it's through me that you are free.'
The wolf replied most cunningly,
'Your tongue and your hands certainly
Should have,' he said, 'my gratitude.
28 But I'll say this with certitude –
Were I to have it all my way,
Your eyes would be smashed out for aye!
Your tongue, your hands they rescued me;
32 Your eyes put me in jeopardy!'

31 Del poün

D'un poün cunte que fu iriez
Vers sei memes e curucez,
De ceo que tele voiz ne aveit
4 Cum a lui, ceo dist, avendreit.
A la Destinee le mustra;
E la Dame li demanda
S'il n'ot asez en la beauté
8 Dunt ele l'aveit si aürné –
De pennes l'aveit fet plus bel
Que ne veeit nul autre oisel.
Le poün dit qu'il se cremeit,
12 Que de tuz oiseus plus vi(e)l esteit
Pur ceo que ne sot bel chanter.
Ele respunt, 'Les mei ester!
Bien te deit ta beauté suffire.'
16 'Nenil,' fet il, 'bien le puis dire –
Quant li ruissinol petiz
Ad meillur voiz, jeo sui huniz.'
    Issi est il de plusurs:
20 Cum plus unt, plus sunt coveiturs.

31 The Peacock

Once there was a peacock who
Was discontented, angry too,
Because his voice, he said, was not
4 Befitting or appropriate.
He told all this to Destiny;
That Lady asked him then if he
Weren't with his beauty satisfied –
8 Such fine adornment she'd supplied!
His feathers lovelier made she
Than any bird's he'd ever see.
The peacock answered that he feared
12 He was, of all, the vilest bird,
For he could not sing prettily.
Then she responded, 'Let me be!
Your beauty should suffice for you.'
16 'Oh, no!' he said. 'I tell you true –
Because the nightingale petite
Has finer voice, my shame's complete.'
        This is how many folks behave:
20 The more they have, the more they crave.

32 De l'aignelet e de la chevre

Une berbiz ot aignelé,
E li bercher l'en ad osté
Sun aignelet, si l'en porta;
4 A une chevre le bailla,
Que de sun leit l'ad bien nurri;
Al bois l'en meine ensemble od li.
Quant ele ert creüe e grant,
8 Puis l'apela, si li dist tant:
'Va t'en a la berbiz, ta mere,
E al mutun, que est tun pere.
Asez te ai nurri lungement.'
12 Ele respundi sagement,
'M'est avis que meuz deit estre
Ma mere, cele que me sot pestre;
Meuz que cele ke me porta
16 E qui de li me desevera.'

33 Del bucher e des berbiz

Issi avient que [en] un pastiz
Ot grant cumpaine de berbiz.
Un bucher s'alot od sa muiler
4 Par mi le champ esbanïer.
Les berbiz sanz garde trova;
Un en ocist, si l'en porta.
Chescun [jur] el champ rev[en]eit,
8 Sis en porta e ocieit.

32 The Lamb and the Goat

A sheep produced a lamb one day.
And then a farmer took away
Her little lamb; and after, brought
4 The lamb and gave her to a goat.
With her own milk, the lamb she nourished
And took her with her to the forest.
When lamb had grown big and mature,
8 The goat summoned and spoke to her:
'Time to go to the sheep, your mother,
And to the ram who is your father.
I've nurtured you sufficiently.'
12 The lamb replied sagaciously,
'My reasoning, I think, is good:
My mother's she who gave me food,
For that's a better one than she
16 Who carried, then abandoned me.'

33 The Butcher and the Sheep

There once was in a meadow deep
A goodly company of sheep.
A butcher took his wife and went
4 Into the field for merriment.
He found the sheep without defence;
He killed one and he took it thence.
Repeatedly, he took away
8 A sheep and killed it, one each day.

Les berbiz mut s'en curucerent.
Entre eus distrent e cunseilerent
Que ne se veulent pas defendre;
12 Par dreit ire se laissent prendre,
Ne ja ne se desturnerunt,
Ne pur murir mot ne dirrunt.
Tant atendirent le bricun
16 Qu'il n'i remist fors un mutun.
Quant sul seeit en la pleine,
Ne put müer que ne se pleigne:
'Grant laschesce,' fet il, 'fesimes,
20 E trop mauveis cunseil creïmes –
Que grant cumpainie esteiums,
Quant nus nus ne defendïums
Vers cest humme, que a grant tort,
24 Nus ad tuz pris e jeté mort.'
　　Pur ceo dit hum en repruver:
Plusurs se leissent damager
Que cuntr'ester n'osent lur enemis
28 Que ne facent a eus le pis.

34 **Del singe ki se fist reis**

Un empereres nurri ja
Un singe que forment ama.
E li singes bien atendeit
4 Quanque as humes fere veeit –
Cum l'empereür vit servir,
E ses festes li vit tenir,
Cum tuz le tiendrent a seignur.
8 A la forest se mist un jur.
Tuz les singes fist asembler –
Petiz e granz – qu'il pot trover.
Sur tuz se fist lever a rei;
12 Puis sis retient ensemble od sei.
Des plusurs fist ses chevalers,
E des asquanz ses cunseillers
E les sergaunz de sa meisun;
16 Establi il chescun par nun.

The sheep were quite infuriated.
They met and talked, and advocated
That they should put up no defence.
12 Let them in angry righteousness
Be seized, for they would never flee
Nor say a word, though they might die.
They bore so long this scoundrel's theft
16 That there was only one sheep left.
Knowing that he was all alone,
He could not help but thus bemoan:
'We did,' he said, 'a cowardly deed,
20 And such bad counsel we did heed –
When we, a company immense,
Did not provide for self-defence
Against this man who wronged us thus,
24 Who's captured and then murdered us.'
    Therefore the author's admonition:
Many get hurt by their submission;
They dare not enemies defy
28 Lest they'd fare even worse thereby.

34 The Monkey King

An emperor raised, in times bygone,
A monkey whom he doted on.
Monkey attentively would view
 4 Whatever he saw people do –
The way the emperor was served;
His celebrations he observed,
And how all held him as their lord.
 8 One day he to the forest fared.
He bade the monkeys congregate –
All he could find – the small and great.
He had himself crowned king. Then he
12 Chose six to keep him company.
Some monkeys were his chevaliers,
Others he made his counsellors.
The household servants he installed:
16 Each one by his own name was called.

Dunc prist femme, si ot enfanz,
E tient festes riches e granz.
Dui humme erent al bois alé;
20 Mes il esteient esguaré
La u li singe converserent.
Utre lur volenté alerent
La u il erent assemblé:
24 Nel firent mie de lur gré.
Li uns esteit forment leials,
E li autre trichere e faus.
Quant en lur curt furent entré,
28 Des singes sunt mut bien apelé.
Li lëaus hum les esguarda.
L'emperere li demanda
Quei lui semblot de sa meisnee –
32 Si ele esteit bele e enseignee.
Li leals hum ad respundu
Que avis li ert que singes fu.
'De mei e de ma femme di –
36 E de mun fiz, que tu veiz ici –
Quei t'en semble? Nel me celer!'
'Ceo que m'en deit,' fet il, 'sembler:
Tu es singe, e ele singesse –
40 Leide, hiduse, e felunesse.
Par tant poez saveir de tun fiz
Que ceo est un singe tel petiz.'
Al tricheür, sun cumpainun,
44 Dist memes ceste raisun:
Demanderent de mot a mot.
E il lur dit ke li semblot
Que unc ne vit plus bele gent,
48 Ne meuz feussent a sun talent.
Aprés lur dist de lur seignur
Que bien semblot empereür.
Dunc l'unt entre eus si honuré,
52 De tutes parz li unt encliné.
Le leal hume unt dunc pris,
Si l'unt desiré e maumis.
    Pur sun veir dit li firent hunte.

He took a wife, had children small,
Held many a lavish festival.
Two men into the woods one day
20 Went out, but then they lost their way
There where the monkeys make their home.
The two men did not mean to roam
Right where the monkeys held convention:
24 In no way was it their intention.
One man was very virtuous;
The other false and villainous.
When they entered the monkeys' meeting,
28 They both were given a fine greeting.
The man of virtue looked at them.
The emperor then questioned him
About his court – Now did he find
32 That it was lovely and refined.
To this the honest man returned,
That they were monkeys he discerned.
'Of me and of my wife, let's hear –
36 And of my son, whom you see here –
What do you think? Now nothing hide!'
'Here's how it seems,' the man replied.
'You're monkey and she's monkeyess –
40 Ugly, wicked, hideous.
As for your son, all folks can see
He's just a very small monkey.'
Then to the comrade who was base
44 The monkey posed the selfsame case:
The same inquiry word for word.
It seemed to him, this one averred,
A lovelier folk he'd never seen,
48 Nor one on whom he was more keen.
At this, they all said their seignior
Was truly like an emperor.
The monkeys paid him honour, and
52 Everyone bowed throughout the land.
The good man they did apprehend;
They tore him up, a wretched end.
    They shamed the man for speaking true.

56 Oëz l'essample de cest cunte:
 Ne peot mie od le tricheür
 Li lëaus hum aver honur
 En curt u l'em voille tricher
60 E par mençunge faus juger.

un afne dir qui en contra
·l·lion fil falua

35 De l'asne e del leün

 D'un asne dit ki encuntra
 Un leün fier, sil salua:
 'Deus te saut, frere! Deus te saut!'
4 Li leüns vit l'asne baut,
 Si li respunt hastivement,
 'Des quant sumes si pres parent?'
 Dist li asnes, 'Merveilles oi!
8 Mut preisez autres bestes poi!
 Tu quides bien, si est faile,
 Que nuls ne te cuntrevaile.
 Vien ore od mei en sum cel munt,
12 U les bestes ensemble sunt,
 E jeo te frai ja bien veer
 (E si purrez aparcever)
 Que eles averunt poür de mei
16 Autresi grant cum de tei.'
 Li leüns est alé od lui;
 Sur le munt vunt amdui.
 Desuz le munt en la valee
20 Ot de bestes grant assemblee.
 Li asnes prist a rechaner

56 This lesson is worth listening to:
   There's no respect for honesty
   Against a liar's treachery.
   Deceitfully he testifies;
60 He wins false justice by his lies.

35 The Ass and the Lion

There was an ass who chanced to meet
A lion fierce and thus did greet:
'God save you, brother! God save you!'
4 This hearty ass the lion viewed
And, in reply, abruptly stated,
'You seem to think that we're related?'
Then said the ass, 'What marvel's this!
8 You hold the other beasts worthless!
You seem convinced, though it's not true,
That there is none that equals you.
Come, hear, with me, atop that mound,
12 Where animals are gathered round,
And I will make you well discern
(And thus accordingly you'll learn)
That they will be afraid of me
16 Just as they fear you – equally.'
The lion then set off with him;
They climbed the hill, the two of them.
Below the hill, down in the valley,
20 Animals held a great assembly.
And now the ass began to bray

E si leidement a crïer
Que les bestes se departirent,
24 Tel poür eurent, sil fuïrent.
Li asnes dit, 'Veiz tu, amis,
Ceo que jeo te aveie pramis.'
Li lïuns li ad respundu:
28 'Ceo n'est mie pur ta vertue,
Ne pur fierté – k'en tei as –
Mes pur le cri que tu crias,
Que tant lur semble espoëntable
32 Que tuz te tienent pur deable.'
   Si est del orguillus felun
Que par menace e par tençun
E espoënte la fole gent
36 E quide bien a escïent
Que nuls nel deie cuntrester,
Des qu'il orrunt en haut parler.

36 **Del leün malade e del gupil**

Un lïuns fu mut travaillez,
E de cure tut ennuiez.
En une grave fist sun lit;
4 Mut fu malades a sun dit.
Les bestes fist a sei venir;
Kar il voleit, ceo dist, choisir
Ki meuz purreit en bois chacer
8 E sa viande purchacer.
Uns e uns les mandot;
Sis ocieit e devurot –
Meuz les voleit issi manger
12 Que aprés cure ne travailler.
Li gupilz fu od eus alez.
Hors de la grave est arestez;
Des noveles voleit oïr,
16 Ainz qu'il vousist avant venir.
Li lïuns sist, si l'esguarda;
Irïement li demanda
Pur quei il ne volt venir avant.

And cry in such an ugly way,
That all the animals took flight
24 And left the place, they'd such a fright.
Said ass, 'My friend, you see it's true.
It's just the way I promised you.'
Here's what the lion told the ass:
28 'It's surely not your sturdiness,
And not your strength – I grant you that –
But it's the cry which you cried out
Which seemed to them to be so awful
32 That they all think that you're a devil.'
    It's thus with one who's arrogant,
Whose threats and nasty argument
Give foolish folk a dreadful fright.
36 He's certain his conception's right:
That none will ever him defy
Once they have heard his raucous cry.

36 The Sick Lion and the Fox

This tells of lion's weariness:
For him, the hunt was tedious.
So in a grove he made his bed;
4 He was quite ill, or so he said.
He bade the animals collect
Because, he said, he would select
The one best able in the wood
8 To hunt – and get the lion food.
He called them one by one to him;
He killed each one; devoured them –
For he preferred to eat them thus
12 Than run in hunts laborious.
Fox came along with them one day.
Outside the grove he wished to stay
So he could hear what would betide
16 Before he'd choose to go inside.
The lion sat and fox did eye;
Then angrily he asked him why
He did not wish to come inside.

20 E li gupilz li respunt tant:
   'Sire,' fet il, 'n'i os aler,
   Kar n'en vei nul returner –
   Des bestes que einz entrerent
24 E pur vus veer i alerent.'
       De curt a rei est ensement:
   Teus i entre legerement,
   Meuz li vaudreit en sus ester
28 Pur nuveles escuter.

37 Del leün e del vilein

   Ci recunte d'un lïun
   Que prist un vilein a cumpainun.
   Entre eus cunterent lur parage,
 4 Si parlerent du lur lignage.
   Li lïuns dist, 'Fiz sui a rei.'
   Dist li vileins, 'Va ore od mei!'
   A un mur sunt amdui venu.
 8 Ileoc ad li leüns veü
   Defors la porte une peinture
   Cum un vilein par aventure
   Od sa hache oscist un leün.
12 Si apela sun cumpainun:
   'Ki fist ceste semblance ici?
   Humme u lïuns – Itant me di!'
   'Ceo fist un hum,' dist li vileins,
16 'Od ses engins e od ses meins.'
   Dunc ad li lïuns respundu,
   'Ceo est a tut puple coneü
   Que hum seit entailler e purtrere,
20 Mes li leüns nel seit pas fere.
   Ore en irums ensemble ça!'
   Li vileins veit; sil l'en mena
   A un chastel l'empereür.
24 Issi avient que en cel jur
   Aveient il jugé en plet
   Un barun, que ot mesfet.
   Pruvez esteit de traïsun,

20 And this is how the fox replied:
  'My lord, I do not dare go near,
  For I see no one reappear –
  No beasts who entered here and who
24 Thought they would pay a call on you.'
    At royal court the scene's akin
  For those who lightly go within.
  Better to keep away a pace
28 And listen first to what takes place.

37 The Lion and the Peasant

  This story tells about a lion
  Who took a peasant for companion.
  The two discussed their heritage;
4 They talked of rank and lineage.
  Said lion, 'A king's son I be.'
  The peasant said, 'Now come with me!'
  They soon came to a wall, those two.
8 The lion there could clearly view
  A painting at the entrance way
  Which did by chance a man display
  Using his axe to kill a lion.
12 The lion questioned his companion,
  'This painting here – How was it done?
  By man or lion – Say which one!'
  The peasant said, 'The work is man's.
16 He used his implements and hands.'
  At this the lion did declare,
  'It is a fact known everywhere:
  A man can paint, sculpt pictures, too.
20 These things a lion cannot do.
  Now come with me!' the lion said.
  The peasant was by lion led;
  They to a castle made their way.
24 The emperor there, that very day,
  Was passing judgment on a case:
  A baron and his deed most base.
  The king convicted him of treason

28 Sil fist geter a sun lïun –
   A lung tens ot esté gardez
   Dedenz sa curt enchaënez –
   E il l'ocist ignelepas;
32 Mes n'i garda armes ne dras.
   Li lïuns atant s'en depart
   E li vileins que mut fu tart
   Qu'il s'en fuissent de ileoc turné.
36 En la gastine s'en sunt alé.
   Par mi les landes trespasserent,
   Un autre lïun encuntrerent.
   A celui dit qu'il fet desrei
40 Qu'il meine le vilein od sei,
   Ki seit la fosse apareiller –
   U il purreient trebucher.
   Autresi seivent tut si parent –
44 Ja l'ocireit, si le cunsent.
   Li lïuns dist qu'il l(es) escharnist;
   Ne suffera pas qu'il ocesist
   Pur nule rien unc ne pensa!
48 Li vileins l'ot, sil mercia:
   Mut par li ad dit bon gré.
   Li lïuns li ad dunc demandé
   Si lui semblot cum einz ot fet.
52 Dit li vileins, 'Autrement vet!'
   'Jo vus dis einz,' fet li lïuns.
   'Ainz que fussums cumpainuns,
   Me mustrastes une peinture
56 Sur une pere par aventure.
   Mes jeo te ai plus verrur mustree,
   A descuvert l'as esgardee.'
      Par essample nus veut aprendre
60 Que nul ne deit nïent entendre
   A fable, ke est de mençuinge,
   Ne a peinture, que semble sunge.
   Ceo est a creire dunt hum veit l'ovre,
64 Que la verité tut descovre.

28 And had him thrown in with his lion –
A lion who'd been long constrained
Within the court where he was chained –
This lion killed him straightaway;
32 No heed of arms or of array.
The other lion now departed.
The peasant, anxious to get started,
To join with lion fled in haste.
36 The two soon came unto a waste.
And as they went across the heath,
Another lion they chanced to meet,
Who told our lion it was wrong
40 To travel with a man along;
The man knew how to make a pit –
And lions could fall into it.
This holds for all man's family –
44 He'd kill him now, if they'd agree.
Our lion said he did but taunt;
The peasant's murder he'd prevent,
For he would never thus behave!
48 The peasant heard, and thanks he gave:
May lion evermore be blessed.
The lion asked the peasant next
If all seemed as it was of yore.
52 Said he, 'Quite different from before!'
Said lion, 'Talking in the past,
Before our comradeship was fast,
I was, by you, a painting shown,
56 Which chanced to be upon a stone.
But what I've shown is far more true:
It's what you see in front of you.'
From this example we should know
60 Not to accept that something's so
From fables which are but false seeming
Or paintings similar to dreaming.
Believe only in what you see:
64 The truth revealed openly.

38 De la pulce e del chameil

Une pulce, ceo dit, jadis munta
Sur un chamail, sil chevacha
De si que en un autre cuntree.
4 Dunc s'est la pulce purpensee,
Si ad mercïé le chameil,
Que si süef dedenz sun peil
L'aveit ensemble od li portee;
8 Jamés par sei ne fust alee.
Pur sun travail la servireit
Mut volenters, si ele poeit.
Li chamel li ad respundu,
12 Que unc de li chargiez ne fu.
Ne ne sot que ele fust sur lui;
Ne que ele li fesist nul ennui.
    Issi vet de la povre gent:
16 Si as riches unt aprisement,
Forment les quident curucier,
Damage feire e ennuier.

39 Del hulchet e de la furmie

D'un hulchet cunte la maniere,
Que desque a une furmïere
El tens d'yvern esteit alez.
4 Par aventure est einz entrez;
Viande demanda e quist,
Kar n'en aveit nent, ceo dist,
En sa meisun n'en sun recet.
8 Dist la furmie, 'Quei as tu dunc fet,
Quant viande deüssez guainer
En aüst e tei purchacer?'
'Jeo chant,' fet il, 'e si deduis
12 A autres bestes, mes ore ne truis
Ki le me veule reguerduner:
Pur ceo m'estut ici arester.'
Dist la furmie, 'Chant ore a mei.
16 Par cele fei que jeo te dei

38 The Flea and the Camel

Once long ago there was a flea
Who climbed a camel; thus rode she
Until they reached another land.
4 The flea thought for a moment, and
She thanked the camel because he
Within his fur, so graciously
Had carried her; for she alone
8 Could never on that trip have gone.
Because he'd laboured hard, she would
Now serve him and do what she could.
The camel answered her to say
12 She'd been no burden anyway.
He had not known that she was there;
She had not been an irksome care.
  The same is true with poor folk when
16 They seek access to wealthy men:
They are convinced that they provoke,
Cause trouble, and annoy rich folk.

39 The Cricket and the Ant

A cricket, in a former time,
Onto an anthill once did climb,
And this took place at winter tide.
4 The cricket chanced to go inside,
And there he sought and asked for bread,
For he had none at all, he said,
Not in his household or his haunt.
8 'What were you doing,' asked the ant,
'In August, when you should procure
Your food and make yourself secure?'
'I sing,' he said, 'bring pleasure to
12 All creatures, but I find none who
Will now return the same to me;
I've stopped by of necessity.'
The ant replied, 'Sing to me now.
16 In all good faith, I say to you

Meuz fust que tu te purchassasses
El meis d'aüst e si guainasses,
Que fussez si de freit murant
20 E a nului us viande querant!
Pur quei te durreie a manger,
Quant tu a mei ne puz aider?'
Pur ceo defent que nul ne vive,
24 En nunchaler n'en udive;
Sulum ceo que chescun deit feire
Se deit pener de bien atreire.
Plus est cheri s'il ad quei prendre,
28 Que si a autrui se deit entendre.

40 De la corneille e de la berbiz

Plest vus oïr de une corneile
Que s'asist sur le dos de une oeile.
Od le bek la feri durement,
4 Sa leine li toli asprement.
La berbiz li ad dit, 'Pur quei
Chevaches tu issi sur mei?
Remue tei! Si feras bien!
8 Seez une piece sur le chien,
Si fai a lui cum fez a mei!'
Dist la corneile, 'Par ma fei,
Ne t'estut mie travailler
12 Que tu me deies enseigner.
Jeo sui pieç'a tut enseignee –
Tant sui sage e veizïee –
Bien sai sur ki jeo puis sëer
16 E a seür tut remaner.'
Pur ceo nus mustre par respit
Que ceo est veirs ke l'em dit
Par essample e par repreche:
20 Bien seit chaz ki barbe il lecche!
Bien s'aparceit li vezïez
Les queils il peot aver suz piez.

It would in August have been best
To seek and store the year's harvest
And not be dying from the cold
20 Seeking your food at each household.
Now why should I give food to thee
When you cannot give aid to me?'
  Do not live lives indifferent,
24 Nor let yourselves be indolent.
For everyone should do his share;
To bring in goods must be your care.
What you provide is worth far more
28 Than what you turn to others for.

40 **The Crow and the Ewe**

So hear about this crow: to wit,
Upon a ewe's back she did sit.
Quite sharply with her beak she struck,
4 And cruelly the wool she plucked.
The ewe addressed her, thus spoke she:
'Why do you ride like this on me?
Get off at once! That would be well!
8 And go stay on the dog a spell,
And treat the dog as you have me!'
The crow replied, 'Well, glory be!
You need not be quite so perturbed
12 That you must spell out every word.
I understand what you advise –
I am that cunning and that wise –
I know upon whom I can be
16 And stay in great security.'
    This story serves to demonstrate
That it is true what folks relate
In lessons and fine rhetoric:
20 A cat well knows which beard to lick!
The sly are never at a loss
To know whom they can walk across.

41 Del riche humme e de dui serf

Un riches hume chevacha ja
Par mi un champ, si esgarda
U dui serf ensemble parloënt.
4 E si estreitement cunseiloënt –
Cum s'il fussent entre grant gent.
Vers eus turna delivrement.
Demanda lur pur quel mester
8 Voleient si estreit cunseiller,
Quant nul humme pres de els n'aveit
Ne nul lur parole n'en oeit.
Li un respundi al seignur
12 Qu'il n'aveient nule poür –
Einz lur semblot vezeüre
Qu'il parloënt de tel mesure.
   Ceo funt suvent li nunsavant:
16 De teu chose mustrent semblant,
Pur autre gent suzvezïer,
Que lur ne peot aver mester.

42 Del mire, del riche humme, e de sa fille

D'un mire cunte, ki segna
Un riche humme, qu'il garda
En une grande enfermeté.

41 The Rich Man and the Two Serfs

A rich man long ago did ride
Across a field, and there he spied
Two serfs engaged in conversation,
4 Huddled quite close in consultation –
Acting as if among great men.
The rich man turned toward them amain.
He asked them what was the affair
8 That brought them close in counsel there
When no one else was at all near
Nor any word they spoke could hear.
One answered the seignior and said,
12 It wasn't that they were afraid –
They thought that they appeared quite clever
When they conversed like that, however.
    The ignorant will oft act so
16 And will affect an outward show:
They think they outwit other folks,
Though they've no need of such a hoax.

42 The Doctor, the Rich Man, and His Daughter

There was a man of medicine
Who served a rich man, cared for him
During a malady most grave.

4 Puis aveit le sanc comandé
A sa fille, que ele l'esgardast
Que nule rien n'i adesast.
Par le sanc, ceo dist, conustreit
8 Quel enfermeté ses pere aveit.
La meschine porta le sanc
Enz sa chambre desuz un banc.
Mes mut li est mesavenu:
12 Kar tut le sanc ad espandu.
Ne l'osa dire ne mustrer;
Ne autre cunseil ne sot trover,
Mes se memes fist segner.
16 E sun sanc lessa refreider,
Tant que li mires l'ot veü;
E par le sanc aparceü
Que cil ert preinz qu'il ot lessé.
20 Le riche humme ad mut esmaié,
Qu'il quidot bien aver enfant.
Sa fille fist venir avant.
Tant par destreit, tant par amur,
24 Li estut cunustre la verrur:
Del sanc li dist que ele espandi,
E que li autre esteit de li.
    Autresi vet des tricheürs,
28 Des laruns, des boiseürs:
En ki la felunie meint,
Par eus memes sunt ateint.
Quant meins se gardent de estre pris,
32 Si sunt encuntré e ocis.

43 **Del vilein e de l'escarbot**

D'un vilein dit ki se giseit
Cuntre le soleil, se dormeit.
A dens giseit tut descovert,
4 E ses pertus esteit overt.
Uns escharboz dedenz entra,
E li vileins s'en esveilla.
Grant mal li fist, tant que a un mire

4 He drew some blood, and then he gave
   It to the daughter, trusted her
   To watch and keep the sample pure.
   For by that blood, he'd know, said he,
8 What was her father's malady.
   The young maid took the sample thence
   Into her room and to a bench.
   Alas, her fate did badly fare:
12 She spilled the blood she'd taken there.
   This deed she dared not tell or show
   And did not know what else to do
   Except to draw more blood – her own.
16 She got some blood, let it cool down
   Before the doctor came and viewed it.
   The doctor, seeing it, concluded
   It had from someone pregnant come.
20 At this, the rich man was struck dumb.
   He really thought he would give birth.
   And so he called his daughter forth.
   As much from love as from distress,
24 The daughter must the truth confess:
   She said she spilled what had been drawn;
   This other blood – it was her own.
      And thus it is with all beguilers;
28 The same holds true for thieves and liars:
   Those who with wickedness are fraught,
   By their own deeds they will be caught.
   Escape attempts will be in vain,
32 For thwarted they will be and slain.

43 The Peasant and the Beetle

The peasant of this story lay
Asleep out in the sun one day.
He lay face down, completely nude,
4 His anus could be clearly viewed.
A beetle into him did creep;
The peasant woke up from his sleep.
He went, for he was in such pain,

8 L'esteit alez cunter e dire.
  Li mires dist qu'il esteit preinz.
  Ore fu mut pis que ne fu einz,
  Kar le vileins bien le creï.
12 E li fous people quil l'oï.
  Dïent que ceo est signefiance.
  En poür sunt e en dutance –
  N'i ad celui ki bien ne creit,
16 Que grant mal lur avenir deit –
  Tant est fol peoples nuncreables,
  Que en veines choses nunverables
  Unt lur creance e lur espeir.
20 Le vilein gueitent pur saveir
  Par unt cil enfes deveit nestre.
  Li escarboz par la fenestre,
  U il entra, s'en est eissuz.
24 Dunc furent il tuz deceüz.
     Par ceste essample le vus di:
  Del nunsavant est autresi,
  Ki creient ceo que estre ne peot,
28 U vanitez le oste e muet.

44 Del vilein ki vit un autre od sa femme

D'un vilein cunte que gueita
Dedenz sun hus, si espia.
Un autre humme vit sur sun lit,
4 Od sa femme fist sun delit.
  'Allas!' fet il 'Quei ai jeo veü!'
  Dunc li ad la femme respundu:
  'Quei avez vus, beau sire, amis?'
8 'Un autre humme! Ceo m'ert avis,
  Sur le lit vus tient embracee!'
  Dunc dit la femme tut curucee,
  'Bien sai,' fet ele, 'ne dut mie,
12 Que ceo est vostre vielle folie;
  Tu ve[u]ls mençoinge tenir a veire.'
  'Jel vi,' fet il, 'sil dei bien creire.'
  'Fous es,' fet eles, 'si tu creiz

8 To see a doctor and complain.
  The doctor said that he was pregnant.
  Now worse than ever felt the peasant,
  For he believed the doctor's word.
12 And when the foolish people heard,
  They said they had an omen here,
  And all were filled with dread and fear –
  Because of him, of faith untrue,
16 Misfortune great would be their due –
  The foolish folk are so naïve
  That vanities they will believe,
  And put their faith in falsity.
20 They watched the peasant now to see
  Just how the baby's birth would go.
  The beetle, through the man's window
  Where it had entered, took its leave.
24 The foolish folk were thus deceived.
    This example serves to say
  The ignorant are oft this way:
  Believing that which cannot be,
28 They're swayed and changed by vanity.

44 The Peasant Who Saw Another with His Wife

It's said a peasant lay in wait
And spied within his household gate.
A man in his own bed he sighted
4 Who there with his own wife delighted.
'Alas!' he said. 'What have I spied!'
And this is how his wife replied:
'Fair lord, dear love, what do you see?'
8 'Another man! It seems to me
That he embraces you in bed!'
Then angrily the woman said,
'I'm very sure, it is no guess,
12 That this is your old foolishness;
You cling to lies as verity.'
Said he, 'I must trust what I see.'
'You're crazy,' she replied, 'if you

16 Pur verité quan ke tu veiz.'
   As mains le prent, od li l'en meine
   A une cuve de ewe pleine;
   Dedenz la cuve le fist garder.
20 Puis li cumence a demander
   Qu'il veit dedenz; cil li dit
   Que sun ymagine memes vit.
   'Pur ceo,' dist ele, 'n'iés tu pas
24 Dedenz la cuve od tuz tes dras;
   Si tu veies une semblance.
   Tu ne de[i]z pas aver creance
   En tes oilz, que mentent si sovent.'
28 Dist li vileins, 'Jeo me repent!
   Chescun deit meuz creire e saver
   Ceo que sa femme li dit pur veir
   Que ceo que cis faus oilz veient,
32 Que par veüe le foleient!'
      Par ceste essample nus devise
   Que meuz vaut sen e quointise –
   E plus aide a meinte gent –
36 Que sis aveirs ne si parent.

45 Del vilein ki vit sa femme od sun dru

   D'un autre vilein voil ci cunter,
   Que od sa femme vit aler
   Vers la forest sun dru od li.
 4 Aprés eus vet; cil s'en fuï,
   Si s'est dedenz le bois musciez,
   E cil returne tut iriez.
   Sa femme leidist e blasma;
 8 E la dame li demanda
   Pur quei parlast issi vers li.
   E ses baruns li respundi
   Qu'il ot veü sun lecheür,
12 Ki li fist hunte e deshonur,
   E aler od li vers la forest.
   'Sire,' fet ele, 'si vus plest,
   Pur amur Deu, dites me veir!

16 Believe all that you see is true.'
   She took him, led him by the hand
   Unto a vat of water and
   She made him peer into the vat.
20 The woman next demanded that
   He tell her what he saw inside.
   He saw his image, he replied.
   'Just so. And you are not,' she said,
24 'Inside that vat completely clad.
   What you see here is but semblance,
   And you ought not to give credence
   To eyes which often lies present.'
28 The peasant said, 'I do repent!
   Each one had best believe and know
   Whatever his wife says, is so!
   And not believe what false eyes see;
32 Their vision can be trickery!'
      From this example comes this lore:
   Good sense and shrewdness are worth more –
   And will, to many, more help give –
36 Than wealth or any relative.

45 The Peasant Who Saw His Wife with Her Lover

   Another peasant I'll tell about
   Who saw his wife once venture out
   Into the forest with her lover.
 4 He chased; the man ran off for cover
   And hid among the shrubbery.
   The peasant went back angrily;
   He cursed his wife, took her to task.
 8 What could the lady do but ask
   Why he addressed her in this way.
   Her husband answered her, to say
   Her paramour he had just seen,
12 And thus disgraced and shamed he'd been.
   He'd seen them go among the trees.
   'My lord,' she said, 'now if you please,
   For love of God, tell me the truth!

16 Quidastes vus humme veeir
   Aler od mei? Nel me celer!'
   'Jel vi,' fet ele, 'el bois entrer.'
   'Lasse,' fet il, 'morte sui!
20 Demain murrai u uncore hui!
   A ma aiole avient tut autresi –
   E a ma mere – ker jel vi:
   Un poi devant lur finement
24 (Ceo fu sceü apertement)
   Que uns bachelers les cundueient
   E que od eus autre rien n'aveient.
   Ore sai jeo bien, pres est ma fins.
28 Mandez, sire, tost mes cusins,
   Si departirums nostre aveir;
   N'os el secle plus remaneir!
   Od tute la meie partie
32 Me metrai en une abeïe.'
   Li vileins l'ot, merci li crie.
   'Lessez ester, ma bele amie!
   Ne departez de mei einsi!
36 Mençunge fu quanque jeo vi!'
   'N'i os,' fet ele, 'plus arester,
   Kar de m'alme m'estut penser,
   Ensurketut pur la grant hunte
40 Dunt tu as fet si grant cunte.
   Tuz jurz me sereit repruvé
   Que vilement avereie vers vus erré
   Si vus ne me jurez serement,
44 Si quil veient mi parent,
   Que n'en veïstes hume od mei.
   Plus afïerez la vostre fei
   Que jamés mot n'en sunerez
48 Ne jamés nel me repruverez.'
   'Volunters, dame,' il li respunt.
   A un muster ensemble vunt.
   La li jura ceo que ele quist –
52 E plus asez qu'il i mist.
      Pur ceo dit hum en repruver
   Que femmes seivent enginner;
   Les vezïez e li nunverrable
56 Unt un art plus ke deable.

16 You think you saw a man forsooth
   Go off with me? Now be quite honest!'
  'I saw him go into the forest.'
  'Oh, woe!' she said. 'I'm dead! For I
20 Tomorrow – even today – shall die!
   It happened to my grandmother –
   I saw it, yes – and to my mother,
   That just before the time they died
24 (This was well known both far and wide),
   A young man led the two away
   Though they'd no cause to go that way.
   I know for sure, my end is near.
28 My lord, call all my cousins here.
   Now let's divide our goods of worth;
   I dare not waste my time on earth!
   With all the share that comes to me,
32 I'll go into a nunnery.'
   The peasant heard and cried for peace.
  'My lovely sweetheart dear, now cease!
   Do not take leave of me this way!
36 It was a lie I saw today!'
  'To wait here longer, I don't dare,'
  She said; 'my soul must be my care.
   Especially after the dishonour
40 You've done to me by your false rumour –
   People will ever chastise me
   For wronging you so wickedly.
   Unless you swear an oath to me,
44 Which all my relatives can see,
   That you saw no man with me there.
   Upon your faith you must now swear
   That you'll not speak of this again
48 And will from chiding me abstain.'
  'Gladly, lady!' he gave consent.
   Together to a church they went.
   He swore to all she'd asked him for –
52 Whatever he could do – and more.
    And so, forewarned all men should be
   That women know good strategy.
   They've more art in their craft and lies
56 Than all the devil can devise.

46 **Des oiseaus e del cuccu**

Des oiseaus dit que s'asemblerent
A parlement, si esgarderent
Que entr'eus deüssent aver rei
4 Quis governast par dreite fei.
Chescun de eus numa le sun
A fere cele electïun.
Tuz esteient dunc esbaï,
8 Quant del cuccu oient le cri.
Ne surent quels oiseus ceo fu,
Mes que tut tens diseit, 'cuccu.'
Mut le peot l'um de loinz oïr,
12 Kar tut le bois fet retentir.
Tuz diseient en lur gargun
E afermerent par raisun
Que cil oisel, ke si chauntout,
16 E si grant noise demenout,
Deveit bien estre rei e sire
De governer un grant empire.
S'il fust si pruz e si vaillanz
20 En ses ovres cum en ses chanz,
A seignur le voleient aver.
Mes il voleient primes saver
Sun estre e sun cuntenement.
24 Pur ceo gardent communement
Ki deit aler en lur message:
La mesenge, que mut est sage.
A parceivre en verité

46 The Birds and the Cuckoo

It's said that birds, a multitude,
Did hold a meeting and conclude
That they should have a king, one who
4 Would govern and be just and true.
The birds agreed that sound of voice
Should be the basis of their choice.
They all were taken by surprise
8 When first they heard the cuckoo's cries.
What bird this was, nobody knew,
But that all day he said, 'cuckoo.'
From far he could be heard with ease;
12 His call would echo in the trees.
Each in his parlance, every bird,
Set forth his reasons and averred
This bird with song so clamorous,
16 So noisy and vociferous,
Should well their king and lord become
And govern thus a great kingdom.
Were he as worthy and as strong
20 In actions as he was in song,
They wanted him their lord to be.
Before that, though, they wished to see
His nature and his habitude.
24 They met on this and did conclude
Which bird they ought to send as page:
The titmouse, who was very sage,
With facts a shrewd discoverer,

28 L'unt d'ici qu'a li enveié.
La mesenge vola tut dreit
D'ici a l'arbre u il esteit.
Mut s'esteit pres de li asise,
32 Si l'esgarda par grant quointise.
Ne preisa gueres sa manere,
Kar il feseit mauveise chere.
Uncore vodra plus haut munter,
36 Sun curage volt espruver.
Sur une branche en haut saili,
Desur le dos li esmeulti.
Unc li cuccu mot ne dist
40 Ne peiur semblant ne l'en fist.
Arere s'en vet la mesenge;
Le cuccu leidist e blastenge –
Ja de lui ne ferunt seignur!
44 As autres dist la deshonur
E la hunte qu'il li fist grant:
'Unc ne mustra peiur semblant!
Si uns granz oiseus li mesfeseit,
48 Mauveisement s'en vengereit –
Quant envers li ne se osa prendre,
Ki est de tuz oiseus la mendre.
Eslisent tel ki seit vaillant,
52 Pruz e sage e enpernant.
Reis deit estre mut dreiturers,
En justise redz e fiers.'
A cel cunseil se sunt tenu,
56 E si unt esgardé e veü
Que de l'egle ferunt rei.
E si vus sai bien dire pur quei:
Li egles ad bele grandur,
60 Si est asez de grant valur;
Mut est sobres e atemprez.
Si une feiz est bien saülez,
Bien repeot juner aprés,
64 Qu'il n'est de preir trop engrés.
Prince se deit bien reposer,
Ne se deit mie trop deliter,
Lui ne sun regné aviler,

28 Was sent out as their messenger.
   The titmouse left immediately
   And flew straight to the cuckoo's tree.
   She perched in close proximity
32 And gave him careful scrutiny.
   His manner gave her no delight:
   He was indeed a dreadful sight.
   Yet higher still she wished to settle
36 So she could verify his mettle.
   She jumped up to a higher limb
   And defecated over him.
   The cuckoo did not say a word
40 And did not seem the least disturbed.
   The titmouse to the rest returned;
   The cuckoo bird she cursed and spurned –
   Never should he be made seignior!
44 She told them of his dishonour
   And how, by her, he'd been disgraced:
   'He did not seem to mind the least!
   Were a large bird to do him wrong,
48 This bird's revenge would not be strong –
   Considering that he has not stirred
   Against the very smallest bird.
   We ought to choose one stout of heart,
52 Who's noble, valorous, and smart.
   A king should be one very righteous
   Who's firm and stern in dealing justice.'
   With this advice, all did agree,
56 For everyone could clearly see
   That they should make the eagle king.
   And I'll give you the reasoning:
   The eagle's grand and glorious,
60 And he's especially valorous,
   And very staid and dignified.
   And once the eagle's satisfied,
   He fasts again quite easily
64 And does not lust too much for prey.
   A prince should be well-rested, too;
   In his delights not overdo;
   Nor shame himself or his domain,

68 Ne la povre gent eissilier.
   Issi l'unt fet cum jeo vus di.
      Par cest essample nus mustre ici
   Que hum ne deit pas fere seignur
72 De mauveis humme jangleür,
   U n'i a si parole nun.
   Tel se nobleie par tençun
   E veut manacer e parler,
76 Que mut petit fet a duter.

47 Del vilein e de sun cheval

   D'un vilein nus cunte ici,
   Que aveit un cheval nurri.
   Tant l'ot gardé, qu'il le vot vendre,
4 Deners volt aver e prendre.
   Pur vint souz, ceo dist, le durra.
   Un sun veisin le bargena,
   Mes ne vot mie tant doner;
8 Al marché les covient aler.
   Cil a ki le cheval esteit,
   Otri l'autre qu'il le larreit
   Al pris que cil humme le metreit
12 Que encuntre eus primes vendreit,
   Desqu'il vendreient al marché
   De tutes parz l'unt otrïé.
   Quant el marché furent entre,
16 Un humme borne unt encuntré.
   Qui le destre oil aveit perdu.
   Ensemble od eus l'unt retenu;
   Si li demandent sun avis
20 Que del cheval die le pris.
   Il lur respunt ke dis souz vaut –
   S'il est ignels e süef e haut
   Cil ki le cheval bargena,
24 De la sue part l'otria –
   Mes li autre le cuntredit,
   Kar trop l'aveit preisé petit.
   Tant l'en ad dit e chastïé,
28 Que a la justise l'en ad mené,

68 Nor cause the poor folk undue pain.
  The birds did what I said they'd do.
      And so this lesson's shown to you:
  Do not have as your lord someone
72 Who's wicked and a charlatan.
  For all his words, he's but verbose;
  In argument, he's grandiose.
  Although he'll talk and threaten harm,
76 He cannot stir up much alarm.

47 The Peasant and His Horse

  Here's one more story from my source:
  A peasant once had raised a horse.
  He'd kept the horse for quite a spell,
4 But now he felt he had to sell.
  'For twenty sous! A gift!' he said.
  A neighbour tried a lower bid
  And would not to his price consent;
8 So off to market they both went.
  The horse's owner posed this course:
  He'd let the other have the horse –
  And as for price, it would be set
12 By the first man that they would meet
  When they got to the market-place.
  That, they agreed, would be the case.
  They reached the market, went inside,
16 And met a man who was one-eyed.
  He'd no right eye, for he had lost it.
  By our two men he was accosted.
  They asked him now for his advice:
20 What ought to be the horse's price?
  He answered it was worth ten sous –
  If it was fast and rode well, too.
  The man who wished the horse to buy
24 Was fully ready to comply –
  But now the other man said no,
  Claiming the price was set too low.
  The buyer then complained so much
28 He took the matter to a judge.

Si li mustra cument il fu.
E li vileins ad respundu,
Ja sun cheval n'avra pur tant:
32 Ne li tendra cel covenant.
Cil vot mustrer raisnablement
Que bien li deit tenir covent –
Quant pur lui ne fu mespreisez
36 Ne pur l'autre plus avilez;
Unc nel cunut ne nel vit mes.
Li vileins li ad dit aprés
Qu'il ne deit tenir sun esgart,
40 Kar il nel vit fors de l'une part.
Pur ceo l'aveit demi preisié,
Qu'il n'en veeit fors la meité.
Ne pot mie d'un oil veeir
44 Quei li chevals deveit valeir.
Icil, ki entre eus esteient
E le vilein parler oieie(e)nt,
Le turnerent en gaberie;
48 N'i ad celui ki ne s'en rie.
Od sun cheval s'en est alez:
Par bel parler s'est deliverez.
Pur ceo volt ici enseigner
52 E mustrer bien e doctriner:
Ki que unc se sent entrepris
E n'eit od sei ses bons amis
Ki sacent cunseil doner,
· 56 Que bien deit contreguaiter,
Si parler deit devant justise,
Que en sa parole ait tel cointise –
Par mi tute sa mesprisun,
60 Que seit semblable a la reisun.
Li sages hum en grant destreit
Turne suvent sun tort en dreit.

48 Del larun e de la sorcere

D'un larun cunte ki se giseit
Suz un buissun, si se dormeit.
Une sorcere le trova;

The situation he explained.
The peasant, in reply, maintained
The horse, for that, could not be sold:
32 He'd not to their agreement hold.
The buyer started to expound
On how by contract each was bound –
He thought the horse not wrongly priced
36 Nor that its worth was minimized.
The peasant said, this one-eyed man
We're never going to see again.
They ought not with his view abide
40 For he could only see one side.
His price was just a moiety
For half was all that he could see.
One eye could simply not suffice
44 To estimate the horse's price.
And then the people who were near
And who, this peasant's speech did hear,
Thought that it was but silly chaff;
48 Not one among them did not laugh.
Then off the man and horse did walk;
He'd saved himself through fancy talk.
   This story serves to educate,
52 To show us well and demonstrate
That if one finds he's in a snare
And none of his good friends is there
Who could provide some wise direction,
56 He'd better act with circumspection
When he should speak before the court,
And make quite cunning his report –
So what he's done, however awful,
60 Should thereby seem both right and lawful.
The wise man in a dreadful plight
Can often turn his wrong to right.

48 The Thief and the Witch

This is the story of a thief
Who lay under a bush, asleep.
It chanced a witch found him; she stopped,

4 Lez lui s'asist, si l'esveilla.
Sil cumença a cunseiller
Que tuz jurs tienge sun mester.
Ele par tut lui aidera
8 En tuz les lius u il irra.
Ne lui estut nïent duter,
Pur quei la voille reclamer.
Dunc fu li leres sanz poür.
12 Eissi avient que par un jur
Fu entrepris a larecin,
Si l'i troverent si veisin.
Si li dïent qu'il ert penduz,
16 Kar malement s'est cuntenuz.
Il ad la sorcere mandee,
Si l'ad a cunseil apelee,
Si li prie ke lui aidast.
20 Cele li dist qu'il ne dutast,
A seür fust e tut en pes.
Quant des furches esteient pres,
Si l'apela li leres a sei.
24 'Dame,' fet il, 'deliverez mei!'
'Va,' fet ele, 'ne dutez rien;
Jeo te deliverai tresbien.'
Quant el col li mistrent la hart,
28 Cil cria de l'autre part –
La terce feiz – a la sorcere
Que li membrast en queile manere
L'aseüra suz le buissun.
32 Ele respunt par faus sermun:
'Puis cel hure te ai bien aidé –
E meintenu e cunseillé.
Mes ore te vei si demener,
36 Que ne te sai cunseil duner.
Purpense tei quei tu feras –
Ja par mei cunseil n'averas!'
Pur ceo chastie tute gent
40 Qu'il ne creient – Deus le defent! –
En augure n'en sorcerie;
Kar trahiz est ki s'i afie!
Le cors en est mis en eissil;
44 E l'alme vet en grant peril.

4 And sat down near, and woke him up.
  She started trying to persuade
  The thief to keep for aye his trade.
  She said she'd help him constantly
8 No matter where he chanced to be.
  He need fear nothing more at all
  If he would just give her a call.
  Thus was the thief afraid of nought.
12 And then one day it came about
  That he was caught midst thieving labours
  And was discovered by his neighbours.
  They said that hanged this thief must be
16 For he had acted wickedly.
  He called the witch and asked her to
  Advise him now what he should do.
  He prayed for her to give him aid.
20 She told him not to be afraid;
  He should stay calm and confident.
  As toward the gallows next they went,
  The thief called for the witch. Said he,
24 'Ho! Lady! Now deliver me!'
  'Go on,' she said, 'and don't you worry,
  For I will rescue you most surely.'
  Soon after, when a rope was tied
28 Around his neck, once more he cried –
  Now for the third time – to the witch
  That she remember those things which
  She'd promised him beneath the bush.
32 With lying tongue, she answered thus:
  'Since then, I've been much help to you –
  Supported and advised you, too.
  But when I see you act this way,
36 I don't know what wise words to say.
  Decide, yourself, what you should do –
  I'll no more be advising you!'
    All folks this warning should receive:
40 They ought not – God forbid! – believe
  In witchcraft or in augury;
  Such faith brings only treachery!
  The body is in torment cast;
44 The soul, it goes in peril vast.

49 Del fevre e de la cuinee

Uns fevres fist une cuinee
Bien trenchante e bien forgee.
Mes ne s'en pot de rien aider
4 N'od li ne sot cument trencher,
De ci que ele fust enmancee
De aucun fust e aparaillee.
Al bois ala pur dema(u)nder
8 A chescun fust qu'il pot trover,
Al quel il li loënt entendre,
Del queil il puisse mance prendre.
Quant ensemble en eurent parlé,
12 Communement li unt löé
Qu'il prenge de la neire espine;
Neïs l'escorce e la racine
Est mut dure a depescer –
16 De cel la peot bien enmancer.
Li fevres ad lur cunseil creü,
Kar ne l'unt mie deceü.
De l'espine ad la mance pris,
20 Si l'ad a sa cuinee asis.
Od memes icele cuinee
Ad puis l'espine detrenchee.
Mal guerdun li ad rendu,
24 Que de lui ot sun mance eü.
　　Tut autresi est des mauveis,
Des tresfeluns e des engres:
Quant uns produm les met avant
28 E par lui sunt riche e manant,
S'il surpuient meuz de lui;
Tuz jurs li frunt hunte e ennui.
A celui funt il tut le pis
32 Ki al desus les ad mis.

50 Del lu e del mutun

Jadis avient que un lu pramist
Que char ne mangereit, ceo dist,
Les quarante jurs de quareme;

49 The Blacksmith and the Axe

Next of a blacksmith I will tell
Who made an axe – quite sharp, forged well.
But for his use it was not fit;
4 He could not chop his wood with it
Until a handle could be fashioned
To which his axe could then be fastened.
So off into the woods went he
8 To ask whatever trees he'd see
For their advice on which tree could
Supply a handle from its wood.
The trees consulted on this question
12 And then came up with this suggestion:
That it be from the blackthorn wrought,
For even this tree's bark and root
Were very hard to break or split –
16 A handle could be made from it.
The blacksmith their advice believed,
And by them he was not deceived.
He from this thorn a handle made
20 Then fixed it to the axe's blade.
And with this very axe, now he
Chopped to the ground the blackthorn tree.
He gave it thus poor recompense
24 In that his handle had come thence.
    With wicked folks the same holds true –
With those corrupt and evil, too:
When someone good helps them advance,
28 So they gain wealth and affluence,
They think they're better now than he;
They bring him harm and infamy.
To him they do the worst disgrace
32 Who set them up in their high place.

50 The Wolf and the Sheep

A wolf once promised, long ago,
That eating meat he would forgo,
Said he, for forty days of Lent;

4 A tant aveit mis sun esme.
En un bois trova un mutun
Cras e refait, sanz la tuisun.
A sei memes demanda,
8 'Quei est ceo,' fet il, 'que jeo vei la?
Ceo est un mutun, m'est avis!
Si pur ceo nun que jeo ai pramis –
Que nule char ne mangereie –
12 De sun costé me referee!
Ore ai,' fet il, 'dit grant folie!
Jeol vei tut sul sanz cumpainie.
Ceo m'est avis, si jeo nel gart,
16 Teus vendra d'aucune part,
Que l'en merra ensemble od sei –
Si nel larra nïent pur mei!
Jeol puis bien prendre pur un mutun,
20 Sil mangerai pur un saumun;
Meuz vaut li saumun a manger,
E sil peot l'um vendre plus cher.'
   Si vet de humme de mauveis quer:
24 Il ne peot lesser a nul fu[e]r
Sun surfet ne sa glutunerie.
Ja encuntre sa lecherie
Humme ne femme lecheresse
28 Ne gardera vou ne pramesse.

51 De la singesse e de sun enfant

Une singesse ala mustrant
A tutes bestes sun enfant.
Cil la teneient pur fole
4 E par semblant e par parole,
Tant que a un lïun le ala mustrer.
Si li comence a demander
S'il fu mut beus, e il li dit
8 Une plus leide beste ne vit.
Porter li ruve a sa meisun,
E si recorde ceste reisun:
'Chescun gupil prise sa cue,

4 Exactly that was his intent.
  He found a sheep among the trees,
  All plump and fat, not too much fleece.
  The wolf now asked himself, said he,
8 'And what is this that here I see?
  Why, I believe it is a sheep!
  If I had not my pledge to keep –
  That from all meat I would abstain –
12 I'd look at those fat flanks again!
  How stupidly I've talked!' said he.
  'The sheep is all alone, I see.
  I think that if I don't take care,
16 Someone will come and grab a share,
  Then off with it that one will flee –
  And there'll be nothing left for me!
  I'll make that sheep a tasty dish
20 And think of it as salmon fish;
  For salmon tastes superior
  And also costs a great deal more.'
    With one of wicked heart, it's so:
24 He's never able to let go
  Of surfeit or of gluttony.
  Responding to this lechery,
  A man or woman lecherous
28 Will not keep vows or promises.

51 The Monkey and Her Baby

Once there was a monkey-lady
  Who showed all animals her baby.
  They thought this mother quite absurd
4 Both in her manner and her word,
  But then she did to lion go.
  She asked him first if it weren't so –
  That it was beautiful. Said he,
8 An uglier beast he'd yet to see.
  He ordered her to take it home
  And keep in mind this axiom:
  'Every fox his tail does prize,

12 Si se merveille que ele est sue.'
   Cele s'en va triste e dolente.
   Un urs encuntre enmi la sente.
   Li urs estut, si l'esgarda.
16 Par quointise l'areisuna.
   'Vei jeo,' fet il, 'ileoc l'enfant –
   Dunt les bestes parolent tant –
   Que tant par est beus e gentilz?'
20 'Oïl,' fet ele, 'ceo est mes filz.'
   'Bailez le ça, tant que jo le bes.
   Kar jeol voil veer plus pres.'
   Cele le baile, e il le prent,
24 Si l'ad mangé hastivement.
      Pur ceo ne devereit nul mustrer
   Sa priveté ne sun penser.
   De tel chose peot humme joïr,
28 Que ne peot mit a tuz pleisir.
   Par descoverance vient grant mals;
   N'est pas li secles tut leals.

52 **Del dragun e del vilein**

   Ore cunterai d'un dragun,
   Que un vilein prist a cumpainun;
   E cil suvent li premetteit
 4 Que lëaument lui servireit.
   Li dragun le vout esprover,
   Cum il se poeit en lui fïer.
   Un oef li cumanda a garder,
 8 Si dist qu'il voleit errer.
   De l'oef garder mut li preia.
   E li vileins li demanda,
   Pur quei li cumandot einsi.
12 E li draguns li respundi
   Que dedenz l'of ot enbatu
   Trestut sa force e sa vertu;
   Tost sereit mort, s'il fust brusez.
16 Quant li dragun fu esloinez,
   Si s'est li vileins purpensez:

12 And marvels greatly that it's his.'
Sad and depressed, she went from there.
Along the way she met a bear.
Stock still the bear stood and assessed her.
16 Then cunningly the bear addressed her,
'Do I see here that infant small –
The talk of every animal –
The beautiful and noble one?'
20 'Indeed,' she said, 'this is my son.'
'Oh let me hold and kiss the dear.
I'd like to see it closer here.'
She gave it to the bear, and he
24 Took it and ate it hastily.
      And for this reason you should not
Disclose your secret or your thought.
Some things can bring delight to one,
28 Which to some others prove no fun.
Disclosure brings iniquity;
This world has no integrity.

52 The Dragon and the Peasant

Now to a dragon's tale attend
Who had a peasant for a friend.
This peasant promised frequently
4 To serve the dragon faithfully.
The dragon wanted to make sure
The man's allegiance was secure.
He asked the man an egg to shield
8 And said he wished to go afield.
He begged the man to watch it well.
The peasant asked him then to tell
Why he was making this request.
12 The dragon, answering, confessed
That in that egg he had closed tight
All of his potency and might.
Were it to break, he soon would die.
16 But when the dragon went away,
The peasant thought to this effect:

Que l'of n'ert pur lui gardez.
Par l'of ocira le dragun,
20 Sun or avera tut a bandun.
Quant l'of esteit depesciez,
E li dragun fu repeirez,
L'escale vit gisir a tere.
24 Si li cumença [a] enquere
Pur quei ot l'of si mesgardé.
Ore seit il bien sa volenté,
Bien aparceit sa tricherie.
28 Departi est lur cumpainie.
    Pur ceo nus dit en cest sermun,
Que a tricheür ne a felun
Ne deit l'um comander sun or,
32 Ne sa vie, ne sun tresor.
En coveitus ne en aver
Ne se deit nul trop afïer.

53 **Del reclus e del vilein**

D'un reclus cunte ki aveit
Un vilein, que od lui esteit.
Quant li reclus de Deu parlat,
 4 E li vileins li demandat,
Pur quei Adam manga le fruit,
Par quei le people aveit destruit –
E, quant il la pume manga,
 8 Pur quei Deu ne li parduna.
Al reclus suvent en pesa,
Tant que a une feiz se purpensa
Que le vilein apeisereit
12 De la demande qu'il feseit.
Une grande gate demanda,
Sur une table l'adenta,
Une suriz ot desuz mise.
16 Puis defendi que en nule guise
Al vilein qu'il n'i adesast
Ne ke desuz ne [re]gardast;

That he would not that egg protect.
He'd make the dragon die by this,
20 And all the gold would then be his.
He smashed the egg to smithereens.
The dragon, back from venturings,
Sees on the ground that egg shells lie.
24 And so he starts by asking why
His egg has been so poorly tended.
He sees now what the man intended
And understands his treachery.
28 Thus ended camaraderie.
    You've heard this story for this reason:
To men of wickedness and treason
Do not your precious gold consign,
32 And not your life, or treasure fine.
The greedy and penurious
Are never to be trusted much.

53 The Hermit and the Peasant

Here is a hermit's tale of old.
A peasant stayed with him, I'm told.
And when the hermit God would mention,
 4 The peasant then would always question
Why Adam ate the fruit that day
Corrupting all humanity –
And when he ate the apple, then
 8 Why God had not forgiven him.
This plagued the hermit constantly
Until he figured out one day
How he an answer could provide;
12 The peasant would be satisfied.
The hermit a large bowl requested,
And face down on the table placed it,
And under it a mouse put he.
16 Then this he forbade utterly:
The man must not go near the bowl,
And must not look beneath at all;

Kar il ireit a un muster
20 A ureisun pur Deu preer.
Quant li reclus s'en fu alez,
S'est li vileins purpensez
Que grant merveille li sembla
24 De la gate qu'il garda.
Ne se pot mie astenir
Qu'il ne la voille descovrir
Pur veer i ceo ke desuz fu.
28 Quant la osta, si ad veü
La suriz – ke lui eschapa.
Mes quant sis sires repeira,
Mut s'en curuça durement,
32 Si demanda par maltalent
Pur quei ot la gate ostee,
N'ot sa defense pru gardee.
Le vilein li respunt aprés,
36 'Sire' fet il, 'jeo ne poi mes.
U li queors me deüst partir,
U jeo l'alasse descoverir.'
'U est la suriz devenue?
40 Pur quei ne l'as detenue?
La folie vus fust pardonee.'
'Tost,' fet il, 'me fu eschapee.'
'Ami,' fet il, 'ore les ester!
44 Ne voilez mes Adam blamer,
Si le fruit de l'arbre manga,
Que nostre sire li devea.
Li deables li cunseilla,
48 Que par sa femme l'enginna,
E li pramist si grant honur,
Que per sereit al Creatur.'
Pur ceo ne deit nul encuper
52 Autrui fesance ne blamer
Ne mettre fame sur sun preme;
Chescun reprenge sei meme!
Tel quide blamer le fet d'autrui,
56 Que meuz devereit reprendre lui.

For he was off to church that day
20 Where unto God he wished to pray.
   Then when the hermit had set out,
   The man began to think about
   How good it seemed, how marvellous,
24 This bowl that in his keeping was.
   The peasant now could not forbear:
   He must discover what was there
   By seeing what was under it.
28 He raised the bowl, and found, to wit –
   The mouse – who quickly ran away.
   But when his lord returned that day,
   The hermit was upset and mad,
32 Asking to know, in temper bad,
   Why he had raised the bowl up, and
   Why he had done what had been banned.
   Then this reply the peasant made:
36 'I could not stand it, sir,' he said.
   'My heart and body would have split,
   If I had not looked under it.'
   'Now what has happened to the mouse?
40 If you at least had kept him close,
   I'd pardon your stupidity.'
   'It ran away so fast!' said he.
   'Friend, let it be!' his lord exclaimed.
44 'Now Adam should no more be blamed
   If from the tree he ate the fruit
   Although our Lord forbade he do it.
   It was the devil who advised it
48 And slyly through his wife devised it,
   And promised him such majesty
   His Maker's equal he would be.'
      One ought not others inculpate
52 Nor others' deeds denunciate,
   Nor of one's neighbour, spread false news.
   Let everyone himself accuse!
   He who condemns another's deed
56 Ought to reproach himself instead.

54 Del vilein ki ura aver un cheval

D'un vilein cunte ki entra
En un muster e si ura.
Un sun cheval aveit mut cher;
4 Si l'atacha hors del muster.
A Deu requist qu'il li aidast
E que un autretel cheval li donast.
Tant cum [il] fist ceste ureisun,
8 Sun cheval emblent li larun.
Quant il fu del muster eissuz,
Si esteit si cheval perduz.
Arere vet hastivement,
12 Si prie Deu devotement
Que autre chose ne requereit –
N'autre cheval mar le dureit –
Mes face li aver le suen –
16 Kar il n'avera jamés si buen!
   Pur ceo ne deit nul hum preier
De plus aver qu'il n'a mester;
Ceo gart ke Deus ad doné,
20 Si li suffise en lëauté.

55 Del vilein ki pria pur sa femme e ses enfanz

Un vilein ala al muster
Suventefeiz pur Deu prier.
A Deu requist qu'il li eidast
4 E que sa femme cunseillast –
E ses enfanz – e nului plus.
Ceste preere aveit en us.
Sovent le dist od si haut cri
8 Que un autre vilein l'entendi,
Si li respunt hastivement:
'Deus te maudie omnipotent,
Ta femme e tes enfanz petiz –
12 E nuls autres ne seit maudiz!'
   Par ceste essample volt retreire:
Chescun deit tele priere feire,
Que a la gent seit pleisable
16 E a Deu seit acceptable.

54 The Peasant Who Prayed for a Horse

Next is a peasant's tale: One day
He went into a church to pray.
He had a horse he treasured much;
4 He tied this horse outside the church.
He sought God's help, asked if He would
Provide a second horse as good.
But while he offered up this prayer,
8 Thieves stole the peasant's horse from there.
And when out of the church came he,
His horse had vanished utterly.
In haste the man went back inside,
12 And very piously he prayed
That God not grant him anything –
Another horse He need not bring –
Just let him his own horse regain –
16 He'd not have one as good again!
　　Nobody ought to pray, therefore,
To have more than his needs call for.
He ought to keep what God hands out
20 Which should suffice beyond all doubt.

55 The Peasant Who Prayed for His Wife and Children

A peasant, in an olden day,
Would often go to church to pray.
He prayed that God would aid provide
4 And asked the Lord his wife to guide –
His children, too – but no one more.
He always made this very prayer.
He often raised his voice so high,
8 Another peasant heard him cry
And answered him thus hastily:
'May God omnipotent curse thee,
Your wife, and those small babes of yours –
12 And to nobody else, this curse!'
　　Thus this example serves to say:
Each one must pray in such a way
That folks will think agreeable
16 And God will find acceptable.

56 Del vilein e de sa caue

D'un vilein cunte ki aveit
Une caue qu'il nurisseit.
Tant la nurri que ele parla.
4 Un sun veisin la li tua.
Cil s'en clama a la justise,
Si li cunta en queile guise
Icil oisel suleit parler
8 Les matinees e chanter.
Li juges dit qu'il ot mesfet;
Celui fist sumundre a pleit.
De cordewan prist une pel,
12 Si l'ad mise suz sun mantel.
L'un des chés leise dehors pendre,
Que li juges deüst entendre
Qu'il li aporte pur luier,
16 Que de sun pleit li deive aider.
Le mantel suvent entreovri,
Tant que li juges le choisi.
L'autre vilein fist apeler,
20 Que ert venu a lui clamer.
De la caue li demanda,
Quei ceo esteit que ele chanta
E queile parole ele diseit.
24 Cil respundi qu'il ne saveit.
'Quant tu,' fet il, 'rien ne saveies,
Ne sa parole n'entendeies,
Ne nïent n'esteit sa chançons,
28 Ne tu n'en deiz aver respuns.'
Cil s'en ala sanz sa dreiture –
Pur le lüer dunt cist prist cure.
    Pur ceo ne deit prince ne reis
32 Ses cumandemenz ne ses leis
A coveitus mettre en bailie;
Kar sa dreiture en ert perie.

56 The Peasant and His Jackdaw

There was a peasant, as I've heard,
Who once brought up a jackdaw bird.
The bird could speak, so well he'd raised her.
4 Then she was murdered by a neighbour.
Our man complained about his daw
In court, and told the judge there how
His bird was wont to talk away
8 And, in the mornings, sing each day.
The neighbour, said the judge, was wrong;
He summoned him to trial ere long.
The neighbour got a leather hide,
12 Put it beneath his cloak, inside,
And then he let hang down an end
So that the judge could comprehend
That it was brought as bribery
16 If he would help him in his plea.
His cloak he opened frequently
Until the hide this judge did see.
He called the other man amain,
20 The one who'd come there to complain.
The judge asked, in his questioning,
What songs the daw was wont to sing
And what great words she'd say also.
24 The man replied he did not know.
'If you,' he said, 'don't know a thing,
Don't understand her chattering,
And if her songs you do not know,
28 To you my judgment should not go.'
Without his due the man went out –
Thanks to the bribe; the judge took that.
    And thus it is, a king or prince
32 Should not his law or ordinance
Entrust to people covetous:
Destroyed will be all righteousness.

57 **Del vilein e del folet**

D'un vilein cunte ke prist ja
Un folet, que lung tens gueita.
Cil lui dona treis uremenz,
4 Pur quei nel mustrast as genz.
Le vilein fu joius e lez.
Quant [a] sa femme est repeirez,
Les deus uremenz li dona;
8 Un en retient, pru nel garda.
Eissi furent bien lungement,
Qu'il ne firent nul urement –
Desque a un jur qu'il aveient
12 A un manger, u il esteient
De une berbiz, l'eschine e l'os –
Dunt la meüle apareit fors.
La femme en ot grant desirer –
16 Volenters la vousist manger!
Mes ne pot aver as meins,
Si ad uré ke li vileins
Eüst tel bek, mut li plereit –
20 Lung cum li witecocs aveit.
Eissi avient cum ele ura.
E li vileins s'esmerveila,
Si ad uré que en veie fust
24 E que sun vis meme eüst.
Deus uremenz unt ja perduz,
Que nuls n'en est a bien venuz.
    A plusurs est si avenuz –
28 Suventefez unt perduz
Ki trop creit autri parole,
Que tut les deceit e afole.
Li fous quide del veizïé
32 Quel voille aver conseillé
Si cum sei – mes il i faut:
Kar tant ne seit ne tant ne vaut.

57 **The Peasant and the Goblin**

A peasant caught, in times of yore,
A goblin he'd been waiting for.
He gave three wishes to the man
4 If he would not tell anyone.
This made the peasant blithe and gay.
And when his wife came home that day,
He gave two wishes to her; one
8 He kept, not thinking what he'd done.
And then a long time passed in which
Neither of them made a wish –
Until one day it chanced they were
12 Both at a feed, and they saw there
The back and bones of a plump sheep –
And marrow fat from these did seep.
The woman such a craving had –
16 She wanted so that marrow fat!
She could not grasp some in her hand,
And so she wished that her husband
Should have a beak now for her pleasure –
20 Long, like a hornbill's beak in measure.
The woman's wish materialized.
The peasant, who was quite surprised,
Now wished to leave that place and then
24 To have his own face back again.
Two wishes were already gone;
No good had come from either one.
    And so with many it will be –
28 Those people lose out frequently
Who trust too much in what they hear,
In speeches that beguile and blear.
The fool believes chicanery
32 And hopes that thus advised he'll be
In how things are – But he errs, surely:
A man's no wiser than he's worthy.

58 Del gupil e de la lune

D'un gupil dit que une nuit
Esteit alez en sun deduit.
Sur une mare trespassa.
4 Quant dedenz l'ewe garda,
L'umbre de la lune ad veü:
Mes ne sot pas quei ceo fu.
Puis ad pensé en sun curage
8 Qu'il ot veü un grant furmage.
L'ewe comence a laper;
Tresbien quida en sun penser,
Si l'ewe de la mare ert mendre,
12 Que le furmage peüst bien prendre!
Tant ad beü qu'il creva;
Ileoc cheï, puis ne leva.
    Meint humme espeire, utre dreit –
16 E utre ceo qu'il ne devereit –
(A) aver tutes ses volentez.
Dunt puis est morz e afolez.

59 Del lu e del corbel

D'un lu cunte ke vit jadis
U un corbel s'esteit asis
Sur le dos de une berbiz.
4 Li lus parla od nobles diz:
'Jeo vei,' fet il, 'grant merveille –
Le corp sur le dos d'une oweille!
S[i]et la u siet, dit ceo que dit,
8 Fet ceo que fet – sanz cuntredit!
Mal ne cr[i]ent de nule rien.
Si jeo i seisse, jeo sai bien
Que tute gent me hüereient;
12 De tutes parz m'escrïereient,
Que jeo la vodreie manger;
Ne me larreient aprismer.'
    Issi est del tricheür:
16 En esfrei est e en poür

58 The Fox and the Moon

A fox, it's said, one night went out
To have some fun and prowl about.
His path took him across a mere.
4 He looked into the water there
And he beheld the moon's reflection:
This was beyond his comprehension.
He thought, with all his heart construed,
8 It was a great cheese that he viewed.
He starts to lap the water next,
Thinking his reasoning's correct:
Were there less water in the lake,
12 How easily that cheese he'd take!
He drank until he burst, and then
He fell, never to rise again.
    Many people thus expect –
16 Beyond what's fitting and correct –
To have whatever they desire.
They're thus destroyed and they expire.

59 The Wolf and the Crow

The story goes that long ago
There was a wolf who saw a crow.
Upon a sheep's back crow did sit.
4 Then nobly spoke the wolf, to wit:
'I can't believe that this is so –
Upon the ewe's back there's a crow!
Sits where he wants, says what he will,
8 Does what he wants – protest is nil!
He fears no animosity.
If I sat there, 'tis certainty
That everyone would shout me down;
12 They'd yell at me from all around.
    – I'm going to eat the sheep! – they'd cry.
They'd not permit me to draw nigh.'
    Thus with the trickster it is clear:
16 He's terrified and filled with fear

(Sa cunscience le reprent)
Que tuz cunuissent sun talent.
Forment li peise del leal,
20 Que hum ne tient ses fez a mal.

60 Del cok e del gupil

D'un cok recunte ki estot
Sur un femer e si chantot.
Par delez li vient un gupilz
4 Si l'apela par muz beaus diz.
'Sire,' fet il, 'mut te vei bel!
Unc ne vi si gent oisel!
Clere voiz as sur tute rien –
8 Fors tun pere – que jo vi bien,
Unc oisel meuz né chanta –
Mes il le fist meuz, kar il cluna.'
'Si puis jeo fere,' dist li cocs.
12 Les eles bat; les oilz ad clos;
Chanter quida plus clerement.
Li gupil saut e sil prent;
Vers la forest od lui s'en va.
16 Par mi un champ, u il passa,
Curent aprés tut li pastur;
Li chiens le hüent tut entur.
'Veit le gupil, ki le cok tient!
20 Mar le guaina, si par eus vient!'
'Va,' fet li cocs, 'si lur escrie
Que sui tuens, ne me larras mie!'
Li gupil volt parler en haut,
24 E li cocs de sa buche saut –
Sur un haut fust s'est muntez.
Quant li gupilz s'est reguardez,
Mut par se tient enfantillé,
28 Que li cocs l'ad si enginné.
De mal talent e de dreit ire
La buche cumence a maudire,
Ke parole quant devereit taire.
32 Li cocs respunt, 'Si dei jeo faire:

(His conscience brings this apprehension)
That everyone knows his intention.
Good people cause him much distress:
20 He fears they'll take his deeds amiss.

60 The Cock and the Fox

And now a cock you'll hear about;
Atop a dung heap he sang out.
Then up to him there came a fox
4 Who with fine words addressed the cock.
Said fox, 'How lovely you are, sir!
I've never seen a nobler bird!
Your voice the clearest of them all –
8 Save for your sire's (as I recall);
No bird could better vocalize
Than he – for he would close his eyes.'
'I'll do the same,' the cock proposed.
12 He flapped his wings; his eyes he closed;
He thought to make his song shine bright.
The fox leaped up and clutched him tight
And took off toward the forest; and
16 As he passed through some open land,
The shepherds tried to run him down;
Dogs barked at him from all around.
'Look at the fox! He's caught a cock!
20 If he comes near, woe to the fox!'
The cock said, 'Shout to them just so –
I'm yours and you'll not let me go!'
But as the fox began to shout,
24 From fox's mouth, the cock leaped out –
And up the trunk of an old tree.
And when the fox all this did see,
He felt himself most infantile
28 To have been duped by rooster's guile.
Outraged and in a dreadful wrath,
The fox began to curse his mouth
For speaking when it ought to hush.
32 The cock replied, 'I'll do as much

Maudire l'oil, ki volt cluiner,
Quant il deit guarder e guaiter,
Que mal ne vienge a lur seignur.'
36   Ceo funt li fol: tut li plusur
Parolent quant deivent taiser,
Teisent quant il deivent parler.

61 Del gupil e del colum

D'un columb cunte ke jadis
Sur une croiz s'esteit asis.
Un gupil vient desuz, sil vit;
 4 En haut parla, si li dit:
 'Pur quei seiez tu,' fet il, 'la sus
 En si grant vent? Kar descent jus,
 Si seez od mei en cest ab[r]i!'
 8 'Jeo nel os fere!' ceo respundi.
 'Pur nïent as poür de mei,
 Si te sai bien dire pur quei:
 Jeo fu ore ainz a un cunté,
12 U grant people ot asemblé.
 Un brief i vient de part le rei,
 Que ad mandé par dreite fei
 Que beste a autre ne mesface
16 N'a nul oisel – ja Deu ne place –
 Que entre eus n'eit mes si feite guere.
 Pes veut mettre dedenz sa tere;
 Ensemble purrunt mes aler
20 Oiseus e bestes, en pes jüer.'
 'Dunc descendrai,' fet li culums.
 'Mes jeo vei la lez cez buissuns
 Deus chevalers mut tost aler;
24 Si funt deus chiens od eus mener.'
 Dist li gupilz, 'Sunt il bien pres?'
 'Il chevachent,' fet ele, 'adés.'
 'Meuz est que en cele grave voise
28 Que par eus eie estrif u noise.
 Il n'unt pas tuz le bref oï –
 Ki vient del rei. Jol vus afi,

And curse the eye that thinks to shut
When it should safeguard and watch out
Lest the seignior should suffer ill.'
36   And thus with fools, for they all will
Speak out when they their tongues should check
And check their tongues when they should speak.

61 The Fox and the Dove

Once long ago it happened that
A dove atop a signpost sat.
A fox walked by and saw him there
4 And spoke out to him, loud and clear:
'Why do you sit up there,' he said,
'In such high wind? Come down instead
And sit with me quite sheltered here.'
8 The dove replied, 'I do not dare!'
'You should not be afraid of me,
I'll tell you why assuredly:
At council meeting I've just been
12 Where many people did convene.
A letter from the king arrived
Which by his royal right prescribed
The animals to harm no bird
16 Or other beast – So help me Lord –
Let war forever more be banned.
Desiring peace throughout the land,
He said that henceforth birds and beasts
20 Should all, together, play in peace.'
Said dove, 'Then I'll come down to thee.
But there beside that bush, I see
Two knights approaching hastily;
24 Two dogs are in their company.'
The fox asked, 'Are they very near?'
The dove replied, 'They're almost here.'
'Into that grove I'd better dash
28 Than suffer clamour or a clash.
The proclamation they've not heard –
The one the king sent. You've my word,

Ne m'estuvereit pas remüer,
32 Si tuz l'eüssent oï cunter.'
       Si vet des feluns veizïez.
    Par eus sunt plusurs enginnez
    Par parole, par faus sermun,
36 Cum li gupilz fist le colum.

62 De l'egle, de l'ostur, e des colums

    Li egles est des oiseus reis;
    Pur ceo qu'il est pruz e curteis.
    Li osturs est sis senesçaus,
 4 Que n'esteit mie del tut leiaus.
    Li egles sist par un grant chaut
    Sur la branche d'un cheine en haut.
    Li ostur sist plus bas de lui.
 8 Garda aval, si ot ennui
    Des colums, que desuz vol(et)oent,
    Jus a la tere entre eus jüoent.
    'Vus vus jüez,' fet il, 'suz mei.
12 Mes si li egles, nostre rei,
    Se fust d'ici un poi remüez
    E sur un autre fust volez,
    Li gius ireit en autre guise –
16 Jeo fereie de vus justise!'
       Pur ceo ne deit princes voler
    Seneschal de grant fierté aver
    Ne coveitus ne menteür –
20 Si nel veut fere sun seignur.

63 Del cheval e de la haie

    Un cheval vit u herbe crut
    Dedenz un pré, mes n'aparut
    La haie dunt fu clos li prez.
 4 Al saillir enz s'est esteillez.
       Ceo funt plusurs, bien le savez:
    Tant coveitent lur volentez,
    Ne veient pas queile aventure
 8 En vient aprés pesante e dure.

I would not have to run away
32 If they'd heard all he had to say.'
   And so it goes with scoundrels sly.
For many folks are hoodwinked by
Their crafty words and lying talks
36 Just as the dove was by the fox.

62 The Eagle, the Hawk, and the Doves

The king of all the birds is eagle;
His strength and virtue make him regal.
The hawk is eagle's seneschal.
4 He is, however, less than loyal.
The eagle, when heat bothers him,
Perches upon a high oak limb.
The hawk sits farther down the oak.
8 He looks below and is provoked
By doves down there who fly around
And play together on the ground.
Said hawk, 'You're down there frolicking.
12 But if the eagle, who's our king,
Would go away from here, if he
Would fly off to another tree,
Your game would go another way –
16 For I would have with you fair play!'
   Therefore a prince ought not to want
A seneschal who's arrogant
Or greedy or of lying word –
20 Unless he wants him made his lord.

63 The Horse and the Hedge

A horse once saw where grasses grew
In meadow land, but failed to view
The hedge which was the meadow's rim.
4 He jumped in – thorns impaled him.
   You know, with many folks it's thus:
They want a thing so very much
They do not see what consequence,
8 Heavy and hard, will follow thence.

64 Del riche humme, del cheval, e del buc

Un riches hum, ceo dit, aveit
Un cheval, que vendre voleit
E sun buc – tut a un pris.
4 Pur vint souz, ceo dist a ses amis,
Chescun d'eus voleit duner,
Si nul les vousist achater.
Uns marchanz les bargena:
8 Le cheval dit qu'il retendra,
Mes li bucs n'en valeit nent.
Li riches hum par maltalent
Dit que ambedeus achatereit
12 U ambesdeus les larreit.
   Veer poëz del nunsavant,
Que sun mal us prise autretant
Cume sun bon tut oëlement –
16 Ne peot lesser sun fol talent.

65 Del lu e de l'escarbot

Ci nus recunte cum uns lus
En une grave jut tut suls.
Desuz la cue aval li entre
4 Un escarboz de ci al ventre.
Li lus saut sus, si s'esveilla;
Mut anguissusement cria.
Tant se vultra e tant sailli
8 Que li escarboz s'en (r)eissi.
Quant li lus le garda e vit,
Mut par li fu en grant despit:
'Allas,' fet il, 'dolenz cheitifs –
12 Que dedenz mei t'esteis mis!'
Li escarboz ad respundu:
'Certes,' fet il, 'bien est sceü
Que jeo vail asez meuz de tei,
16 Quant tu demeines tel buffei.
Ore asemble ta cumpainie
E ceus que te serunt en aïe.
E jeo asemblerai mes genz

64 The Rich Man, the Horse, and the Billy Goat

About a rich man I will tell
Who had a horse he wished to sell,
And billy goat – one price the two.
4 He told his friends, for twenty sous
He'd give the two of them away
To anyone who wished to pay.
A merchant tried a deal to make:
8 The horse alone, he said, he'd take;
The goat, however, had no worth.
The wealthy man, now waxing wroth,
Said that the man must buy the two
12 Or else the two he must forgo.
    Thus, one who's ignorant you see:
He thinks his bad ways equally
As prized as his good ways will be –
16 He can't give up stupidity.

65 The Wolf and the Beetle

This story's of a wolf who lay
Alone within a grove one day.
Under his tail a beetle then
4 Went up, into his abdomen.
Awakening, wolf jumped about
And with great anguish he cried out.
So frantically he hopped and leaped
8 That out again the beetle creeped.
And when the wolf did beetle see,
He spoke out most disdainfully:
'Oh woe! Unhappy wretch!' said he –
12 'For crawling up inside of me!'
To this the beetle answered so:
'Indeed,' he said, 'and we all know
I'm just as good as you are, yes,
16 When you act with such haughtiness.
Now go and gather each consort,
All those who'll give you their support.
My people I will gather here,

20 E mes amis e mes parenz.
  Demain tenum une bataille –
  Enmi cel champ seit sanz faille!'
  Li lus l'ad issi otrïé;
24 Pur ses eidanz ad enveié.
  E li escarboz mandat les ees;
  N'i aveit un sul remés,
  Ne grosse musche, ne cornet,
28 Ne bone wespe, ne wibet.
  Quant il deveient aprismer,
  Li lu volt les suens enseigner:
  Cunseil, ceo dit, lur estut prendre;
32 S'il se veut vers eus defendre.
  Chescuns estut garder sa cue,
  U il irrunt a male voue.
  Li cerfs lur dist, 'E nus nus bendums;
36 De cele part nus estupums,
  Qu'il ne puissent de la entrer;
  Dunc purrum plus ferm ester.'
  Issi l'unt fet communement;
40 Bendé se sunt mut feremement.
  Mes quant ceo vient a l'asemblee,
  Une wespe s'est drescee,
  Si puint le cerf par les costez;
44 E il sailli tut esfreez,
  Qu'il se mesfist vileinement
  E la bende desrump e fent.
  Ceo dit li lus, ki esteit pres,
48 'Seignurs, pur Deu, n'i esteium mes!
  Mut par nus est mesavenu,
  Quant li lïen sunt rumpu.
  Fuium nus en hastivement!
52 Si nus demurum ici neient,
  N'i avera ja un sul de nus
  N'eit suz la cue treis u deus.'
    Cest essample nus dit de ceus
56 Que despisent les menurs de eus.
  Tant les avilent de lur diz
  Que al grant busuin sunt honiz.
  E meuz se seivent cil eider
60 La u il unt greinur mester.

20 My friends and my relations dear.
   Tomorrow we will fight it out –
   We'll battle on this field, no doubt!'
   To this, the wolf gave his consent,
24 And for auxiliaries he sent.
   The beetle summoned all the bees;
   There stayed behind not one of these,
   Nor any wasp, nor horsefly fat,
28 Nor able hornet, nor one gnat.
   When it was time for confrontation,
   Wolf gave his troops this information:
   They'd need some good advice, he sensed,
32 So they could have a strong defence.
   Each one must his own tail patrol,
   For there they'd be most vulnerable.
   'Let's bind ourselves up,' said a hart,
36 'And thereby we can plug that part
   So that they cannot get inside;
   And thus we'll be well fortified.'
   Exactly this was what was done:
40 They bound themselves tight, everyone.
   And when they reached the battle site,
   One wasp came forth to start the fight,
   And stung the hart along his side.
44 The hart leaped up so terrified
   He suffered injuries most sore,
   His band was pulled apart and tore.
   Then said the wolf, for he was near,
48 'God help me, lord! Let's not stay here!
   Now all of us are most forlorn
   When all our bandages are torn.
   We must get out of here in haste!
52 If we stay longer in this place,
   There won't be any of us who
   Won't have up in him three or two.'
   This example shows the way
56 That some hate lesser folk than they.
   They rail at them so wickedly,
   They're shamed in an emergency.
   The lesser know best how, indeed,
60 To aid themselves in times of need.

66 Del gris lu

Par veille essample recunte ici
Que tuit li lus sunt enveilli
En cele pel, u il sunt né;
4 La remainent tut lur eé.
Ki sur le lu meist bon mestre,
Quil doctrinast a estre prestre,
Si sereit il tut dis gris lus,
8 Fel e engrés, leiz e hidus.

67 De l'ostur e del ruissinol

Ci nus recunte d'un ostur,
Que sur le fust s'asist un jur,
U li ruissinol ot sun ni
4 E sis oiselez bel nurri.
A sei la prist a rapeler,
Si li cumanda a chanter.
'Sire,' fet il, 'jo ne purreie,
8 Tant cum si pres de mei vus veie.
Si vus pleseit a remüer,
E sur un autre fust voler,
Jeo chantereie mut plus bel –
12 Ceo seivent tuit cist autre oisel.'
     Autresi vet de meinte gent:
Ne püent pas seürement,
La u il dutent, bien parler,
16 Si cum la u n'estut duter.

68 Del corbel ki s'aürne des pennes al poün

Del corbel cunte ki trova
Par un chemin, u il ala,
Plumes e pennes d'un poün.
4 Si s'esguarda tut envirun;
Plus vil se tient que nul oisel,
Pur ceo qu'il ne se vit si bel.

66 The Grey Wolf

An ancient story here is told
Of how all wolves grew very old
Inside the skin they were born in,
4 Spending their whole life in this skin.
No matter who might be his teacher
And tell him how to be a preacher,
A grey wolf's what he'll be for aye,
8 Mean and ugly, base and sly.

67 The Hawk and the Nightingale

About a hawk this tale will be
Who sat one day up in a tree
Where nightingale had made her nest
4 And there her baby birds had raised.
The hawk began by summoning
The nightingale to come and sing.
'Oh sir, I can't do that,' said she,
8 'When I see you're so close to me.
Yet if to move, you would agree,
And fly off to another tree,
Most beautifully I'd sing for you –
12 All other birds know this is true.'
    With many folks this will occur:
They can't be confident and sure,
When frightened, that they speak as well
16 As when they have no fears to quell.

68 The Crow in Peacock's Feathers

In olden times there was a crow
Who chanced along a road to go
And peacock plumes and feathers found.
4 Studying himself, up and down,
He thought he was the worst bird e'er
For he had never looked so fair.

Tutes ses plumes esraça
8 Que une sule n'i leissa;
Des pennes al poün s'aürne.
Trestut sun cors bel aturne.
Puis s'asembla od les poüns.
12 Ne semblot pas lur cumpainuns:
Od les eles le batirent,
Si pis purent, pis li firent!
Dunc revolt as corps aler –
16 Si cum einz fist – corp resembler.
Mes il l'unt tut descunu,
Si l'unt ocis e debatu.
   Ceo peot veer de plusurs,
20 Ki aveir unt e granz honurs;
Uncore vodreient plus cuillir
Ceo qu'il ne poënt retenir.
Ceo qu'il coveitent n'unt il mie,
24 E le lur perdent par folie.

69 Del leün e del gupil

Un lïun fu mut desheitez,
De mal suspris e empeirez.
Tutes les bestes i alerent.
4 Entre eus distrent e [es]garderent
Que hum le deüst mediciner –
Si nuls en seüst cunseil trover.
Al gupil se tiendrent plusur,
8 Que de bestes set le retur
E as oiseus reset parler –
Mecine quere e demander.
Par message le funt somundre;
12 E le gupil estut respundre:
Lez la sale s'esteit mucez;
Kar quointes ert e veizez.
Le leün mut se curuça.
16 Le lu, sun provost, apela;
Demanda lui pur quei ne vient.
Li lus respunt: 'Rien nel detient
Fors l'engresté de sun curage;

He plucked out all his plumes; when done,
8 He had not left a single one.
He did in peacock feathers dress
To make his body beauteous,
And went to join the peacock flock.
12 To them, he seemed like no peacock
And was, by their wings, buffeted.
What worse things they could do, they did!
He wished to be a crow again –
16 As he had been – and look like one.
But no one recognized him, so
They beat him up; they killed the crow.
And this with many folks, you'll see:
20 They've honour and prosperity,
And yet they want to get much more
Than their capacity to store.
They gain nought from their greediness
24 And lose their goods to foolishness.

69 The Lion and the Fox

There was a lion languishing,
Extremely ill and worsening.
The animals all congregated,
4 And they consulted, contemplated
What medicine to give the lion –
Did someone know what should be done?
Most thought that fox was best of all:
8 Knew how to cure an animal
And how to talk with any bird –
He'd tell how lion could be cured.
By messenger the fox was summoned,
12 And this is how the fox responded:
He reached the chamber, hid nearby,
For he was cunning and most sly.
The lion, in a dreadful wrath,
16 Now called the wolf, his provost, forth,
And asked why fox had not arrived.
'Nothing has kept him,' wolf replied,
'Except his heart maleficent;

20 Kar jeo li enveia mun message.
   Amener le frai e prendre;
   Vus le feites defeire u pendre.
   Sil chastïez si fierement
24 Que sample prengent si parent.'
   Li gupil ot qu'il fu jugez;
   Mut durement s'est esmaiez.
   Pas pur pas est avant venuz,
28 Que des bestes fu bien veüz.
   'U as esté tant?' fet li leüns.
   E cil li dit en sun respuns,
   'Si m'aït Deus, beus sire reis,
32 Ne sai quei fesisse ainceis
   Que mescine eüsse trovee.
   Puis ai erré meinte jurnee,
   Que oï vostre comandement.
36 En Salerne fui vereiment;
   Si vus unt li mire mandé,
   Ki oïrent vostre enfermeté:
   Que un lu seit escorcié tut vifs,
40 Si seit li sanc en la pel mis
   Sur vostre piz desque a demain –
   De vostre mal vus rendra sain!'
   Le lu prenent, ke ileoc fu;
44 Vif l'escorcent, tant l'unt tenu.
   Al lïun unt la pel bailé,
   Cil s'en vet a grant hasché.
   Al soleil se sist pur garisun.
48 La vindrent musches e taün,
   Sil depuinstrent mut malement.
   Li gupilz i vient tut quointement,
   Si li demanda quei la fesist
52 E que sanz chapel ileoc s'asist.
   'Tes guanz,' fet il, 'vei depescez.
   Autre feiz seez chastïez
   Que autre ne deiz par mal tenir,
56 Que sur tei deive revertir!'
       Tel purchace le mal d'autrui,
   Que cel meme revient sur lui,
   Si cum li lus fist del gupil –
60 Qu'il voleit mettre en eissil.

20 To him your message I have sent.
   The fox I will go catch and fetch,
   Then you can hang or kill the wretch.
   His punishment will be so grim,
24 'Twill be a lesson to his kin.'
   Fox heard the sentence thus declared
   And was indeed extremely scared.
   Then step by step he neared, until
28 The animals could see him well.
   The lion said, 'You're so late! – Why?'
   Thus spoke the fox in his reply:
   'May God help me, most noble king;
32 I knew not what to do or bring
   Till I could find some medicine.
   I've wandered many days since then,
   When your command I heard decreed.
36 I've to Salerno been, indeed,
   Where doctors sent you this prescription
   When they had heard of your affliction:
   First flay a wolf alive, and then
40 Collect his blood within his skin
   And put it on your chest. Be sure,
   Tomorrow you will have your cure!'
   They grabbed the wolf, for he was near,
44 Skinned him live as they held him there.
   To lion with this skin they went,
   While wolf ran off in great torment.
   For his relief, he sought the sun.
48 Then flies and gadflies fat did come
   To sting the wolf most nastily.
   The fox approached wolf craftily
   And asked him what he meant to do
52 Without his hat on, sitting so.
  'I see your gloves in shreds,' said he;
   'The next time, punished you will be
   So no more wicked things you'll do
56 Lest they should all come back to you!'
    Those who plan ill for other men
   Will get the same thing back again.
   Just like the wolf and fox, you see –
60 Wolf thought he'd bring fox misery.

70 Del gupil e de l'urse

D'un gupil nus recunte e dit,
Que une urse trova e vit.
Forment li preia e requist
4 Que ele suffrist que li fesist.
'Teis!' fet ele, 'mauveis gupilz!
Mut par iés cheitifs e vilz!'
'Jeo sui,' fet il, 'tel cum jeo suil –
8 Sil te ferai estre tun voil.'
'Fui!' fet ele, 'leis me ester!
Si jeo t'en oi mes parler,
Tenir te purras pur bricun;
12 Jeo te baterai od mun bastun!'
Tant l'a li gupilz enchacié,
Que l'urse s'est mut curucié,
Aprés curut pur lui ferir,
16 E il fuï, pur lui trahir –
Tant qu'il meine en un buissun.
E les espines tut envirun
L'unt entaché e encumbré,
20 E par le pel l'unt detiré,
Si ke ne pot avant aler
Pur nule rien ne returner.
Dunc revient li gupil par derere;
24 Sur li sailli cume trichere.
L'urse cumence dunc a crïer,
Puis si li prist a demander:
'Mauveis gupil! Quei fras tu?'
28 Li gupilz li ad tost respundu:
'Ceo que t'oi,' fet il, 'preié,
Dunt tu m'aveies manacié.'
    Ceo deit ester e remaner –
32 Que li pruz hum dira pur ver:
As vezïez est bien avis,
Que lur parole est en tel pris
Cum li engins de meinte gent –
36 Que par cunsel venquent suvent.

70 **The Fox and the Bear**

And now you'll hear what did betide
When fox one day a she-bear spied.
Urgently fox did beg and pray
4 For her to let him have his way.
'Shut up! You wicked fox!' she said;
You are contemptible and bad!'
'That's just the way I am,' said he;
8 'I'll make you want it, too – you'll see.'
'Get out of here! Now let me be!
If I hear more such talk,' said she,
'You will be thought a thieving knave,
12 And I will beat you with my stave!'
The fox kept trying to engage her
Till finally he did enrage her.
She chased the fox so she could strike.
16 The fox kept running, as a trick –
Into a bush he led the bear.
A mass of thorns all 'round her there
Stuck to the bear, entangled her,
20 And made a frazzle of her fur,
So she could not gain any ground
Try how she might, nor turn around.
The fox approached her from the rear;
24 Cheat that he was, he jumped on her.
At this, the bear began to cry,
And then she questioned him this way:
'You wicked fox! What will you do?'
28 The fox made this reply thereto:
'Just what I'd asked you for,' said he,
'When earlier you threatened me.'
And it must always be this way –
32 As worthy men forsooth will say:
Wise people think it's clearly true
That their words will be equal to
Some other person's stratagems.
36 Yet they'll be vanquished by these schemes.

71 **Del leün malade, del cerf, e del gupil**

Un lïun fu de mal grevez,
Si ad tuz ses baruns mandez:
Mires voleit que li quesissent,
4 Que de sun mal le guaresissent.
Tuz li dïent, ja ne guarra(t)
Si queor de cerf mangé n'en a(t).
Dunc assemblent lur parlement,
8 Mandez i fu, n'i vient nent –
Kar si parent e si ami
L'en aveient devant garni.
Un autre fez i fu mandez;
12 E il vient tut esfreez.
Dunc li distrent qu'il voleient
Sun queor aver – si l'ocireient!
Li cerfs l'oï, si s'en ala;
16 A grant peine lur eschapa.
La terce fez le remanderent;
E il vient, dunc le tüerent.
Einz qu'il par fust escorcez,
20 S'est li gupilz tant aprismez,
Qu'il lur aveit le quor emblez,
Si l'ad mangé e devorez!
Quant il voleient avant porter,
24 Si nel porent mie trover!
Entr'eus tienent mut grant pleit,
Si demandent ki ceo ad feit:
Ki le quor lur aveit emblé,
28 Grant hunte ot fet e vilté.
Les bestes ki esteient pres
Surent le gupil mut engrés,
A felun e a mur veizïé –
32 Dïent qu'il ad le quor mangié.
Dunc unt le gupil apelé,
Si li unt le quor demandé.
Il lur jura par serment
36 Qu'il ne l'ot emblé nent.
'Seignurs,' fet il, 'jeo afierai
Que unc le quor ne mangai.

71 **The Sick Lion, the Deer, and the Fox**

Lion was ill, in great torment.
To all his lords, a call was sent.
He asked if doctors could be found
4 Who'd know a way to make him sound.
All said he'd not recuperate
Until a deer's heart he would eat.
They called a meeting, talked it out;
8 They sent for deer, but he came not –
Because his friends and family
Had given warning previously.
A second time they called the deer;
12 This time he came, in dreadful fear.
They told him what the council willed:
To have his heart – he must be killed!
The deer heard this; off he did flee,
16 Barely managing to get free.
A third time now the deer was called;
This time he came, and he was killed.
Even before they'd flayed the deer,
20 A fox there was who crept so near
That from their midst, the heart he stole
And ate it up, devoured it whole!
Thus, when they wished to take the heart,
24 They could not find it – not one part!
They held a hearing, questioning
Which animal had done this thing:
Whoever stole that heart away
28 Should be disgraced for this foul play.
The animals who were close by
Knew fox was violent and sly,
A wicked rogue, though very smart –
32 'Twas he, they said, who ate the heart.
They sent the fox a summons, and
For the deer's heart they made demand.
On oath the fox swore, warranting
36 That he'd not stolen anything.
'My lords,' he said, 'I hearby swear
I never ate that heart of deer.

Pire sereie d'autre beste –
40 Hum me deust trencher la teste,
Si encuntre le mal mun seignur
Eüsse fet tel deshonur.
Ore en irum devant le rei!
44 Venez! Si seez ensemble od mei!
Jeo me derainerai bien,
Que ne me mescrerra de rien.'
Dunc [en] vunt devant le leün,
48 Si li mustrent la raisun.
Del quor dïent qu'il unt perdu.
Dunc ad li gupil respundu:
'Sire,' fet il, 'ceo m'est avis,
52 Il veulent mettre en cest païs
Ceo que ja n'ert, ne unc ne fu,
Ne que jamés n'i ert veü!
Quant li cerf fu a curt mandé,
56 E pur oscire areisuné,
A grant peine s'en eschapa.
Quant terce feiz [i] repeira,
Sacez qu'il n'aveit point de quer,
60 Kar il n'e venist a nul fu[e]r!
Mut sereie ke deslëaus,
Trop sereie mauveis e faus –
Si jeo encuntre vostre santé
64 Lur eüsse le quor issi emblé.'
Li lïuns respunt que verité dist:
S'il queor eüst, ja n'i venist.
'Bien devum le gupil lesser,
68 Que seins s'en puisset repeirer.'
    Par memes ceste raisun,
Quant fols prent sage a cumpainun,
Si nule rien deivent partir,
72 Li sages se set al meuz tenir,
Par parole l'autre deceit;
Sa mençunge pur verité creit.

The worst of animals I'd be –
40 My head you should chop off,' said he,
'If I, despite my lord's disease,
Had ever done a deed so base.
Now let us go before the king!
44 Come with me! Let's get travelling!
I'll clear myself so suasively
That he will have no doubts of me.'
With this, they to the lion went,
48 And there they did their case present.
They told him they had lost the heart;
To which the fox gave this retort:
'It seems to me,' the fox said, 'sire,
52 They wish that in this land there were
What n'er will be, has never been,
And what has never yet been seen!
When summoned to your court was deer,
56 And his death sentence he did hear,
He barely managed to break free.
But when the third time, back came he,
You can be sure he had no heart,
60 Or he would not have come to court!
And I would be indeed untrue,
Extremely wicked, faithless, too –
If risking your good health, I'd dare
64 Ever to steal that heart from there.'
He spoke the truth, lion confirmed:
With heart, he'd never have returned.
'We ought to let the fox be free,
68 To go back safe and sound,' said he.
   It's often like this in the end,
Whene'er a fool has a wise friend.
If something should be portioned, then
72 The wise man has more acumen.
His talk deceives the other, who
Believes the smart man's lies are true.

72 Del lu e del heriçun

Del lu dit e del heriçun,
Que jadis furent cumpainun.
Li hiriçuns deveit ester
4 Cuntre les chiens e desturber;
A lui les deveit fere entendre,
Quant li lus ireit preie prendre.
Un aignel prist li lus un jur.
8 Si l'escrïerent li pastur,
Les chiens li vunt aprés huant,
E il s'en vet al bois fuiant:
Li heriçun, leist entrepris.
12 Quant il l'apele e dit, 'Amis!
Pur amur Deu, vien mei aider!
Tu ne me deiz mie lesser!'
Li lus respunt, 'Aïe tei!
16 Kar ja cunseil n'avras pur mei.'
Li hiriçuns li ad prïé,
'Baisez mei, par cherité!
A mes enfanz purras cunter –
20 E par enseines remembrer –
Que ore sunt povres e orphenin,
Ke mei leissastes el chemin.'
Li lus beisa le hyriçun –
24 E il s'aert a sun mentun;
A ses levres s'est atachez
E od ses ferm afichez.
U il vousist u ne deinast,
28 Al lu estut qu'il l'aportast.
Quant el bois fu od lui venu,
Li hyriçun est descendu;
Sur un aut chene est munté.
32 Dunc s'esteit li lu recordé,
Si li pria qu'il descendist
Devant les chiens sil defendist.
Li hyriçuns li respunt tant,
36 'Amis,' fet il, 'va t'en avant –
Si te jois de tun aignel!
La char aïes e la pel,

72 **The Wolf and the Hedgehog**

Of wolf and hedgehog this is told,
And their companionship of old.
Here is the task that was hedgehog's:
4 He'd hinder and distract the dogs;
They'd listen to what he had to say
While wolf went out to seize his prey.
It chanced one day wolf seized a lamb.
8 The shepherds shouted out at him,
By howling dogs he was pursued,
And off he fled into the wood
Leaving the hedgehog sorely pressed.
12 'My friend!' the hedgehog cried, distressed.
'For love of God! Help me I say!
You can't abandon me this way!'
'Oh, help yourself!' the wolf then said,
16 'For I will never give you aid.'
The hedgehog begged, and thus spoke he:
'Then kiss me now, for charity!
So you can tell my children small
20 (This token will remind them all)
They're orphans now, in poverty,
For on this road you stranded me.'
The wolf then gave hedgehog a kiss –
24 Who grabbed wolf by the chin at this.
Then to his lips he held on fast,
And with his mouth he stayed attached.
Whether wolf wanted to or no,
28 Where e'er he went, hedgehog must go.
They reached the woods, hedgehog on wolf,
There the hedgehog let go, got off
And climbed high up a tree, an oak.
32 The wolf, remembering, now spoke,
Begged him to come down right away
And help him keep the dogs at bay.
And this is what the hedgehog said:
36 'My friend, now you may go ahead –
Enjoy your little lamb! For you
May have its flesh, the lamb skin too,

Si tu te puis des chiens garir;
40 Kar jo ne quer rien partir.
Sul me eüssez ore einz lessé,
Mes jo t'ai bien suzveizïé!'
   Ceo peot hume veer del felun,
44 Ke veut trahir sun cumpainun:
Il memes est encumbrez
La u li autre est deliverez.

73 Del vilein e de la serpent

Del vilein e de la serpent
Nus cunte ici, cumfeitement
Eurent ensemble cumpainie
4 E lëauté e fei plevie.
La serpent al vilein preia
E par amur li demanda
Que leit li aportast suvent
8 Deus feiz le jur par tel covent;
Que grant sen li enseignereit
E ke riche hume le fereit.
Si li mustra sun estre u fu,
12 E u lung tens aveit jeü:
Dedenz une piere cavee
U ele s'esteit arestee.
Li vilein ne l'ad pas ublïé
16 Que li ne ad lait aporté.
Ele li duna mut grant or,
Si li enseigna un tresor:
Sa tere li fist bien arer;
20 Si li enseigna a semer.
Tant li duna or e argent
Que merveille fu a la gent.
Mes bien li dist qu'il le perdreit,
24 De quel hure ke li plareit,
Si de rien li mesfeseit;
Kar bien e mal fere poeit.
Li vilein, quant vient a meisun,
28 A sa femme cunte la raisun

If you can keep the dogs away.
40 But I will have no part, I say.
Before, you left me destitute,
But this time I have bested you!'
    You'll see this in a criminal:
44 He'll make plans to betray his pal,
But he himself entrapped will be
Just where the other one goes free.

73 The Peasant and the Snake

A peasant and a snake is now
The subject of our tale, and how
They swore, those two, camaraderie
4 And pledged their trust and loyalty.
One day the snake made inquiry,
Asking the man most courteously
If he to her would milk convey
8 By covenant, two times each day.
She'd then impart great knowledge and
Would make him rich, a wealthy man.
She showed him where her home was made,
12 Where she for many years had stayed.
In hollow rock it was located:
Here's where she'd long been situated.
The peasant now did not neglect
16 To bring her milk as he had pledged.
She gave to him great stores of gold,
And of a treasure he was told:
His land, she said, should be well plowed;
20 She told him how it should be sowed.
He reaped such gold and silver thus,
That people thought it marvellous.
But snake told him he'd lose all this
24 At any time she might so wish
If ever wickedness he'd do:
For she both good and evil knew.
The peasant went back to his house
28 And told the story to his spouse,

Qu'il ot oï de la serpent.
Ele li respunt hastivement:
S'il voleit sun cunseil feire,
32 Qu'il en purreit a bon chef treire.
Ocie la, si fera mut bien.
Puis ne la crendra de nule rien.
En dute en est ore en sa merci,
36 Bien se deit deliverer de li;
N'avera dute de sun mesfet.
Le buket li porte plein de leit,
Puis si l'asise a tere jus,
40 Si s'en traie un poi en sus.
Quant la serpent vendra avant,
Sa hache tienge bien trenchant,
Si la fierge si durement
44 Que n'i ait mes recovrement.
Li vilein dit ke si fera.
Le leit ad pris, od tut s'en va.
Le buket mist devant la piere,
48 Puis se traist un poi ariere.
La serpent [vint] si voleit beivre,
[E li vilains la volt decoivre;
La hache haute por ferir.]
52 E ele oï le cop venir,
En la piere se met dedenz,
E li vileins s'en va dolenz.
Ne demurra mes que al demein,
56 Tuz les berbiz a cel vilein
Furent en la faude trovees –
La serpent les ot acurees.
Sun enfant ocist en sun bercel,
60 Dunt li vileins ot mut grant doel.
Par maltalent, par dreite ire,
A sa femme cumença a dire:
'Femme,' fet il, 'cunseille mei!
64 Cist mal m'est venu par tei.
Tu me donas cunseil de mal –
Fol e felun e desleal!'
Ele respunt a sun barun:
68 'Jeo ne sai cunseil ne mes un –

All that the snake to him did say.
Quickly the wife replied this way:
That he would come out well ahead
32 If he would do what his wife said.
Go kill the snake; that's right, I'm sure.
Then he'd have nought to fear from her.
He's at her mercy, and afraid;
36 He must get free of her, she said.
In doing so, he must not quail.
Take her some milk, a brim-full pail.
Down on the ground he should put it
40 And then step back a little bit.
And when the snake would venture out,
Should seize his axe, all sharp and stout,
And strike the snake so forcefully
44 There could be no recovery.
To this the peasant gave consent.
He took the milk, and off he went.
He put the pail before the rock
48 And stepped a little distance back.
The snake went out to drink; the man,
Thinking he'd tricked her with his plan,
Raised high his axe to strike at her.
52 She heard the deadly swing come near,
So back into the rock went she.
The peasant went home woefully.
And then just one day after that,
56 Every single sheep he had
Was found within the peasant's shed.
The snake had killed them – all were dead.
She killed his cradled infant, too,
60 Which he most painfully did rue.
With bitter heart and furious,
The man unto his wife spoke thus:
Said he, 'Advise me now, wife dear!
64 It's your fault this misfortune's here.
For your advice to me was bad –
Deceitful, wicked, indeed – mad!'
The wife responded to her lord:
68 'I've no advice except this word –

Fors tant que tu voises a li,
Si li crïez pur Deu merci.'
Al vilein est tart qu'il i aut,
72 Plein buket prent de leit chaut.
Devant la piere a la serpent
En est venu dutusement.
Sa cupe bat, merci cria.
76 E la serpent li demanda
Quei il quert la a tut sun leit.
'Merci,' fet il, 'de mun mesfeit,
E que nus fuissums ici amis,
80 Cum nus avums esté jadis.'
'Nenil, nenil,' fet ele, 'mestre,
Ceo ne purreit en nul sens estre.
Autrement poüm nus entreamer –
84 Si tu me veuls leit aporter
Issi cum tu einceis fesis,
Bien t'ert rendu, jol te plevis.
Le buket metras devant mun us,
88 E puis si te trarras en sus.
Ne te voil pas veer si pres;
Kar jeo ne te crerrai jamés.
Ne sai cument te crerreie,
92 Tant cum en ceste pere veie
Le cop ke ta hache i feri.
E jeo le sai tres bien de fi,
Quant le berz verras devant tei,
96 U tes enfes fu mort par mei,
Que de mei t'estut remembrer.
Tu ne me purras ublïer
Sulunc iceste mesestance.
100 Tel amur e tel bienvoillance,
Cum entre nus devum aveir –
Sanz mal fere, sanz mal voleir –
Icest otrei que nus aiums;
104 Si ke jamés ne nus creüms.'
Issi est suvent avenu –
De plusurs femmes est sceü:
Que si cunseillent lur seignur
108 Ke lur reverte a deshonur.

You ought to go now to her place
And beg her pardon through God's grace.'
The peasant, eager to set out,
72 A bucket of warm milk he brought.
Up to the stone cave where the snake was
The man went, terrified and anxious,
Confessed his guilt, for mercy cried.
76 The snake asked him, when she replied,
What was he with that milk pursuing?
'Mercy,' he said, 'for my wrongdoing.
I'd like us to be friends once more
80 Just as we used to be of yore.'
'Sir, nothing of the kind!' said she.
'There's no way that can ever be.
We can be friends another way –
84 If milk you will to me convey
Exactly as you used to do,
You'll be repaid, I promise you.
Outside my door, deposit it,
88 And then you must back off a bit.
I do not want to see you near;
I will not trust you more, that's clear.
For how, indeed, can I trust you
92 As long as on this rock I view
The mark your axe made on impact.
And this I know well for a fact:
Whenever you the cradle see
96 There where your child was killed by me,
You'll have to think about me yet.
You won't be able to forget
How I caused that calamity.
100 Such friendship and such amity
We'll have between the two of us –
No thought or deed injurious –
I grant that this we can attain.
104 But there will be no trust again.'
    It's often like this, as we know –
Of many women this is so:
Their men they counsel in such ways
108 That turn on them and bring disgrace.

Meinte femme cunseille a feire
Ceo dunt a plusurs nest cuntreire.
Sages hum ne deit pas entendre
112 Ne a fole femme cunseil prendre,
Cum fist icist par sa vileine,
Dunt il ot puis travail e peine.
Mut [e]üst grant aveir guainé,
116 Si ele ne l'eüst forscunseillé.

74 Del mulez ki quist femme

Jadis fu [si] enorguilliz
Li mulez, que resemble suri,
Qu'il ne voleit en sun parage,
4 En sun semblant, en sun lignage,
Femme quere, qu'il preisist.
Jamés n'avera femme, ceo dist,
S'il ne la treve a sun talent –
8 Fille al plus haut element
Vodra li mulez demander.
Al soleil en ala parler;
Pur ceo qu'il esteit plus haut
12 E en esté puissant e chaut.
Lui prie sa fille a muiller;
Kar ne sot a plus haut aler.
Li soleil dist qu'il voist avant,
16 Si trovera un plus puissant –
La nue – que l'enumbre e fet obscure;
Ne put parer, quant sur lui cure.
Li mulez a la nue vient,
20 Dit que si puissant le tient,
Que sa fille volt demander.
Ele li rova avant aler;
Par raisun lui vodra mustrer
24 Que plus puissant purra trover:
Ceo est li venz, ki bien esgart,
Que, quant il vente, la depart.
Fet li mulez, 'A lui irai;
28 Jamés ta fille ne prendrai!'

Many a woman's guiding word
Will prove for other folks untoward.
A man of wisdom ought not listen
112 Or heed advice from foolish women
As did this peasant from his wife,
Bringing him misery and strife.
Great wealth he would have realized
116 Had he not been so ill advised.

74 The Vole Who Sought a Wife

There once was so vainglorious
A vole (which is a kind of mouse)
That he'd not of his lineage,
4 Of his own kind or heritage,
Look for or choose a wife to wed.
He'd never have a wife, he said,
Unless he found one very pleasing –
8 The daughter of a most high being
Was what the vole thought he should seek.
So to the sun he went to speak:
The sun, highest of all, he guessed,
12 Hottest in summer, mightiest.
Vole wished to wed sun's daughter now;
He'd gone as high as he knew how.
If he looked further, said the sun,
16 He'd find an even stronger one –
The cloud – who shades and makes a cover –
Sun can't come out when cloud takes over.
The vole went to the cloud erelong
20 And said that since she seemed so strong,
Her daughter he would like to wed.
He'd better look some more, she said,
For she would like to demonstrate
24 That he'd find someone stronger yet:
It was the wind, she did believe;
Whene'er wind blew, he made cloud leave.
'I'll go to him,' thus vole did speak,
28 'Your daughter's hand I will not seek!'

Idunc en est alez al vent,
Si li ad dit cumfeitement
La nue l'i ot enveié.
32 Si li ot dit e enseigné
Qu'il ert la plus forte creature;
En sa force n'aveit mesure.
Tutes autres riens departeit,
36 Quant il ventot – tut destrueit.
Pur ceo voleit sa fille prendre;
Ne voleit mes aillurs entendre,
Pur ceo qu'il ot [oï] cunter
40 Que rien nel pot cuntre ester.
Li venz respunt, 'Tu as failli –
Femme n'averas pas ici.
Plus fort i a ke jeo ne sui,
44 Que mut sovent me fet ennui.
Encuntre mei si fort esteit,
Ne li chaut rien de mun forfeit.
Ceo est li granz murs de piere,
48 Que tuz jurz est forte e entiere.
Unc nel poi depescer
Ne par vent afiebler,
E me rebut si fort ariere –
52 Que n'ai talent ke la requere!'
Li mulez li respundi tant:
'De ta fille n'ai dunc talant;
Ne dei plus bas femme choisir –
56 Que a mei ne deie apurtenir!
Femme prandrai a bon eur!
Ore en irai desque al mur.'
Alez i est, sa fille quist.
60 Le mur l'esguarde, si dist:
'Tu as,' fet ele, 'meserré –
Si n'as mie bien esgardé.
Ki pur ceo ça t'enveia,
64 Ceo m'est avis, qu'il te gabba.
Plus fort verras uncore hui,
A ki jo unc ne cuntre estui.'
'Ki est ceo dunc?' li mulez respunt,
68 'A dunc plus fort en tut le mund!'

On to the wind the vole went now.
Addressing him, the vole told how
By cloud he'd been directed there.
32 The wind in answer made it clear
He was, indeed, the strongest creature,
His power was beyond all measure.
He'd force all other things to scatter
36 Whene'er he blew – destroy all matter.
Vole sought his daughter's hand, therefore;
He'd had enough, would hear no more,
For he had heard what people say:
40 That no one dared get in wind's way.
The wind replied, 'You are misled –
'There's no wife for you here,' he said.
'There is an even stronger one
44 That I find very bothersome.
She put up such a strong defence,
My force was of no consequence.
I'm talking of the great stone wall
48 Who stands so strong and sound through all.
The wall no force can devastate,
Nor all my wind debilitate.
She hurls me back so powerfully –
52 Another visit won't please me!'
The vole replied to him just this:
'Your daughter's hand I do not wish.
I'll choose no wife of lesser station –
56 That would not suit my situation!
I'll have a wife of quality!
So now the wall I must go see.'
He went to wall and sought to wed
60 Her daughter; eyeing him, wall said,
'You certainly do misconstrue –
It seems that nothing's clear to you.
Whoever sent you on your way
64 Has made a fool of you, I'd say.
Today one stronger yet than I
You'll see – one whom I can't defy.'
The vole responded, 'Who is this?
68 The strongest in the world, I guess!'

'Ore,' fet ele, 'ceo est la suriz.
Dedenz mei [gist e fet] ses niz.
Il n'ad en mei si fort morter
72 Que ele ne puisse trespercer.
Desuz me fuet, par mi mei vient,
Nule chose ne la detient.'
Li mulez dit, 'Coment? Ch[a]ëles!
76 Ore ai oï dures noveles!
Ja est la suriz ma parente!
Ore ai perdu tute m'entente!
Jeo quidoue si haut munter;
80 Ore me covient a returner
E encliner a ma nature.'
'Teus est le curs de aventure.
Va a meisun, e si te retien
84 Que ne voilles pur nule rien
Ta nature mes despiser.
Teus se quide mut eshaucer
Utre sun dreit e relever,
88 Que plus estut bas returner.
Mespreiser ne deit nul sun dreit
(Si ceo n'est mal) ki k'il seit.
Ja ne saveras si luinz aler
92 Que tu puisses femme trover,
Que meuz seit a tun [ués] eslite
Ke la suricette petite.'
    Issi avient as orguillus –
96 As surquidez, as envïus –
Que requerent qu'il ne devereient:
La revertent u ne vodreient.

75 De l'escarbot

D'un escarbot nus cunte e dit,
E jeo l'ai trové en escrit,
Que ot jeü en un femer.
4 Quant il fu saül de manger,
Hors s'en eissi; a munt garda,
E vit l'egle cum il vola.

'You're right, and that's the mouse,' said she,
'Who makes her nest inside of me.
There's no mortar – with which I'm made –
72 So strong that she cannot invade.
She digs below and runs through me;
Nought hinders her activity.'
The vole replied, 'What's this? Oh dear!
76 Oh this is dreadful news to hear!
The mouse and I are family!
My mission's ruined utterly!
I thought that I would rise so high,
80 But now I must turn back, so I
Can bow to my own kind,' said he.
Said wall, 'That's what your lot must be.
Go home, and keep in mind for aye,
84 That you should never, come what may,
Your nature ever again despise.
Whoever thinks that he can rise
Beyond his rightful situation
88 Must come back to a lower station.
Never should one his birthright scorn,
Whate'er he knows (unless baseborn).
Because so far you cannot go
92 To find yourself a wife, you know,
Who would be better in your house
Than this – the little lady mouse.'
  With prideful folks it's often thus –
96 Those arrogant and envious –
Who seek what they should not; for they
End back where they don't want to be.

75 The Beetle

A beetle's story I'll relate
That I found written down of late.
This beetle lay in a dung hill.
4 One day, when he had had his fill,
He went outside; his dung hill eyeing,
He saw, above, an eagle flying.

Mut par l'en tient a orguillus;
8 Enz en sun quor fu mut envïus.
As autres escarboz le dist
Que lur Sepande lur mesfist;
L'egle veit curteis e bel,
12 Il n'esteient um ne oisel.
Saül, ne poeient voler;
Jeün, ne sorent aler.
'L'egle ai esguardé tut en jur,
16 Que nus tenums a seignur;
Si haut vola que nel vi pas,
E quant il volt, si revient bas.
Mes sa voiz est basse e quoie,
20 N'est pas plus haut que la moie.
Autresi est mis cors luisanz
Cum est li suens, tut seit il granz.
Une chose ai en mun pensé:
24 Ne en yvern ne en esté
Ne voil mes el femer entrer!
Od autres oiseus voil voler –
Si viverai cum il viverunt
28 E irai la u il irunt!'
Idunc cumence a chanter
Mut leidement e a crïer.
Derere l'egle prist un saut;
32 Car il quida voler plus haut.
Ainz que gueres fust luinz alez,
Esturdi fu e estunez;
Ne poeit mie haut munter
36 Ne a sun femer puis asener.
Feim aveit, manger voleit.
Par grant destresce se pleineit;
Ne li chaleit si oiseus le oëit
40 Ne si nul de eus l'escharneit.
(Nent plus que fet al gupil,
Que autres bestes tienent vil.)
'Ore ne chaut que hum me tienge
44 Verm u oisel – mes que jo vienge
Dedenz la fiente del cheval;
Kar de feim ai dolur e mal.'

So proud this eagle seemed to be,
8 His heart was filled with jealousy.
To other beetles he observed,
They'd by their Maker been disserved:
She'd made the eagle courtly, grand,
12 But they were neither bird nor man.
When full, the beetles can't take wing;
Hungry, they can't be journeying.
'This whole day long, I fixed my gaze
16 On eagle, whom we deem our liege.
He flew so high up, out of view,
And came down when he wanted to.
His voice, of soft and easy tone,
20 Is yet no louder than my own.
My body glistening is, likewise,
As much as his, despite his size.
One thing is absolutely clear:
24 No matter what the time of year
I won't stay in a dung heap more!
With other birds I'd rather soar –
And I will live just as they do
28 And go wherever they go, too!'
With these words he began to sing
And make a dreadful clamouring.
After eagle, the beetle hopped;
32 To fly the higher was his thought.
Before the beetle far had gone,
He found himself bewildered, stunned,
And neither could fly higher still
36 Nor yet go back to his dung hill.
And he was famished, wanted food,
Sorely complained, loud as he could,
And did not care if any heard
40 Nor if they mocked him, any bird.
(No more than fox did long ago
When other beasts thought him so low.)
'I don't care whether I am thought
44 A worm or bird – or even that
I come in horse's excrement.
I'm sad and sick from famishment!'

Issi avient des surquidez:
48 Par eus memes sunt jugez;
Ceo enpernent que ne poënt fere,
Dunc lur covient a retrere.

76 Del sengler e de l'asne

D'un sengler cunte que encuntra
Par un chemin, u il ala,
Un asne, que ileoc estut.
4 Merveilla sei que ne se mut,
E qu'il li ne leissa la veie,
E que vers li ne s'asupleie!
A lui se hurtot malement.
8 Dunc l'apela par maltalent:
'Bien sai,' fet il, 'quei jeo fereie,
Si mes denz aguiser voleie!'
Par ceste essample nus assume
12 Que si est de l'orguillus hume,
Que quide bien en sun penser
Ke nul ne li deive cuntre ester.
Tant par sa fie en sa prüesce
16 Qu'il memes se hurte e blesce.

77 Del teissun e des pors

Issi avient que par un an
Ot en bois plenté de glan.
Les pors i (s)unt mis e chaciez.
4 Li teissuns s'est acumpainiez
Ensemble od eus, si recunut
Que porc esteit e estre dut.
Quant li porc viendrent a meisun,
8 E il vit fere l'occisïun,
Li teissuns comence a crïer,
A reneer e a jurer
Que teissuns fu! – ses piez musça,
12 Quant od les porcs al bois ala.

And thus with prideful folk we see
48 That their own judges they will be:
What they can't do, they undertake,
And then find out they must turn back.

76 The Boar and the Ass

There was a boar, as it is told,
Who met, while walking down the road,
An ass. Boar thought it curious
4 That ass budged not from where he was.
He would not yield and let boar go.
No deference would this ass show!
The boar then jabbed him viciously
8 And spoke to him maliciously:
'I know what I would do, forsooth,
If I should want to hone my tooth!'
Let this example be our guide.
12 When someone is all swelled with pride,
So sure he is of his position,
He thinks he'll meet no contradiction.
He trusts so his own might and sway
16 That he just hurts himself this way.

77 The Badger and the Pigs

Long ago the acorns were
Abundant in the woods one year.
To track them down, the pigs were sent;
4 Along with them, the badger went.
A pig he was, badger would say;
He must, therefore, behave that way.
But when the pigs came home, the badger
8 Saw what awaited them – mass slaughter!
The badger started crying there
And to renounce his deeds and swear
He badger was! – His feet he'd hid and
12 Gone with the pigs into the woodland.

Ceo est custume dasquanz genz
Si est oï e veü suvenz:
Teles custumes veulent enprendre
16 Dunt plusurs funt a eus entendre.
Mes quant il sunt aparceüz,
Tuz jurz sunt plus mescreüz.

78 Del lu e del heriçun

Un lu s'esteit acumpainez
Al hyriçun e bien afiez.
Puis avient si que li lus fu pris.
4 Al hyriçun ad dit, 'Amis,
Aïe meie! Si Deus te aït!'
Li hyriçuns respunt e dit,
['Je ne te puis noient aidier.
8 Au saintuaire va proier
Par cui tu iés pris e lïez
Que tu par euz soies aidiez.
Je cuit que tu lor prameïs
12 Tel chose que pas ne feïs.]
Tun vou t'estut ainz aquiter,
Que nuls te puisse deliverer.
Ja ne t'en aiderai ainceis;
16 Tel est la custume e la leis.'
Ceo veit hum suvent del felun:
Tant enchantet sun cumpainun
Qu'il memes est enginnez,
20 E ja par lui n'ert aidez.

79 Del lu e del bateler

Un lu vient a une rivere,
Mes ne sot en queile manere
Utre l'ewe puisse passer.
4 Un vilein vit ileoc ester
En un batel, si l'apela;
Que utre le past, ceo li pria.

With such folks that's how it will be
And this we often hear and see:
They will behave with such pretension
16 That they'll have everyone's attention.
But when they truly are perceived,
They find that they are not believed.

78 The Wolf and the Hedgehog

Wolf once was in the company
Of hedgehog; each pledged loyalty.
It happened wolf was captured and
4 He cried out to the hedgehog, 'Friend,
Come help me now! As God's my aid!'
The hedgehog, answering him, said,
['I can't help you in any way.
8 You'd better go to church and pray
That he by whom you're bound and tied
Will help you out and be of aid.
You promised, I believe, someone
12 To do a thing you haven't done.]
And from that vow you must get free,
Or nobody can rescue thee.
There's no way I can help you now;
16 Such is the custom and the law.'
      In one who's wicked it is thus:
This one will charm his friend so much
He gets himself ensnared, instead!
20 His friend will never give him aid.

79 The Wolf and the Boatman

Wolf to a river came one day
But now he couldn't find a way
Or any means to get across.
4 He saw a peasant then who was
Down at the river. Wolf called out –
Take him, he begged, across by boat!

Li vileins dist qu'il ne fereit,
8 Si bon lüer de lui n'aveit.
'Jo l'otri bien,' ceo dit li lus.
El batel entrent ambesdous;
De la tere sunt esluiné.
12 Li lus ad le vilein prïé
Qu'il li desist qu'il fera.
E li vileins li cumanda
Que treis paroles de saveir
16 Il deüst dire al sun espeir.
'Jeo volenters,' li lus respunt.
Idunc dresça la teste a munt;
'Bien fet, ki bien fet, ceo savez.'
20 Dist li vileins, 'Ceo est veritez.'
Quant il furent un poi alez,
Si li ad le vilein rovez,
Que un veir deist, e il retreit
24 'Mut fet pis, ki ne feit.'
Fet li vileins, 'Ore di le terz!'
Li lus esteit mut veizez;
Ne li voleit dire plus,
28 Ainz qu'il venist a tere sus.
Quant li lus esteit arivez,
Al vilein dist, 'Ore entendez!
Tut est perdu e luinz e pres
32 Quan que l'em fet pur mauveis!'
Fet li vileins, 'Si Deu m'eït,
De treis choses m'avez veir dit.
Pur quei ne vousis ainceis dire?'
36 Dunc comença li lus a rire:
'N'osai,' fet il, 'kar jeo cremeie
Que de la nef geté sereie.'
    As prudes hummes e as leiaus
40 Avient suvent damage e maus
De la cumpainie as feluns;
Mauveis en est lur guerduns.

No, he would not! the peasant said,
8 Unless he should be well repaid.
'I promise! Done!' wolf gave consent.
Into his boat the two then went
And soon were distant from the land.
12 The wolf then asked the peasant man
To tell him how he could repay.
The peasant laid it down this way:
That three wise sayings he should cite,
16 And do so when the time was right.
'Most willingly,' the wolf then said.
And straightaway wolf raised his head:
'He does well who does well, you know.'
20 The peasant said, 'That's surely so.'
A little farther from the land,
The peasant did of wolf demand
A truth; the wolf replied to that:
24 'He does far worse, whoe'er does naught.'
'Now tell the third!' the peasant said.
The wolf was very sly indeed.
He thought he'd better speak no more
28 Until he'd reached the other shore.
Then when the wolf was safely there,
He told the peasant man, 'Now hear! –
Both far and near you lose all when
32 You minister to evil men!'
The peasant said, 'So God help me!
You've told me three true things today.
To say such things, why wait till now?'
36 The wolf began to laugh aloud:
'I did not dare! I was afraid
You'd throw me off the boat!' he said.
To true men of integrity
40 Come anguish and adversity
When they consort with evil men:
They'll be rewarded poorly then.

80 De l'ostur e del huan

D'un ostur recunte ici
Que sur un fust aveit sun ni –
E li huan ensemble od lui.
4 Tant s'entreamerent ambedui
Que en un ni ensemble puneient,
E lur oiseus ensemble aveieint.
Ore avient si que un an
8 Li osturs les os al huan
Aveit duiz e [es]cha(r)piz
Od les suens oiselez petiz.
Puis lur ala quere viande,
12 Si cume nature le demande.
Mes quant a eus fu repeirez,
Fu sis niz orz e suillez:
Li huan l'aveient malmis!
16 Quant li ostur fu asis,
Ses oiseus leidi e blama;
Par maltalent lur repruva
Que vint ans ot eire tenue,
20 Unc si grant descuvenue!
Si oisel ne li firent mes!
Cil li respundirent aprés
Qu'il nes deit mie blamer,
24 Lui memes deit encuper:
Kar lur derere ont eü foire,
Pur ceo est dreit que en sun ni paire!
Il lur respunt, 'Vus dites veir.
28 Legere chose est a saver:
De l'oef le poeie bien geter –
Par chalur e par cover –
Nel poi fors mettre de nature –
32 Maudite seit tel nureture!'
Pur ceo dit hum en repruver
De la pum del duz pumer,
Si ele cheit desuz le fust amer.
36 Ja ne savera tant rüeler,
Que al mordre ne seit recunue,
Desur quel arbre ele est crue.
Sa nature peot hum guenchir,
40 Mes nul ne put del tut eissir.

80 **The Hawk and the Owl**

About a hawk I'll tell you next
Who in a tree trunk made her nest.
There was an owl in that tree, too.
4 They got along so well, those two,
That these birds did the same nest share,
They laid their eggs and hatched them there.
And then one year it happened that
8 The hawk upon the owl's eggs sat
And soon she hatched the eggs of owl
Along with her own birdies small.
And then she went to look for food
12 Just as her nature said she should.
But when she came back to her nest,
She found it all befouled and messed:
The owls had badly dirtied it!
16 And as the hawk in nest did sit,
She cursed and blamed the little birds
And scolded them with angry words:
This nest for twenty years kept she
20 With never such indecency!
Nor been by birds so mortified!
To her the little owls replied,
They weren't to blame for what was done.
24 Instead, she was the guilty one:
They'd diarrhea out the rear;
Of course that would in nest appear!
(S)he answered, 'What you say is so;
28 It is an easy thing to know:
For I can hatch owl's egg – I sit
And keep it warm and cover it –
But I cannot change nature's course –
32 Upon such nurturing, a curse!'
 An apple, we can likewise see,
Once fell from a sweet apple tree.
Under a bitter tree it lay.
36 But it can't roll so far away
That someone biting it won't know
The tree that did this apple grow.
From one's kind, one can deviate
40 But one can never abdicate.

81 De l'egle, de l'ostur, e de la grue

Un egles esteit mut iriez
Envers un ostur e curucez.
Tuz les oiseus fet asembler;
4 Aprés l'ostur les fist voler,
Saver s'il le purreient prendre.
Mes ne lur volt pas atendre:
El crus d'un chesne s'esteit mis.
8 Les oiseus l'unt entur asis.
Puis esgardent ki l'a(s)saudra
E ki avenir i purra.
Dunc unt la grue enveié
12 Pur le lung col l'unt preié.
La grue lance bek avant,
E li ostur demeintenant
L'aveit par la teste saisie.
16 La grue fu si esbaïe,
Que li mesavient par derere.
Tuz les oiseus fist trere arere –
Que entur lui venu esteieint
20 E ki aider li voleient.
Tuz les ordea e mesbailli,
E il s'en fueient desur li.
Quant ele ot sa teste fors mise,
24 Purpensa sei que en nule guise
Ne volst el païs arester,
Ainz passera, ceo dist, la mer
Pur la hunte que ele aveit fete,
28 Que li sereit tuz jurs retrete.
Quant ele fu en mer entree,
Si ad une maue encuntree,
Si li demanda en enquist
32 U ele alot. E cele li dist
Que de sun païs ert fuïe,
Si li cunta sa vileinie.
Dunc ad la maue respundue,
36 Demanda li si ele est venue
Senz cel usteil quil a huni.
E la grue li respundi:
'Einz l'ai,' fet ele, 'ensemble od mei!'

81 The Eagle, the Hawk, and the Crane

An eagle once was irritated
About a hawk, infuriated!
He called for all the birds to flock
4 And bid them all fly after hawk
To see if they could capture him.
But hawk wished not to wait for them
And hid within a hollow oak.
8 But then the birds surrounded hawk
And they began to talk about
Which one should strike, who'd draw hawk out.
It was crane who received their beck,
12 And this because of her long neck.
And when the crane thrust forth her beak,
The hawk, who was extremely quick,
Seized the crane's head and held on tight.
16 The crane was taken so with fright,
She had a mishap at her rear.
The birds all moved away from her –
Those who'd been round her, in attendance,
20 And who had wished to give assistance.
She'd covered them with excrement
So up they flew and off they went.
Then when she got her head back out,
24 There's one thing she was sure about:
She'd not stay in this land, she said –
She'd go across the sea instead,
For the disgraceful thing she'd done –
28 Which she'd soon hear from everyone.
And then when she had reached the sea,
She met a seagull there, and he
In parley with her, asked the crane
32 Where she was going. She explained
That from her land she'd had to flee
And told of her atrocity.
The seagull, hearing what she'd done,
36 Now asked the crane if she had come
Without her implement of shame.
She could in answer but exclaim:
'I have it with me still!' said she.

40 'Dunc te lo jeo par dreite fei
    Que tu t'en vois en ta cuntree,
    Quant de celui n'es deliveree.
    Greinur mal peot il ailurs fere.'
44 La grue se mist al repeire.
      Cest essample ad pur ceo cunté:
    Cil que sunt plein de mauveisté
    E en lur cuntree mesfunt,
48 Puis la guerpissent, si s'en vunt.
    Pur nent lessent lur païs,
    Aillurs funt il autel u pis!
    Lur mauveis quor deivent changer –
52 Ne mie lur mauveis quor lesser.

82 Del prestre e del lu

    Un prestre volst jadis aprendre
    A un lu lettres fere entendre.
    'A' dist le prestre; 'A' dist li lus,
 4 Que mut ert fel e enginnus.
    'B' dist le prestre, 'di od mei.'
    'B' dist li lus, 'jo l'otrei.'
    'C' dist le prestre, 'di avant.'
 8 'C' dist li lus, 'a i dunc itant?'
    Respunt le prestre, 'Ore di par tei.'
    Li lus li dist, 'Jeo ne sai quei!'
    'Di que te semble, si espel.'
12 Repunt li lus – il dit, 'Aignel!'
    Le prestre dit que verité tuche:
    Tel en pensé, tel en la buche.
    Le plus dit hum sovent:
16 Cel dunt il pensent durement
    E par lur buche est cuneü,
    Ainceis que seit d'autre sceü.
    La buche mustre le penser,
20 Tut deive ele de el parler.

40 'Then I must conscientiously
   Advise you to go home forthwith
   Since you've not gotten rid of it.
   It may yet do worse things elsewhere.'
44 And so crane started home from there.
    Now this example should address
   Those who are full of wickedness,
   Who've done wrong in their native home
48 And think they'll leave it all and roam.
   For nothing do they take this course;
   They'll do elsewhere the same or worse!
   One must first change his wicked heart –
52 One can't forsake it and depart.

82 The Preacher and the Wolf

   A preacher long ago was set
   To teach the wolf the alphabet.
   'A' said the preacher; 'A' wolf said,
4 Who very crafty was, and bad.
   'B' said the priest, 'say it with me.'
   'B' said the wolf, 'and I agree.'
   'C' said the preacher, 'say it o'er.'
8 'C' said the wolf, 'are there yet more?'
   The preacher said, 'You say them now.'
   The wolf replied, 'I don't know how!'
   'Say what you think, spell what you can.'
12 The wolf replied to this, 'A lamb!'
   The preacher told him that rang true,
   For as one thinks, his mouth goes, too.
    And thus, with many men you'll find
16 Whatever's topmost in their mind
   The mouth lets slip, and first they say
   What might come out some other way.
   The mouth exposes what one thinks
20 Though it would speak of other things.

83 De la serpent e del champ

Une serpent trespassot ja
Par mi un champ translança.
Li chans li dist, 'Reguarde tei!
4   Tu n'en portes nent de mei!'
        Autresi est des veisïez
Quant il se sunt acumpainez,
Entre eus se veulent si guaiter,
8   Tant se quident suzveizïer –
Que li uns par l'autre ne perde
Ne autres fors eus ni aerde,
Dunt entre eus seient encumbrez
12 Li uns par l'autre ne blamez.
Li uns de l'autre rien ne prent
Plus que li chans de la serpent.

84 De l'arundele e des muissuns

Un hum, ceo dit, entassot blé,
E l'arunde l'ad esguardé
Cum li muissun defors estoënt,
4   Que al blé asprimer n'osoënt.
L'arunde dunc les apela;
Que avant venissent lur rova.
Tant les aveit aseürez
8   Que en la grange esteient entrez.
Del blé mangerent durement
Dunt le vilein firent dolent!
Idunc jura qu'il les prendreit
12 E qu'il les us estupereit.
E l'arunde les ad garni,
Que le cunseil celui oï;
Li muissun s'en sunt desturnez;
16 Deus jurs entiers n'i sunt entrez.
Li vileins dist a sun sergant
Que merveille li semblot grant –
Ke li muissun sunt devenu.
20 Li bachelers ad respundu,

83 The Snake and the Field

It chanced a snake was on his way
Winding across a field one day.
The field spoke to the snake, 'Watch out!
4 Make sure that from me you take nought!'
    With cunning folk it thus will be
When in each other's company.
Each one keeps such a watchful eye,
8 Hoping the other he'll outsly –
Not losing to the other one
And sure, likewise, that nothing's won
For which he might be obligated
12 Or, by the other, inculpated.
One from another ought not take
More than the field did from the snake.

84 The Swallow and the Sparrows

A man was binding wheat one day.
A swallow, watching, saw the way
The sparrows would outside remain,
4 Not daring to get near the grain.
The swallow called to them and said
She thought that they should go ahead.
She gave them such encouragement
8 That soon into the barn they went.
The wheat they gobbled eagerly
And brought the peasant misery!
He swore he'd capture them for this
12 By plugging all the entrances.
The swallow cautioned every bird
About his plan which she had heard;
And so the sparrows stayed away,
16 Out of the barn for two whole days.
The peasant to his servant said
That this seemed very strange indeed –
The sparrows had all gone away.
20 The young man, in reply, did say

Que l'arundel l'aveit fet
Qu'il s'esteient issi retret.
Mes s'il voleit sun cunseil creire,
24 Teus paroles direit pur veire,
Dunt l'arundele decevereit
E les muissuns li remereit.
En haut parlast que ele l'oïst,
28 E si afermast e bien desist
Que jamés oiseus ne prendreit –
Ne que ja mal ne lur fereit.
Li vileins dist ceste parole,
32 L'arundele, ke fu fole,
As muissuns l'ala recunter,
Sis refist en la grange entrer.
Li vileins ad ses engins fet,
36 Les muissuns ad pris e a mort tret.
Dunc tencerent a l'arundele,
Que ele lur ot dit male novele.
Ele lur respunt, 'Cil me menti,
40 E jeo menti vus tut autresi.
Quant me dist veir, e jeo a vus.
Ore est li maus turné sur nus.'
  Pur ceo mustre par cest escrit,
44 Meintefeiz hum trove e dit:
Meint hum a, ki mentir veut,
A celui ke li mentir solt.
Nul sage hum ne devreit creire
48 Parole, nule si ele ne fust veire.
Tel creit mençunge en sun curage,
Que li turne a grant damage.
Si fist l'arundele le vilein,
52 Que les muissuns prist al demein.

85 Del vilein e des bus

Ci nus recunte en ceste fable,
Que uns vileins treist hors de sa stable
Od ses bus le fiens qu'il firent.
4 Li buf par tençun l'asaillirent,

That swallow made it happen so:
'Twas she who bade the sparrows go.
If he would listen to advice,
24 He'd tell the peasant something wise:
A way that he could dupe the swallow
And thus could bring back every sparrow.
He should speak loud so she would hear;
28 And then he should affirm and swear
He'd never capture any bird –
Not one of them he'd ever hurt.
The peasant spoke as he was bid.
32 Here's what the foolish swallow did:
She told the sparrows what she'd learned;
Thus to the barn the birds returned.
The peasant then did traps prepare,
36 And caught the sparrows, killed them there,
While they the swallow did accuse:
They said she'd given them false news.
'He lied to me,' she then replied,
40 'Accordingly, to you I lied.
When he spoke truth, I did likewise;
Now back upon us are his lies.'
From this example we see well
44 What people often find and tell:
That many men will choose to lie
To one who lies habitually.
A wise man must not trust forsooth
48 A single word that's not the truth.
Who in his heart believes a lie
Will grievously be hurt thereby.
Swallow and peasant were this way:
52 He caught the sparrows the next day.

85 The Peasant and the Oxen

You will be told here in this fable
Of peasant and oxen; from the stable
He made them haul their defecation.
4 So they began an altercation.

Si repruverent al vilein
La bone cerveise e le pein,
Que par lur travail ot eü;
8 Mes malement lur ad rendu;
Kar a grant hunte les demena.
E li vileins lur demanda
Que ceo esteit qu'il lur fist feire?
12 'Fiens funt il fors de l'estable treire!'
Dist li vileins, 'Vus le femastes;
E la meisun encumbrastes.'
Li buf dïent, 'Ceo est veritez!'
16 Dunc s'est li vilein purpensez,
Si lur respunt que hors le traient –
Bien est dreiz que la peine en aient!
  Issi va del mauveis sergant
20 Que tut en jur va repruchant
Sun grant servise a sun seignur;
Ne prent garde del honur.
De ceo qu'il mesfet suvent
24 Ne li peot suvenir nïent.
Quant sun travail veut repruver,
De sun mesfet li deit remembrer.

86 De la musche e de l'ef

Une musche e un es tencerent
E ensemble se curucerent.
La musche dit que meuz valeit,
4 E que en tel liu valeir poeit –
U cele ne se osot veer!
Nis sur le rei poeit seer!
E quanque l'ees tut l'an purchaçot
8 E atraheit e t[ra]veillot,
Li ert toleit, si ert tüé,
E de sa meisun fors geté.
'Jeo e mes cumpainuns mangums
12 De tun miel tant cum volums.'
Li ees respunt, 'Vus dites veir.

The peasant man they did upbraid
For the fine beer and loaves of bread
That by their sweat and toil he had.
8 Yet what he gave as pay was bad;
He treated them with great disdain.
The peasant questioned them amain:
What had he done – What's this about?
12 'You make us haul our ordure out!'
Said he, 'It's what you defecated.
With it the house is saturated.'
The oxen said, 'How true that is!'
16 The peasant pondered over this,
Concluding, 'They should haul it off –
It's their own work – they must not loaf!'
   With a bad servant it's this way:
20 He keeps complaining every day
Of his great service to his lord;
His master's honour is ignored.
His frequent impropriety
24 Goes quickly from his memory.
When he complains of tasks assigned,
He'd best keep his misdeeds in mind.

86 The Fly and the Bee

A fly and bee once disagreed;
Each made the other mad indeed.
Fly said he was superior;
4 Where'er he went, his worth was more –
Where bee dared not be seen, he guessed.
The fly upon the king could rest!
Although bee spent the year procuring,
8 Accumulating and securing,
They'd take her stores and kill the bee –
Cast out of her own house she'd be:
'My friends and I will eat your store
12 Of honey – all we hanker for.'
The bee responded, 'That is so.

Mes il est leger a saveir
Que plus es vils que jeo ne sui –
16 Kar en tuz lius fez [tu] ennui.
Sez u seez, vas la u vas,
Ja par tun fet honur n'avras.
Jeo sui pur le mien fet amee,
20 E mut cheri e bien gardee.'
    Issi fet del natre felun:
Quant il ad bien en bandun,
Vers les meillurs trop se noblee.
24 E de parole s'esrichee;
Par grant desdein les cuntralie.
Neis si nul est que bien li die
La verité de sun afeire,
28 En pleine curt, le(s) fera teire.

87 De l'escufle e del jai

Un escufles jut en sun lit;
Malades est, si cum il dit.
Un jai ot sun ni pres de lui,
4 A ki il fist suvent ennui.
Li escufles se purpensa
Que sa mere i enveera,
Si li fra requere pardun
8 Que pur lui face oreisun.
'Mere,' fet il, 'kar li preez!
Qu'il prie pur mei, li requerez!'
'Jeo,' fet ele, 'cument irai?
12 Ne sai cument li prierai.
Meintefeiz as suillé sun ni
E sur ses oiseus esmeulti.'
    Issi est de la fole gent:
16 La u il unt mesfet suvent
Veulent aler merci crïer,
Ainz qu'il le veulent amender.

But it does not take much to know
You're wickeder than I; that's clear –
16 For you make trouble everywhere.
Sit where you wish, go where you please;
You'll have no honour for your deeds.
Yet I am loved for what I do;
20 I'm cherished and protected, too.'
With greedy, evil man 'tis thus:
Whene'er his goods are copious;
He boasts to his superiors,
24 Exalts himself and puts on airs,
Irking them with his insolence.
But if he's of no consequence,
Whoever tells him the straight truth –
28 And publicly – will shut his mouth.

87 The Kite and the Jay

A kite was lying in his bed;
He was quite ill, and so he said.
A jay had made his nest near by
4 Whom kite did frequently annoy.
Here's what the kite now thought about:
He planned to send his mother out
To beg for pardon of the jay
8 And ask that he, for kite's sake, pray.
'Mother, I ask you now,' said he,
'Go beg the jay to pray for me!'
And she replied, 'How can I go?
12 I don't know how to beg him so.
His nest you frequently have dirtied
And defecated on his birdies.'
With foolish people it's like this:
16 Exactly where they've gone amiss
They cry for clemency and grace
Before they try to mend their ways.

88 De deus lus

Deus lus hors bois s'encuntrerent.
La se resturent, si parlerent
Que nul hum nes osot atendre –
4 Tut ne vousissent il rien prendre.
Ceo dist li uns, 'Kar assaiums
Bien a fere, si nus poüms –
Par quei nus eüssum honur
8 E que nul n'eit de nus poür.'
Li autre dit, 'Jo oi merveilles!
Quant tel chose nus cunseilles!
Di dunc, u nus poüms aler?'
12 'Jeo te sai,' fet il, 'bien mustrer.
Veez la cel champ, u la gent sïent,
U lur garbes cuillent e lïent.
Alums e si lur aidums,
16 E lur garbes ensemble portums.'
'Bien avez dit,' cil li respunt.
D'isci el champ venuz i sunt.
Le blé cuillirent e porterent,
20 Mes les humes les escrïerent.
Li uns des lus ad dunc parlé,
Sun cumpainun ad apelé:
'Veez,' fet il, 'cum nus escrïent!
24 Mal nus veulent, pis nus dïent!
Nostre bienfet ne vaut nïent
Plus que li maus vers ceste gent.
Hastivement al bois alums,
28 Seüms si cum nus sulïums.'
Iluc jurerent e pramistrent,
Jamés bien ne ferunt, ceo distrent.
    Ceo veit hum suvent del felun,
32 Ki a mut petit d'acheisun
Laisse le bien qu'il comence.
Sil ne veit en sa presence
Le lüer que en veut aver,
36 A mal en turne sun esper.

88 **The Two Wolves**

Two wolves met near a wood one day.
They stopped and talked about the way
That none dared be with them – no man –
4 Even when theft was not their plan.
One wolf spoke first and said, 'I would
Like us to try to do some good –
Then we'll become illustrious
8 And none will be afraid of us.'
'My word!' replied the other wolf.
'You think that we could pull that off!
So tell me now, what can we do?'
12 The one replied, 'I will show you.
Look at that field and see those folks
Gathering up and tying stalks.
Why don't we go and help those men.
16 We'll carry sheaves along with them.'
'You've spoken well,' he gave consent,
And down into the field they went.
They gathered up and carried grain.
20 The men cried out at them amain.
The first wolf now must have his say,
And called out to his friend this way:
'See how they shout at us!' he said.
24 'They wish us harm, and speak worse yet!
And our good deed is no more prized
Than wicked ones in those folks' eyes.
Let's run back to the woods,' said he,
28 'And be the way we used to be.'
And they made promises and swore
That they would do good deeds no more!
One sees this in a criminal
32 Who'll find excuse however small –
Whatever good he starts, he'll leave.
Should he not then and there receive
The praises that he thinks are due,
36 His good intentions turn askew.

89 Del gupil e del lu

Un gupil e un lu s'(a)irerent
E ensemble se curucerent,
Si que nul nes pot acorder
4 Ne lur raisun a bien turner.
Nepurec par ceste acheisun
Alerent devant le leün;
La parole li unt mustree
8 De verité tut recordee.
Li lïuns dit que avis li fu,
Que li lus aveit tort eü
E li gupilz aveit raisun.
12 'Mes tant i ot de mesprisun –
E issi cume mei est avis –
Tut eit issi li lus mespris:
Sa mençunge est plus covenable
16 E meuz resemble chose estable
Que del gupil la veritez.'
Nul de eus ne deit estre jugez.
    Issi deit fere li bon sire:
20 Il ne deit pas juger ne dire,
Si si hume, que de lui tienent,
Ireement en sa curt vienent.
Ne deit si vers l'un parler,
24 Que a l'autre deive mut peser,
Mes adrescer a sun poër
E l'ire fere remaner.

90 Del lu e del cheverol

Une chevre voleit aler
La u pasture poeit trover.
Sun cheverol apela a li,
4 Si li pria e defendi
Qu'il ne laissast pur murir
Ensemble od eus beste venir –
Pur parole ne pur preere! –
8 De ci ke ele revienge arere.

89 The Fox and the Wolf

A fox and wolf were furious.
Each irked the other one so much
That no one could bring peace about
4 Or help them reason this thing out.
To help resolve their argument,
The two before the lion went,
Their disagreement to relate
8 And all the facts enumerate.
The lion told them how it seemed:
The wolf was in the wrong, he deemed:
'The fox's case is right enough.
12 I've heard, however, so much guff,
That this, as well, seems clear to me –
Mistaken's how a wolf must be –
For lies and wolf are consonant!
16 Lies better suit his temperament
Than truth does fox's disposition.'
On neither could he bring conviction.
  No good seignior should be this way:
20 No judgment pass, no verdict say,
If men under his sovereignty
Should come to court most angrily.
Unto the one he must not utter
24 Something that might upset the other.
But he must try to put things right,
As best he can, and end their spite.

90 The Wolf and the Kid

A she-goat wished, in olden days,
To find a field where she could graze.
She called her kid to her and said
4 To heed her well: For she forbade
His letting any beast inside –
By this, on pain of death, abide! –
No matter what their prayers or talk,
8 Not until she herself came back.

Quant ele fu al bois venue
E li lus l'ot dedenz veüe,
Al cheverol vet, si li rova
12 Que l'us overist; ceo li pria
Od tele voiz cume la chevre aveit.
E li cheverol li respundeit,
Que la voiz de sa mere oï,
16 Mes sun cors nent ne choisi:
'Va arere,' fet ele, 'lere!
Bien sai que tu n'es pas ma mere!'
Si li cheverol l'[e]üst recuilli
20 En la meisun ensemble od li,
Mangié l'[e]üst e devoré!
    Pur ceo chastie le sené:
Que hum ne deie mal cunseil creire,
24 Ne mençuinge dire pur veire.
Tute gent seivent cunseiller;
Mes tuz cunseilz n'unt pas mester.
Li feluns e li desleial
28 Dunent tuz jurs cunseil de mal.

91 **Del mesurer**

Ci nus cunte d'un mesurer,
Que tere mesurot un jur.
Durement maudist la mesure;
4 Kar ne pot par nule aventure
Od li, ceo dist, dreit mesurer.
La perce dist, 'Lai mei ester!
Jeo ne faz par mei nule rien.
8 Tu me gettes, ceo veit hum bien.
Mes tu es plein de tricherie –
Sur mei turnes ta felunie!'
    Issi funt li nundreiturers.
12 Quant hum aparceit lur mesters,
Les autres veulent encuper
E lur mesfet sur eus turner.

Then as she reached the forest land,
Wolf marked her disappearance and
Went to the kid, there to implore
12 The kid to open wide the door.
He tried to sound like mamma goat.
The kid, in his reply, made note,
While he heard mamma loud and clear,
16 He did not see her body there:
'Get out of here! You plunderer!
You're not my mamma – That I'm sure!'
However, had the kid said yes
20 And let the wolf into his house,
On kid wolf would have had a feed!
  Smart people therefore should take heed:
Do not believe in bad advice,
24 Nor, feigning truth, should you tell lies.
For all can give advice, indeed,
But not all of it should we heed.
And men of falseness, men of vice,
28 Will always give you bad advice.

91 The Surveyor

Hear now of a surveyor's way,
Out measuring some land one day.
He cursed his measure and accused
4 It fiercely: it could not be used
To measure properly, said he.
The measure answered, 'Let me be!
I can't do anything alone.
8 It's clearly you who throws me down.
But you are full of treachery –
To blame your own misdeeds on me!'
  With malefactors it's the same.
12 When someone understands their game,
They'll try accusing someone else
For evil that they did themselves.

92 **De la bisse e de sun feon**

Une bisse chastiot ja
Un suen feon, que ele mena,
Cum il se deüst par tut guarder
4 E des veneürs desturner
E de lui qu'il ne l'encuntrast,
Qu'il ne l'ocesist e mangast.
Quant il aloënt si parlant,
8 Si unt veü un hume errant;
Arc portot, setes e bulzuns.
Sa mere apela li feüns;
Demanda li, que cil hume fu.
12 E la bysse ad respundu:
'C'est cil, dunt plus te deiz cremer;
E greinur poür puz aver.
Mes ore l'esgarde bien de pres,
16 Si tu l'encuntres jamés,
Que de lui te saces garder.'
'Nus n'estut pas,' fet il, 'duter.
Il ne nus veut fere nul mal.
20 De l'autre part del cheval
Est descenduz, si est mucez.
De nus veer est esmaiez.'
'Nenil, beu fiz, de ceo n'i ad nïent.
24 Einz esguarde hardiement,
Si vait sun fust aparaillant –
U ad grant mal el chef devant.
Sil le fet vers nus venir,
28 Bien en purrum le mal sentir!
Meuz est que nus en fuïums.'
Dunc li respundi li feüns:
'Ne fuirai mie, dici qu'il traie –
32 Quel aventure que jeo en aie!'
En reproche dit hum suvent,
Fous ne crent, dici qu'il p[r]ent.
Quant fol ne vuet crere le sage,
36 Suvent i pert par sun utrage.

92 **The Doe and Her Fawn**

In olden days there was a doe.
She warned her fawn, who was in tow,
That he must keep watch everywhere,
4 And of the hunters must stay clear
And of all others he might meet
Who'd kill him for a bite to eat.
As they went walking, talking thus,
8 They saw a man who roving was,
With bolts and arrows and a bow.
The fawn called to the mother doe
And asked her who this man could be.
12 In answer to her fawn, said she:
'Of him you should be most in dread;
Fear him with all your might,' she said.
'Look very closely at that man,
16 So if you meet him once again
You'll know to watch out when he's near.'
Said fawn, 'We have no need to fear.
I'm sure that he no harm intends.
20 Out of our sight he now descends,
Gets off his horse and tries to hide.
He sees us and is terrified.'
'Oh no, dear son, you're wrong,' said she.
24 'At first he watches carefully,
Preparing arrows all the while –
The tips of which indeed are vile.
If he should send one over here,
28 We'd feel it, certainly, my dear!
It's better that we run away.'
The fawn replied to her this way:
'Until his bow's drawn, I won't flee –
32 No matter what my fate may be!'
  For many men these words are apt:
Fools do not cry until they're trapped.
When fools don't heed what wisdom says,
36 They're dupes of their own stupid ways.

93 Del corbel ki enseignot sun oisel

Ci nus recunte d'un corbel
Que enseignot un suen oisel,
Qu'il ne deüst nul humme atendre,
4 Quil vousist encumbrer e prendre.
Sil humme veïst baisser vers tere,
Prendre bastun u piere quere,
Dunc s'en deüst aillurs voler –
8 Que cil nel poïst encumbrer!
ˈSi jeo nel vei,' fet il, 'beisser
N'en ses meins rien manïer,
Dei jeo dunc remüer?'
12 Li corps respunt, 'Laisse m'ester!
Vole par tei, si te (h)aïe!
Ore sui sanz dute de ta vie.
A mes autres oiseus irai,
16 A mun poeir lur aiderai.'
    Par cest essample nus dit tant:
Quant hum ad nurri sun enfant,
Qu'il le veit sage e veizïé,
20 Le queor ad joius e lié!
A sun cunseil le deit leisser
E puis les autres avancer.

94 Del buc e del lu

Par veil essample truis escrit,
E Ysopus le cunte e dit.
Un bucs entra en une lande,
4 Si alot quere sa viande.
Guarda, si vit un lu venir –
Ne pot esturner ne guenchir!
Enmi la lande s'arestut.
8 Li lus demanda, que ceo dut
Qu'il seit en cele lande mis –
E qu'il aveit dedenz quis?
Li bucs respunt, 'Jeo vus fuï,
12 Tant cum jeo poi. Mes ore sai de fi,

93 The Crow Instructing His Child

Next is a story of a crow
Who taught his fledgling long ago
He must not hang about with men
4 Lest they should maim and seize him then.
If he sees someone bending down
To grab a stick or find a stone,
He'd better fly off instantly –
8 Lest the man do him injury!
'If I don't see him stooping and
If I see nothing in his hand,
Then do I have to move away?'
12 The crow replied, 'Enough, I say!
So fly away! Take care, my dear!
For of your life I have no fear.
And I,' he said, 'must go see how
16 To help my other birdies now.'
  A lesson from my tale now hear:
When someone does an infant rear,
Then sees him grow up shrewd and smart,
20 He should be happy, glad of heart!
Let him manage his own affairs,
And go help others cope with theirs.

94 The Billy Goat and the Wolf

This tale was written long ago;
And Aesop spoke and told it so.
A billy goat into a wood
4 Went searching one day for some food.
He looked, saw wolf coming his way –
He can't turn back or run away!
And so he stopped amid some brush.
8 The wolf spoke now, inquiring thus:
Why did he in those bushes fare –
What was he looking for in there?
Said goat, 'From you I tried to flee
12 As best I could. But now I see

Que jeo ne poi fuï[r] avant!
Pur ceo vus sui alé querant.'
Li lus li dist, 'E jeo te ai quis
16 Par tuz les bois de cest païs –
Ceo m'est avis, un an entier.
Mut aveie grant desirer
De manger de ta char, que est saine –
20 Si n'iés mie chargié de laine.'
 'Ore m'avez,' fet li bucs, 'trové!
 Si vus requer par charité
 Que aucune merci e pardun
24 Facez cest vostre cumpainun.'
 Li lus li dist, quant il l'oï,
 'Tu n'averas ja de mei merci!
 Kar ne te puis terme doner,
28 Que jeo te veie vif aler.'
 'Jeo ne quer terme,' dist li bucs,
 'Fors tant que jeo die pur vus
 Une messe, autre pur mei,
32 Sur cel tertre, ke jo la vei.
 Tutes les bestes qui l'orrunt,
 Que as bois e as viles sunt,
 Ferunt pur nus a Deu preere.'
36 Li lus l'otreie en teu manere:
 Hors de la lande amdui en vunt,
 Ensemble vienent tresque al munt.
 Li bucs esteit desus muntez.
40 Li lus fu tut aseürez,
 Desuz remist, si atendi.
 Li bucs leva en haut sun cri.
 Si durement aveit crïé,
44 Que li pastur sunt hors alé
 E cil que pres del munt esteient
 E as viles entur maneient.
 Le lu virent, si l'escrïerent –
48 De tutes parz les chiens hüerent.
 Le lu unt pris e deciré,
 E il ad le buc apelé,
 'Frere!' fet il, 'bien sai e vei,
52 Malement avez prïé pur mei.

It's useless, for I can't flee more!
I've come to look for you, therefore.'
'I've looked for you,' the wolf replied,
16 'Throughout the land, woods far and wide –
For one whole year, it seems to me.
And I have wanted fervently
To eat your flesh, so firm and full –
20 Indeed, you've hardly any wool.'
The goat replied, 'You've now found me!
I ask you, out of charity
To do an act of great compassion –
24 Just one small thing for your companion.'
The wolf responded readily.
'You'll have no charity from me!
For I can't grant you a reprieve
28 And see you running 'round alive.'
'I only ask for this delay
So that for your sake I could say
A mass, and also one for me,
32 Yonder upon that hill I see.
All of the beasts who'll hear my prayer
In towns and forests everywhere
Will say a prayer to God for us.'
36 This plea the wolf acknowledged thus:
They left the woods and walked until
Together they had reached the hill.
On up the hill billy goat went.
40 But wolf, who was so confident,
Remained below and standing by.
The goat now loudly raised a cry.
Indeed so loud and hard he cried
44 That all the herdsmen ran outside
And all folks dwelling near the mound
And those in villages around.
They saw the wolf and raised a shout –
48 From every side the dogs barked out.
They caught the wolf, tore him to shreds,
While he called to the goat and said,
'My brother, it is clear to see
52 That you have badly prayed for me.

Bien poi entendre par le cri,
Que ceo ert preere de enemi.
Mut est mauveise ta pramesse.
56 Unc mes n'oï peur messe!'
'Par ma fei, sire,' dist li bucs,
'Tut autresi priai pur vus,
Cum vus vousistes pur mei feire;
60 Kar fel estes e de put eire.
Ja ne poeie jeo merci aveir,
Que jeo vesquisse tresque al seir;
Pur ceo m'estut de mei penser,
64 E vus leisser e ublïer.'
    Ceo veit hum de meinte gent
Que quident tut a escïent
Que autre deive pur eus preer
68 E lur message bien porter.
Si parolent le plus pur eus
E leissent si ublïent i ceus,
A ki il eurent bel premis –
72 Ne lur fu unc fors li pis!

95 Del vilein e de sa femme cuntrarïuse

Un vilein ot femme espuse,
Que mut esteit cuntrarïuse.
Un jur furent ensemble alé
4 Pur eus deduire par un pré.
Li vileins a sa femme dit
Que unc mes des oilz ne vit
Nul pré fauké si üelement.
8 Ele li respunt hastivement,
'Ainz fu a uns forces trenchez.'
Dist li vileins, 'Einz est fauchez.'
'Einz est,' fet la femme, 'tenduz.'
12 Dunc s'est li vileins irascuz.
'Tu es,' fet il, 'fole pruvee –
Ceste herbe fu od falcs copee!
Me tu iés si engresse e fole –
16 Que avant veus mettre ta parole.

I understand your cry to be
The praying of an enemy.
Your promise is deplorable.
56 I've heard no mass more horrible!'
'In all good faith, my lord, I say
I prayed for you in just the way
You would have prayed for me,' goat said,
60 'For you are evil and low bred.
You wouldn't have the charity
To let me live till eve,' said he;
'I must fend for myself – I thought,
64 And you I forfeited, forgot.'
       With many people this we see –
Those who believe with certainty
That other men for them should pray
68 And bear their message in this way.
They'll speak just for themselves, howe'er,
Forgetting those who sought their prayer
To whom they made fine promises –
72 Yet they will be the worse for this!

95 The Peasant and His Contrary Wife

A peasant man a wife did marry
Who was exceedingly contrary.
One day they to a meadow went
4 Together for their merriment.
Then spoke the peasant to his wife,
He'd seen no meadow, all his life,
Cut with a scythe so evenly.
8 His wife responded speedily,
'Rather, it was cut with shears.'
'Rather, it was a scythe, my dear.'
The wife said, 'Rather, sheared it was.'
12 This made the peasant furious:
'You've proved yourself a foolish ass –
It was a scythe that cut this grass!
You've such a nasty, foolish way –
16 You always have to have your say.

La meie veus fere remeindre;
Par engresté me vols ateindre.'
Li vileins l'ad aval getee,
20 Si li ad la lange copee.
Puis demande quei avis li fu
Que ele en aveit entendu –
Si li prez fu od falcs fauchez
24 U od forces fust trenchez.
La vielle, quant ne pot parler,
Od ses deiz prist a mustrer
Que forces l'aveient trenché,
28 E que falcs ne l'ot pas seié!
    Par cest essample veut mustrer;
Bien le peot hum suvent pruver:
Si fols parole une folie
32 E autre vient, que sens li die,
Nel creit pas, einz s'en aïre;
La u il set que l'en est pire.
Veut sa mençunge mettre avant,
36 Nul nel fereit de ceo taisant.

96 Del vilein e de sa femme tenceresse

D'un vilein cunte ki aveit
Une femme qu'il mut cremeit,
Kar ele esteit mut felunesse,
4 De male part e tenceresse.
Eissi avient que par un jur
Menot ses humes en labur.
Dunc prïerent cil al vilein
8 Que lur dunast cerveise e pein –
Si en purreient le meuz ovrer.
A sa femme les ruve aler
E li prïer que ele lur dunast;
12 Kar pis lur sereit, s'il i alast!
Cil unt a la femme preié;
Puis li unt dit e cunseillé
Que sis sires pas nel voleit.
16 Dunc respundi que ele lur dureit –

You take away whatever's mine;
And me, you vilely undermine.'
Down to the ground his wife he flung,
20 And then the man cut out her tongue.
He asked if this was her intent –
And what, exactly, had she meant –
Was it a scythe that trimmed the sod
24 Or was it shears that clipped the sward?
The woman could not talk, and so
She used her fingers now to show
The meadow had been clipped by shears;
28 No scythe had cut the grasses here!
    From this example we should learn
What people frequently discern:
That when a fool speaks foolishness
32 And someone comes who talks some sense,
The fool will doubt him and get mad
Although he knows his case is bad.
He has to get his falsehoods in
36 And nobody can silence him.

96 The Peasant and His Cantankerous Wife

About a peasant you will hear
Who had a wife whom he did fear,
For she was full of wickedness,
4 Bad-tempered and cantankerous.
One day it chanced to come about
That with his workmen he went out.
The workers sought the man and said
8 They'd like from him some beer and bread –
By this, their work would benefit.
He said to ask his wife for it
And beg she should these things bestow;
12 They'd be worse off were he to go!
They went to ask for bread and beer,
And they explained and said to her
That their seignior had asked for none.
16 So she replied, she'd give them some –

Mes guardassent qu'il n'en eüst –
Ne ne mangast od eus ne beüst!
Ore alassent faucher les prez;
20 Ele lur portereit asez.
Cil s'en alerent lïement,
Ele vient aprés hastivement.
Viande e beivre lur aporta.
24 Que haitié fussent, ceo lur preia.
Ensemble asistrent al manger.
'Pensez,' fet ele, 'del haiter!'
'Si ferums nus,' fet li baruns,
28 'E grant merci que nus l'avums!'
Quant ele vit sun seignur lié,
Mut ot le queor triste e irrié.
De sun barun se treist ariere –
32 E il siwi vers la rivere.
Tant cum ele se traist en sus,
E il la siwi e plus e p[l]us –
Tant que li piez li eschapa,
36 En l'ewe cheit, si enfundra.
Les serganz saillirent aprés;
A val l'ewe curent adés
Pur li tenir, que ele ne passast
40 E que li floz n'en portast.
Li vilein les ad escrïé,
Dit que ne sunt pas bien alé.
Encuntre l'ewe la deüssent quere –
44 La la purrent trover a tere,
La la querunt, si ferunt bien.
Tant ert encuntre tute rien,
Que al val l'ewe n'est pas alee,
48 Od reddur n'est mie turnee –
En sa mort ne feïst ele mie
Ceo que ne vot fere en sa vie.
   Issi avient: plusurs estrivent
52 Vers lur seignurs tant cum il vivent.
Ne saver ne veulent ne sentir,
Quels maus lur peot avenir:
Lur riote tienent avant.

But take care he gets none of it –
He must not eat or drink a bit!
Now go on back, the meadow scythe;
20 She'd bring them plenty, said the wife.
So off they went most happily
And she came after hastily.
She brought the workers drink and food
24 And bade them be of cheerful mood.
Together they sat down and ate.
Said she, 'Cheers! Let us celebrate!'
Their lord replied, 'We will do thus,
28 And thanks for all you've given us!'
Then when she saw her husband glad,
Her heart grew miserable and mad.
And now away from him she drew –
32 Down to the river – he pursued.
The more she tried to flee from there,
Closer, closer he came to her –
Till she lost footing on the ground,
36 Fell in the water and went down.
Then after her jumped in the servants,
Carried swiftly with the currents,
To grab her, try to stop her, so
40 She'd not be carried with the flow.
The peasant called his men; said he,
They were not where they ought to be.
Upstream they ought to look for her –
44 They'd find her on the bottom there.
So there they looked, with great success.
For she'd so much contrariness
That down the stream she would not go,
48 But went against the water's flow –
Behaving in her death, this wife,
Exactly as she'd wished in life.
    And many folks will thus argue
52 With their seignior their whole life through.
They do not think about or care
What trouble this may cause howe'er,
Persisting in their disaccord.

56 Quant il le va aparcevant,
  E il le turne en maltalent,
  Si se venge plus asprement.

97 **Del lievre e del cerf**

  Un lievres vit un cerf ester –
  Ses cornes prist a reguarder.
  – Mut li sembla bele sa teste!
4 Plus se tint vile que nule beste,
  Quant autresi n'esteit cornuz,
  E qu'il esteit si poi creüz.
  A la Sepande ala parler
8 Si li cumence a demander:
  Pur quei ne l'ot tel criee
  E de cornes si aürnee
  Cum ot le cerf qu'il ot veü.
12 La Deuesse ad respundu:
  'Tu mesfez,' fet ele, 'lei mei ester!
  Tu nes purreies guverner!'
  'Si ferai bien!' il li respunt.
16 Dunc ot cornes al chief amunt,
  Mes nes poeit mie porter,
  Kar ne saveit od tut aler;
  Car plus aveit que ne deüst
20 Ne que sa grandur n'estut.
    Par ceste essample veut mustrer:
  Le coveitus e le aver
  Veulent tuz jurz tant comencer

56 When he sees what they do, the lord
   Will turn on them with bad intent;
   His vengeance is more vehement.

97 The Hare and the Deer

A hare once saw a stock-still deer –
And at his horns began to peer.
– This head, thought he, so beautiful!
4 While *his* seemed lowliest of all
Because such horns were not his lot;
Also he was too small, he thought.
He went to talk to the Creator
8 And started to interrogate her:
Why had she not made him that way
With antlers in such fine array
Like those of deer whom he'd just seen.
12 To this the goddess answered then,
'You're wrong! Now stop it! Let me be!
You couldn't manage them,' said she.
'Oh yes, indeed I could!' hare said.
16 Thus he got horns atop his head
But could not carry them around
And could not move with them, he found.
It was more weight than he could bear
20 And much too much for likes of hare.
From this example you should see
Folks covetous and miserly:
They always start such projects as

24 E si se veulent eshaucer,
  Si enpernent par lur utrage,
  Que lur turne a damage.

n leu regarda un coulou
Qui coullott desoiz unbuisso

98 **Del lu e del colum**

  Un lu esgarda un colum,
  Que cuillot desuz un buissun
  Ramels, dunt sun ni voleit fere.
4 Li lus parla (ne se pot tere!) –
  'Mut te vei,' fet il, 'travailler,
  Cuillir merin e purchacer;
  Jeo ne vei meudre ta meisun.'
8 Dunc respundi li culum,
  'E jeo te vei tuz jurs berbiz cuillir,
  Aignel e mutuns retenir;
  E si n'en es meuz avancez
12 Ne plus riches ne plus preisez.'
    Issi vet il des robeürs,
  Des laruns e des tricheürs:
  Quant il asemblent autri aveir,
16 Mut le peot hum sovent veer,
  Qu'il n'en sunt gueres amendé;
  Tuz jurz vivent en poverté.

24 They think will raise their social class.
What they attempt through foolishness
Turns back on them, injurious.

98 The Wolf and the Dove

A wolf one day a dove did see
Gathering beneath the shrubbery
Some little twigs, his nest to build.
4 Wolf spoke (for he could not be stilled!) –
'You're labouring so hard, I see,
Gathering, massing wood,' said he;
'You can't improve your house this way.'
8 The dove responded right away,
'And I see you collecting lambs,
Gathering sheep, amassing rams;
That's not made you superior
12 Or more esteemed or wealthier.'
With thieving men the same is true,
With scoundrels and with tricksters, too:
When they amass another's goods,
16 It can be clearly understood
This won't bring them prosperity;
They'll always live in poverty.

99 **Del gupil e del chat**

Un gupil e un chaz alerent
Par mi un champ, si purparlerent
Qu'il sereient cumpainun;
4 Dunc s'asemblent suz un buissun.
Li chaz al gupil demanda,
Par quels se defendera
La u il erent entrepris.
8 E li gupil li dit, 'Amis,
Cent engins sai, u mut me crei,
E pleine puche en ai od mei.
Mes jo ne voil la puche overir,
12 De ci que cil deivent failir.'
Li chaz respunt par breve raisun,
'Nus n'erums mie cumpainuns,
Kar jeo ne sai fors un engin,
16 Ceo seivent bien tut mi veisin.'
La u il vunt issi parlant,
Deus chiens vienent tost curant.
Li gupil vers le chat escrie,
20 'Ore ai mester de ta aïe!'
Le chaz respunt, 'Aïe tei! –
N'ai que un engin, cel ert od mei!'
Dunc saut le chaz sur l'espine.
24 Le chien saisissent par l'eschine
Le gupil, sil vunt detirant,
E li chaz li escrie tant:
'Cumpain, pur quei esparnies,
28 Que ta puche ne deslïes?
Tu l'esparnies trop lungement –
Li chien te hastent durement!

99 **The Fox and the Cat**

Once long ago a fox and cat
Walked in a field and reckoned that
They now would good companions be;
4 They sat down in the shrubbery.
The cat then asked the fox to tell
In what way he'd defend himself
If he should meet adversity.
8 The fox replied, 'My friend,' said he,
'A hundred tricks I know, I'm sure,
I've got a pouch chock-full, right here.
But I don't want to open it
12 Until I find it requisite.'
The cat replied quite pointedly,
'We never can be friends,' said he,
'For only one trick can I do,
16 And all my neighbours know this, too.'
And while they were conversing thus,
Two dogs ran toward them in a rush.
Then fox to cat did cry and shout,
20 'I need you now to help me out!'
Said cat, 'You must your own help be –
I've but one trick, and it's for me!'
Into a thornbush jumped the cat.
24 The dogs now by his backbone snatched
The fox, to tear him into shreds.
The cat cried out to him and said,
'My friend, why hold back now? Oh why
28 Do you not now your pouch untie?
Already you've held back too long –
The dogs are coming at you strong!

Pur quei n'as tun sac deslïé?'
32 'Jeo l'ai,' fet il, 'trop esparnié.
   Jeol te di bien, meuz amereie
   Tun sul engin, si jeo l'aveie,
   Que ces dunt ai ma puche pleine.
36 Jeo te vei delivere de peine.'
   'Bien me deit,' fet il, 'remembrer
   De ceo que jeo ai oï cunter:
   Suvent est ateint li gupilz,
40 Tut seit il quointes par ses diz!'
      Del menteür avient suvent:
   Tut parot il raisnablement,
   Sil put li sages entreprendre,
44 S'il veut a sa parole entendre.
   Del leial humme est meuz creüe,
   Une parole e entendue,
   E plus put en un grant pleit,
48 Que quanque li mentere feit.

100 Del riche humme ki volt aler utre mer

Uns riches hum voleit aler
Utre mer pur converser.
A Deu pria qu'il amenast
4 A sauveté, qu'il ne dutast.
Einz qu'il se fust aparceüz,
Dedenz la mer est enbatuz.
Lors prie Deus qu'il meint a tere –

Why haven't you your sack untied?'
32 'I've saved too long,' the fox replied;
   'I tell you truly I'd prefer
   Your single trick, if mine it were,
   To all I have in my pouch here.
36 I see that you are safe and clear.'
   Said cat, 'I must remember well
   And keep in mind what I've heard tell:
   A fox will meet his nemesis
40 However smart he claims he is!'
       With lying men the same is found:
   However logical they sound,
   A sage can trip them up, if he
44 But listens to them carefully.
   An honest man is held more true,
   His words more often heeded, too,
   More suasive in a legal case
48 Than anything a liar says.

100 The Rich Man Who Wished to Cross the Sea

A rich man wished to go one day
Across the sea, a call to pay.
For passage safe, to God he prayed,
4 Also that he'd not be afraid.
Before he realized it, he
Had sailed far out upon the sea.
That God would lead him to the shore

8 Ne li volt autre chose quere.
Cum plus comence a crïer,
E plus ala ses nes par mer.
Quant il vit que Deus ne feseit
12 La priere qu'il requereit
Quant a tere ne pot venir,
Dist Deus fetes vostre pleisir.
Apres cel mot tost ariva
16 La u il vot e destina.
   Li sages deit reisnablement
Prier Deu omnipotent,
Que de lui face sun pleisir:
20 De ceo li peot grant bien venir.
Kar meuz seit Deu quei li estut
Que sis queors, change e mut.

101 Del chevaler e del viel humme

D'un chevaler voil cunter
E par essample remembrer,
Que un veil humme encuntra ja.
4 Ensemble od li s'acumpaina.
Pur ceo qu'il le vit remembré
E en meint liu aveit esté,
Li volt cunseil demander,
8 En quele tere deüst converser?
Kar il memes pru ne saveit.
E li vielz hum li respun[d]eit
Que en la tere voilst ester
12 U tute gent le veulent amer.
'E si jeo,' fet il, 'ne la truis,
Cunseillez mei, queil part jeo puis
Aler ester a lung tens.'
16 Cil respundi par grant sens:
'Va la ester e si me crei,
U tute gent eient poür de tei.'
'E si jeo tere ne puis trover,
20 U la gent me veulent duter?'
'Va la, u nul humme ne veies,

8 He prayed – and that's all he prayed for.
The more the man did cry and shout,
The more his ship went farther out.
And when the man became aware
12 That God would not fulfil his prayer,
And that to shore he could not come,
He prayed to God His will be done.
After these words, he came to land
16 Exactly where he'd wished and planned.
   A wise man should be sensible
And pray to God all powerful
To do with him whate'er His wish:
20 Great goodness then can come from this.
Our needs the Lord can better know
Than hearts can, shifting to and fro.

101 **The Knight and the Old Man**

I wish to tell you of a knight,
So heed this lesson I will cite.
The knight met an old man one day
4 And joined with him upon his way.
Thinking that this man's mind was keen
And he'd to many places been,
The knight wished he'd advise him so:
8 Unto which country should he go?
For he himself had not a clue.
The old man answered him thereto:
He should go seek another land
12 Where he'd be loved by every man.
'And if I don't find that,' he said,
'Tell me where I can go instead,
Where I can stay for a long time.'
16 The old man wisely answered him,
'Here's what I think you ought to do:
Go where they're all afraid of you.'
'What if I find no land,' said he,
20 'Where people are afraid of me?'
'Go where you'll see no man, and where

Que nul ne sace que tu seies.'
   Par cest essample nus veut sumundre
24 Que se deit hum a fol respundre,
Ki plus enquert kil ne devereit;
Si ot suvent que ne vodreit.

102 Del chat, del mulet, e de la suriz

Un chaz seeit desur un fur,
U ot gueité tut en jur.
Vit le mulet e la suriz
4 Sis apela par mut beus diz,
E dist que lur evekes fu –
E que mal cunseil unt eü
Que sa cunfermeisun n'aveient.
8 E les suriz li respun[d]eient
Que asez voleient meuz murir
Ke desuz ses ungles venir.
Les suriz s'en turnent fuiant,
12 E li chaz les vet enchaçant.
En la parei se sunt fichees:
Meus voleient estre mucees,
Si que eles ne puissent muveir,
16 Que od lur esveke remaneir.
Mut crement sa cunfermeisun,
Kar il le seivent a felun.
   Par ceste essample nus devise:
20 Nul ne se deit mettre en justise
De celui que mal lui veut fere,
Mes desturner de sun repeire!

103 De la femme e de sa geline

Une femme se seeit ja
Devant sun us, si esgarda
Cum sa geline gratot
4 E sa viande purchaçot.
Mut se travailot tuten jur.

No one will know that you are there.'
And thus this lesson shows a way
24 To deal with what a fool will say:
More than he ought to, he inquires,
He then hears more than he desires.

102 The Cat, the Vole, and the Mouse

A cat sat on a stove, they say,
Watching and waiting there all day.
The vole and mouse he chanced to see
4 And called to them deliciously.
He was their bishop! – so cat said –
Through bad advice they'd been misled
Not to receive his confirmation.
8 The mice replied, in explanation,
Saying they sooner death would choose
Than ever come beneath his claws.
The mice turned tail and fled in haste
12 And after them the cat gave chase.
They went into the wall to hide:
They'd rather be concealed inside
And so confined they could not stir,
16 Than linger with their bishop more.
They sorely feared his confirmation;
They knew his wicked inclination.
By this example we are schooled:
20 No one should let himself be ruled
By one who seeks his injury.
Better to turn around and flee!

103 The Woman and Her Hen

A woman sat herself one day
By her front door and watched the way
Her hen was scratching all around
4 Seeking what food was to be found.
The whole day long thus laboured she.

A li parla par grant amur,
'Bele,' fet ele, 'lais ester!
8 Que ne voilles si grater!
Chescun jur grant a tun talent
Pleine mesure de furment.'
La geline li respundi,
12 'A quei diz tu, dame, issi?
Quides que jeo aime meuz tun blé
Que ceo que ai tut tens usé!
Nenil, nenil!' fet la geline.
16 'Si devant mei estut une mine
Tuz jurs pleine, pas ne lerreie
Ne pur ceo ne targereie
Que jo ne quesisse tuz jurs plus –
20 Sulunc ma nature, sulunc mun us.'
Par ceste essample veut mustrer,
Que plusurs gens poënt trover
Aveir e ceo que unt mester;
24 Mes ne poënt pas changier
Lur nature ne lur usage,
Tuz jurs coveitent en lur curage.

Epilogue

Al finement de cest escrit,
Que en romanz ai treité e dit,
Me numerai pur remembrance:
4 Marie ai num, si sui de France.
Put cel estre que clerc plusur
Prendreient sur eus mun labur.
Ne voil que nul sur li le die!
8 E il fet que fol ki sei ublie!
Pur amur le cunte Willame,
Le plus vaillant de nul realme,
M'entremis de cest livre feire
12 E de l'engleis en romanz treire.
Esope apel'um cest livre,
Qu'il translata e fist escrire,
Del griu en latin le turna.

The woman told her lovingly,
'My dear,' she said, 'please let it go!
8 I wish that you'd stop scratching so!
And I'd give you, your needs to meet,
Each day a measure full of wheat.'
The hen replied, 'Oh lady, dear!
12 Whatever are you saying here!
Do you think I'd prefer your wheat
To what I've always done to eat!
No, absolutely not!' said she.
16 'And if there were in front of me
A basket always full of grain,
I'd not desist, I'd not refrain
From searching for yet more all day.
20 Such is my nature and my way.'
   And thus we see, from hen and grain,
That many people can obtain
Riches and everything they need;
24 And yet they cannot change, indeed,
Their nature or accustomed ways,
The lust within, for all their days.

Epilogue

To end these tales I've here narrated
And into Romance tongue translated,
I'll give my name, for memory:
4 I am from France, my name's Marie.
And it may hap that many a clerk
Will claim as his what is my work.
But such pronouncements I want not!
8 It's folly to become forgot!
Out of my love for Count William,
The doughtiest in any realm,
This volume was by me created,
12 From English to Romance translated.
This book's called Aesop for this reason:
He translated and had it written
In Latin from the Greek, to wit.

16 Li reis Alfrez, que mut l'ama,
   Le translata puis en engleis,
   E jeo l'ai rimee en franceis,
   Si cum jeo poi plus proprement.
20 Ore pri a Deu omnipotent
   Ke a tel ovre puisse entendre,
   Que a lui pusse m'alme rendre.

16 King Alfred, who was fond of it,
   Translated it to English hence,
   And I have rhymed it now in French
   As well as I was competent.
20 I pray to God omnipotent
   To let me to such work attend
   And thus to Him my soul commend.

SHORT TITLE LIST

TEXTUAL EMENDATIONS

TEXTUAL NOTES

TABLE OF MANUSCRIPT CONCORDANCES

Short Title List

Babrius *Babrius and Phaedrus* editor and translator Ben Edwin Perry (Cambridge: MA: Loeb Library, Harvard University Press 1965)

Ewert and Johnston   Alfred Ewert and Ronald C. Johnston editors *Marie de France: Fables* (Oxford: Blackwell 1942)

Hervieux   Leopold Hervieux *Les Fabulistes latins, depuis le siècle d'Auguste jusqu'à la fin du moyen âge* (Paris: Firmin-Didot 1893–9). The first edition (2 volumes) was later completely revised and augmented by three volumes. Citations to volumes I and II are to the second edition.

'LBG'   A collection of Latin fables later than, but related to, Marie's. See introduction, 15. The fables are found in Hervieux II, 564–649.

Perry   Ben Edwin Perry *Aesopica* (Urbana: University of Illinois Press 1952). The numbers refer to the number of the fable. These fables are translated in *Babrius* with the same numbering as *Aesopica*.

Phaedrus *Babrius and Phaedrus* editor and translator Ben Edwin Perry (Cambridge, MA: Loeb Library, Harvard University Press 1965)

Rom. Nil. *The Romulus Nilantii*. The fables are in Hervieux II, 653–755. See introduction, 15.

Rom. Rob. *The Romulus Roberti*.   A collection of Latin fables later than, but related to, Marie's. The fables are found in Hervieux II, 549–62.

Stith Thompson   Stith Thompson *Motif-Index of Folk-Literature* 2nd edition (Bloomington: University of Indiana Press 1955)

Warnke, *die Fabeln*   Karl Warnke *Die Fabeln der Marie de France, mit Benutzung des von Ed. Mall hinterlassenen Materials* Halle: Niemeyer (Bibliotheca Normanica, VI) 1898. Reprint, Geneva: Slatkine 1974

Warnke, *die Quellen*   Karl Warnke, 'Die Quellen des *Esope* der Marie de France,' in *Festgabe für Hermann Suchier* (Halle: Niemeyer 1900) 161–284. Also in separate printing Halle: Niemeyer 1900

Notes

TEXTUAL EMENDATIONS

3.22 jeo] sil
3.92: a periller] apperiller
4.36: puis] pris
6.13: ele] il
6.24: n'esforcera] nel forcera
9.28: cuida] cuit
11.19–20, 35–6 Y
16.15: ne] de
16.18: enz] dedeinz
16.34: sachiez] saudrez
18.31: el] il
23.45: clarté] la char ADM
40.16: seür] suiur
41.10: parole n'en oeit] parole oeit n'en oeit
46.8: oient] dient
47.54: n'eit] veit
72.13: aider] eider
73.52: E ele oï le cop venir Y] Le cop oi venir aneire
74.29: al vent] avant ADV
74.70: gist e fet] e est AD
74.73: fuët] fuit AD
74.93: a tun [ués] eslite] a tun eslite ACD
74.98: La revertent u] La revere u il [erasure] u
75.12: jeün] a leun
76.7: se] sa AD

78.7–12: Q. See note.
80.25: foire] frere
80.26: poire] pere
86.27: la verité] leauté AD
88.13: champ] gent AD
96.28: l'avums] t'avums
97.16: chief] chiel
103.21: ceste] cest ceste
Epilogue.11: M'entremis] meintenur AD

TEXTUAL NOTES

PROLOGUE 4: *essamples*. This word is problematic to translate, for it seems to cover a wide range of meanings, from 'established doctrine' to 'fable and moral.' Warnke suggests a distinction based on grammatical gender; masculine for doctrine, system, or science; and feminine for the fable and its moral (*die Fabeln* xcv). This distinction does not prove to be consistent or significant, however, though it does seem that when *essample*, either masculine or feminine, is used in the moral, it refers to the specific fable and its application, as in the Prologue, l 25. The present translation tends to be conservative, using 'example,' 'model,' or 'lesson' for *essample* regardless of gender.
PROLOGUE 12: A large branch of medieval fables, derived from the classical Phaedrus, contains this added prologue in which a Romulus claims to have translated the fables from Greek to Latin for his son Tiberinus (or Tiberius). Later this Romulus came to be identified as the Emperor.
PROLOGUE 17–20: The precise meaning of these lines is not clear. Marie seems to be saying that Aesop, like Romulus, translated these fables from Greek to Latin. See Epilogue ll 14–15.
PROLOGUE 19: *trovees*, meaning both 'found' and 'created,' encapsulates the dual nature of the fable tradition as well as Marie's own contribution (see introduction 6–11).

1.5: In the Latin versions, the cock finds a pearl.
1.10: *honuree* ADY. Most of the mss have *remuee*, removed; that is: Never will you be removed by me.
1.15: The cock shifts from the formal 'vous' to the colloquial 'tu' as the mockery becomes scorn.
1.20: *humme e de femme*, the majority of mss; *mainte femme*, many women, FOQTY

2.2: *clincel* A; *clintel* D; perhaps from *clin*, slope or bank. The other mss have *duitel*, brook.

2.31: *seignur* ADM. The other mss have *robeur*, robber.

3.22: *musterai* ADM. Warnke, and Ewert and Johnston find *musterai* erroneous. Warnke adopts *metrai* (fut. *metre*, to set, place), Ewert and Johnston, *merrai* (fut. *mener*, to lead), both with support from other mss. It has been kept here as perhaps a deliberate echo of l 2.

3.82: Only in Marie's account is the mouse free and alive at the end. In the Romulus and other Latin versions the mouse is tied around the neck, not the knees, and the mouse (male) dies.

5.3: In Latin versions, the dog carries a piece of meat.

5.7: *Amduis* is unique to A. The majority of mss have the uncontracted *ambedous*, which fits the rhyme.

6.6: *La Destinee* is Jupiter in the Latin versions. Marie's deity, when the fables involve animals only, is always feminine, either la Destinee (here and fable 18), la Sepande (fables 75 and 97), or la Crïere (fable 23).

6.13: *ele* for *il*. *Il* is unique to A and apparently a scribal error.

8.12: *espeldriz* ABD. Warnke puzzles over this word, and suggests a meaning something like tenacious resistance (*hartnäckig widerstanden*). Greimas, however, cites an early 13th-century occurrence (Coincy 1210) referring specifically to puppies, where *espeldri* seems to mean *sevré*, weaned (*Dictionnaire de l'ancien français* 1968). The great variation among mss (*espeudriz* NQT; *espleidriz* Y; *espeudre* C; *espiaurri* RV, *espannis* M; *espani* FHKO; *espelut* P; *esligniez* Z; *petiz* L; *acreu* S) suggests scribal difficulty with this word.

8.31: *e la vigur* ADM. The majority have *en la maisun*, in the house.

8.32: *a deshonur* ADM. The majority have *senz reisun*, without explanation.

9.32: *la suriz s'en fuit* ADV. Most mss have the plural *les suriz fuient*.

11.5: *bugle*, a buffalo or wild ox. *Bubalo* in *Rom. Nil.*

11.19–20: Not in AD. The text here is that of Y. The lines seem to be required, as the deer is divided into four parts (ll 23–4).

11.23: *la quarte part* ADM. The other mss have *se nule beste la perneit*, if any animal took it. A presents a problem of a four-part division among three animals. In *Rom. Nil.*, the deer is divided three ways.

11.27: ABDLN begin a new fable here. In PQY, the initial U is coloured. *Rom. Nil.* treats these as two fables, as they are classically, the first from Babrius; the second, Phaedrus. As the majority of mss treat these as a single fable, and there does seem to be a strong connection between the two, with a single epimythium serving both, they are here considered two versions of the same story.

11.31: Again Marie presents a difficult division of four parts among three contenders. In *Rom. Nil.*, as in Phaedrus, three animals accompany the lion; Marie has omitted the cow.

11.35–6: Not in ADM. The text is Y.

11.37: *Le surplus ai* ADM. The other mss have *la quarte ai. Le surplus* may be a scribal emendation necessitated by the missing ll 35–6.

12.3: *welke.* This word seems to have been problematic, as evidenced by the variety among mss: *welche* E; *wilque* W; *woelca* Y; *guelce* H; *wecle* P; *mole* S; *moulle* RV; *miche* C; *noe* FO; *escaille* T; *oytre* QZ. Q illustrates the fable with a fish! (See introduction, n 15)

12.29: Marie's moral differs considerably from the Latin versions, as does her tale. There the eagle and crow work as partners and share the gains; the moral is that Nature's supposed protection (the shell) proved no match against the two.

13.4: *corf, corbel.* Marie uses *corf* and *corbel* for the Latin *corvus* (raven) of the Phaedrus tradition; and *corneille* for the Latin *cornix* (crow), fable 12.7. Because English readers generally know both 'corvus' and 'cornix' fables as crow fables, I have translated both *corbel* and *corneille* as 'crow.' See also fables 40, 59, 68, 93. (Perry similarly translates both *corvus* and *cornix* as the more general 'crow.')

14.13: *bucs* ABDEY; *tors* L; the other mss have *bués*, ox. In *Rom. Nil.*, as in Phaedrus, the three animals are *aper*, boar; *taurus*, bull; and *asinus*, ass. Warnke suggests that *bucs* may be a scribal mistake for *bués.*

14.14: *asnes*, in the majority of mss; *aigniaus*, lamb, QST

15.10: *sil* ABCDLMQTY. I follow Ewert and Johnston in this reading, assuming that *sil = si le.* Warnke's *si* follows the majority of mss and yields the line: 'And make the others bark.'

15.13: *bunté* ADP; the others, *belté*, beauty

15.42: Here, as in fables 34, 46, 60, and 90, the epimythium begins with the second line of the couplet.

16.34: *sachiez*. *Saudrez*, AD; the meaning is unclear. *Sachiez* is found in the majority of mss.

16.45: *essample* ADHNTVWZ; *escrit* P; the others, *fable*

18.7: Marie's deity is a goddess, *la Destinee*. *Rom. Nil.*, like Phaedrus and the Latin tradition, has the masculine Jupiter.

18.13: *dur* ADM; the others, *le jur*, that day

18.31: *El* is common to the majority of mss. *Il*, found only in ADEOY, is apparently erroneous.

21.23: *Que pur sulement mentir* ADM. Lit.: solely for a lie. This line, as advice to women, is problematic here, for neither the wolf nor the sow has said anything untrue. In the corresponding fable in *Rom. Nil.*, the advice given in the promythium, 'Docet subsequens fabula, quod nullus debet inimico suo cedere, quamvis blanda verba loquatur' – Don't yield to your enemies, no matter how flattering their talk – fits the Latin story: the wolf lies by claiming to be a midwife (*obstetricis*) offering his kindly services. The majority of mss of Marie's fables have 'pur sulement lur cors guarir' – only to save their own skins – a line no more relevant than the reading of the A version, since the sow does not seem to fear for her life. The point of Marie's tale seems to be that men should not be present at childbirth, a sentiment supported in a roughly contemporary medical guide for women, which says that a woman should consult another woman to examine her. 'A man ought to avoid the secrets of women and fly from their intimate association ...' See Beryl Rowland, editor and translator, *The Medieval Woman's Guide to Health* (Kent, OH: Kent State University Press 1981) 9–10.

23.12: The bat's dilemma is justifiable, for while a bat has wings it also has four feet and is, in fact, the only flying mammal.

23.20: *les autres suriz*: the other mice. The Old French for 'bat,' *chalve suriz* (mod. Fr. *chauve-souris*) means literally 'bald mouse.' This is a peculiarly French association. The Latin *vespertilio* connects the bat with the evening.

23.24: *pur fous* ADM. The majority have *poi de lui*, (thought) little of him.

23.34 and 39: *crïere* ADM. Most mss have *la sepande*, which was probably the original word but a problematic one for later scribes, as evidenced by the diversity among mss where scribes either alter sepande: *sespande* H, *serptente* G; or provide a substitution: *nature* EQT, *justice(s)* CFOPW.

23.40: *ele*. Although *crïer* is generally masculine grammatically, Marie renders it feminine. This pronoun is almost uniformly feminine among the mss (*il* only in FOM), no matter what the word for the deity in ll 34 and 39.

23.45: *Tute clarté. Tute la char* (ADM) yields a doubtful line: And then she took all meat away. All the other mss have *tute clarté*.

23.48: *He lose his plumes.* Although unfeathered, the bat was classified among the birds in the Middle Ages.

23.54: *As autres se veut dunc ajuster* AD. The majority of mss have *E il le veie afebleier*: And he sees him weakening.

23.60: After this line, mss other than A add:

Par tut en est a dei mustrez / Avilez mult e vergundez. (D)

And everybody points him out; / He's shunned and held in ill repute.

24.10: *cornant.* Possibly a pun on *cornes*

24.19: *vileins* ADM. The majority of mss have *li huem*, but *vileins* seems apt, since wise sayings were often attributed to peasants; see esp *Li Proverbe au Vilein* (ed A. Tobler, Leipzig 1895) and J. Morawski, *Proverbes français antérieurs au XVe siècle* (CFMA 1925). This fable has no separate moral other than the stag's recollection of the peasant's wisdom.

24.23–4: In *Rom. Nil.*, as in Phaedrus, the stag, while praising his antlers, also criticizes his too slender legs. The comment, 'criticize ... what's to be strongly praised,' seems to refer to the stag's deprecation of his legs, which should have been valued as a means of enabling his escape.

25.1: This story is generally known as 'The Widow of Ephesus' (see Petronius, *Satyricon* xi).

26.9: *gis puis tut le jur* ADM. Most of the mss have *gis, quant pluet le jur*, I lie on rainy days.

26.34: *par li* ADM. The other mss have *par merci*, with his permission.

29.4: *estre* ACDFO. The majority of mss have *eire*, journey.

29.13: In *Rom. Nil.*, as in Phaedrus, a lion, not a wolf, is the bad-breathed king. In *Rom. Nil.*, the animals ask Jupiter for a king; he sends them back to make their own choice, which is the lion. This is the only one of Marie's fables in which the wolf is king, for, as the fable shows, a wolf should not be made king.

29.87: *Ele* (or *il*) *ne saveit* ADM. The majority have *entre dous ert*, between the two. In *Rom. Nil.*, as in Phaedrus, the ape says the lion's breath smells like cinnamon and incense of the gods.

29.93–4: In all mss but AD, the order of these lines is reversed.

29.108: Mss other than ADLG add (order reversed in M):
Je ni doit garder serement / Cuntre son cuer e sun talent. (N)
Never should one his pledge fulfil / If it's against his heart and will.

30.16: *al bois* AD. The other mss have *aillurs*, elsewhere.

31.5: *la destinee* AD; *la nature* Q. The other mss have *la deuesse*, the goddess. In *Rom. Nil.*, as in Phaedrus, the goddess is Juno.
31.19–20: The moral is in ADM only; the other mss end with l 18. Likewise, neither *Rom. Nil.* nor Phaedrus provides a moral.

32.4: The goat foster-mother seems to be new with Marie. In *Rom. Nil.* and the Latin tradition, the lamb, talking with a dog in a field of she-goats, explains that he is looking for the mother who has nurtured him, not his biological mother.

33.3: *bucher* A (mod. Fr. *boucher*, butcher). The word seems to have posed problems for the scribes, as evidenced by the variety among mss: *berker*, shepherd D; *bres* HQTW, *brais* O, *bret* LM, all meaning fool; *home*, man KN; *lerre*, thief R; *chevres*, goat E; *leus*, wolf FPV. Warnke chooses *bres*, Ewert and Johnston emend to *bris*, the nom. of *bricun*, rascal, thief, which also appears in l 15. *Bucher*, however, is closest in meaning to the Latin *lanio*, butcher, of *Rom. Nil.* No wife is mentioned in the Latin; the butcher is simply going out to slaughter sheep.
33.9: In the Latin versions, each sheep is contented as long as he is not the victim.
33.15: *bricun* ADE. Again, there is considerable variety among the mss: *breton* CFGHLMOQTW; *baron* K; *larron*, thief R; *berchon*, woodsman V; *compaignon* I.
33.17: *en la pleine*, in the open ADM; the majority have *en la champaigne*, in the countryside.

34.50: Mss other than ADMY have an additional couplet here:
    E ben pout estre reis sis fiz / Sa femme semble enperiz. (E)
    His son could well be king no less / His wife seemed like an emper-esse.

37.2: *prist un vilein* A. The other mss have *qu'uns vilains prist*, whom a peasant took.
37.9: *defors la porte*, outside the doorway ADM. The other mss have *desur la piere*, on the rock.

39.1: *hulchet* AD (with *criket* written over it in a later hand in D). The original word was apparently problematic for later scribes. The Latin in *Rom. Nil.* is *cicadia*. Most of the mss give various words for cricket: *cricket* BELY, *crisnon* HRVW, *grislet* P, *gresilon* CIKMQT, *crikelon, crekillon* FO. *Hulchet* is not attested to anywhere else, although it almost certainly means cricket. Warnke's suggestion that *hulchet* comes from *hulque*, Eng. hulk, a cargo ship, referring to the shape of the cricket, seems unlikely.

39.11: The cricket answers in the present tense, having no sense of time passing.

40.20: The proverb is contemporary in Latin, French, and English (see Tobler 4, Morawski 264, and F.P. Wilson, *The Oxford Dictionary of English Proverbs* 3rd ed). It is not, however, in the Romulus versions of this fable and seems to be Marie's addition.

41.3: *serf*. Several mss (DELNQT) have *cerf* (stag). The illustration to this fable in Q shows two stags conversing. One of these 'stag' mss may be a source for the slightly later, and probably related, Hebrew collection of fables, the *Meslai Shu'alim*. (*Fables of a Jewish Aesop* translator Moses Hadas [New York: Columbia University Press 1967])

42.26: The anecdote was popular in folk tradition (see Warnke, *Quellen*, 33–4). Marie's moral seems unusually harsh.

43.17: *nuncreables* ADM. The other mss have *muables*, changeable.

46.5: *Chescun de eus numa le sun* AD. The majority of mss have *chescuns duta de mesprisun*, each one feared being wrong (in making this choice).
46.27: *a parceivre en verité* ADM. The majority of mss have *aparcevanz e veziee*, perceptive and shrewd.
46.66: *deliter* AD; *enjurer*, injure M; *penser*, think E. The rest have *pener*, suffer, that is: nor cause too much suffering.
46.67: *aviler* ADM; the rest have *travailler*, work, that is: nor overwork himself or his people.

47.27: *chastïé* AD; *manacié*, menaced M; *lesdenga*, abused P; *est alé*, left L. The others have *hasté*, pressured (him).

52.14: *sa force* ADMQSY seems a valid reading, though Warnke rejects it on the basis of gender agreement with *trestut*. *Son sens*, his intelligence, FIKORV, is also possible, though Warnke believes it not supported by ll 20, 31, and 32.

Warnke adopts *fiu* (wealth, from *fief*), though this reading is supported only indirectly: *feu* GHN, *fui* B. Other variants include *son pooir*, his power P; and *ses privetez e ses presenz*, his secrets and his presence E.

52.32: *ne sa vie, ne sun tresor* AD; *ne ses pensees demoustrer*, nor disclose one's thoughts H. The rest have *n'abondoner son (chier) tresor*, nor abandon one's (precious) treasure.

55.15: *seit pleisable* A, *seit paisable* D; *soit couvenable*, find agreeable M. The others have *ne seit nuisable*, won't find hurtful.

56.10: Mss other than ADMT add the following:
Al jur que cil esteir sumuns / Quil deveit fere sun respuns, (Y)
The day he came before the bench, / The one presenting his defence,

57.25: The granting of three wishes is a common folk motif (see Stith Thompson, J2071). Usually the wife (or husband) makes a foolish first wish, the other responds angrily with a second wish, and the third wish is the resolution, a return to the original state. Marie's tale is unusual (but perhaps not incomplete) in presenting only two wishes, even though the goblin grants them three.

60.19: *Veit.* Ewert and Johnston emend to *vait* based on the scribal tendancy to use *ei* for *ai* (see their introduction xvii). They then translate the line, 'The fox goes (off) holding the cock.' Other mss do not support this verb, however: *veit* AD; *veez* BY; *vers* GIKPRT; *ver* C; the rest have *veiz*.

60.20: *Mar le guaina*, woe what he gained AD. The variety among mss (and many incoherent readings) suggests scribal problems: *le guainna* Y; *le gaira* N; *le garra* R; *l'engarga* O; *en jorra* S; *l'encharai* CK; *l'emporta* M; *l'emporte* P; *l'enquerça* F; *ladese* B; *iert baillis* Q; *est bailliz* T; *bailly est* GI; *le vit* E. Warnke adopts *l'engana*, outsmarted, though without direct ms support.

60.27: *enfantillé* ADM; *a forcillié* Y; *a farcillié* N; *a farrillié* B, all meaning mocked; *a fort truillé*, duped R; *a fannoié*, degraded S; *a cunciié* O, *a conchié* KV, *mal conchiez* L, *a cunchies* F, all meaning dishonoured; *a courechié*, angered P; *a engingnié*, tricked H. Warnke adopts *a farcillié*.

60.37: *taiser* AD; *leisser*, leave E. The rest have *cesser*, cease.

62.18: *de grant fierté* AD. Most of the mss have *en sun regné*, in his kingdom.

63.4: *esteillez* ADM, from *esteil*, presumably *estal*, stake. There is considerable variety among the mss: *esteflez* N; *eschefles*, lacerated HRS; *escliches*, shattered V; *esgenez*, injured W; *acesmez*, adorned CK; *afolez*, destroyed FLOPQT.

65.26: *un sul* ADIKMPT. Warnke adopts *nul frelun*, no gadfly, with only indirect support: *furnun* Y; *fourlon* HN; *felon* CL.

66.1: *Par veille essample* AHNRS. This suggests the beginning of a new fable. Warnke adopts *par cest essample* FMW, believing these words to be the beginning of the epimythium of a lost fable, somehow related to the preceding. Only twelve mss include this passage; five (AKNOP) treat it as a separate fable; the others run it together with the preceding fable. As the only connection between the two is that both involve a wolf, it is clearly a separate story, however fragmentary, and is here treated as such and given a separate number. Warnke numbers it 65b; from this point on, therefore, the numbering in this edition differs from his edition.

68.18: *ocis,* killed AD; *depellei,* skinned M. The majority have *chacié,* chased away.

69.29: *U as esté tant* ADV; *U as esté* M. Warnke follows the majority of mss with *Que quiers tu ci?* – What are you looking for here? – but changes to *U as esté* in his later edition.
69.36: Salerno was famous as the city of the greatest medical school of medieval Europe, well established by the 11th century. Salerno was, moreover, Norman from the 11th to the 13th centuries.
69.47: *Al soleil se sist pur garisun* AD; *la hors s'asist sor le sablon,* he sat outside on the sand M. The others have *a l'eissir fors de la maisun,* on going outside the house...
69.52: *chapel* A, *capel* D. The others have *sa pel,* his skin. The confusion between *sa pel* and *chapel* suggests the possibility of oral transmission.

71.60: Mss other than ADM add the following couplet:
Senz quer fu e senz remembrance / Pur ceo i vint par ubliance. (Y)
Both heart and memory he lacked, / Forgetfulness had brought him back.

72.6: Mss other than ADM include the following couplet here:
E li leus devoit lui aidier / Com (most: quant) il en varroit lou mestier. (C)
The wolf in turn should give him aid / Whene'er he saw he was in need.
Like ADM, a related later Latin version, 'LBG' (Hervieux II, 608; Perry 674) does not mention the wolf's obligation.
72.26: *ferm,* closure (presumably, mouth) AD. Most of the mss have *broches,* quills.

73.50–1: These lines are missing in ADM only. The rhymes support their integrity. The text here is Y.
73.52: *E ele oï le cop venir,* mss other than ADM (the text is Y). The line in ADM, *le*

cop oï venir aneire, is uncertain in meaning, and *aneire* does not rhyme satisfactorily either with *beivre* (ADM) or *ferir* (of the emended text).

73.68: *mes un*, but one (piece of advice) AD; *ne sarmon*, nor sermon K; the others have *ne raisun*, nor explanation.

74.2: *mulez* (mod. Fr. *molez*), field mouse

74.17: *fet obscure*, makes obscure AD. The others have *cuevre*, covers.

74.18: *cure*, (under his) care AD, *ceure* F; the others have *uevre*, (under his) work.

74.45: While *murs* is masculine, the pronouns referring to the wall are feminine, ll 52, 61, 69.

74.47: *murs* AD; *forte* I. The others have *turs*, tower (also ll. 58, 60). While only AD have *murs*, it has been kept as a reading consistent within the ms and plausible in sense. Latin analogues are likewise divided. Odo (63, Hervieux IV, 234–6) has the Castle of Narbo (*castrum Narbonense*); the Berner Romulus (42, Hervieux II, 314), a wall (*murus*).

74.57: *a bon eur*, of good breeding AD; the others, *a grant honur*, of great honour

74.82: *le curs de*, the course of (fortune) AD; the others, *dist la turs*, ... said the tower, (your fortune ...).

75.10: *sepande* AD; *sespande* H, *spande* N; *espondes* C; *diuesse* PW; *encestre* I; *destinee* MRSV; *nature* FOQT

75.12: *um* AD, *home* T; the other mss have *ver*, worm. In l 44, AD conform to the majority, *verm u oisel*, worm or bird.

77.13–14: AD (des granz genz D). The majority have:

Souvent avient des veziez / Com (most: Quant) cuident estre avanciez. (C)

With cunning folks it's oft this way / When their advancement they essay.

78.2: *bien afïez* AD; *aiostez*, allied M. The others have *acuintiez*, acquainted.

78.7–12: The text is Q. Instead of these six lines, AD have the couplet:

Aider pas ne te pus – / Tel vou as fet que ne conus.

I don't know how to help you out. / Your vow I do not know about.

78.20: As it stands, even with the additional lines from other mss, the extant versions of the fable seem fragmentary and cryptic. The meaning is clarified by 'LBG' (Hervieux II, 639–40; Perry 686). When the wolf is caught by chance in a trap and asks the hedgehog to help him out, the hedgehog replies (Perry's translation): 'You have, I suppose, made many vows to the saints, to atone for your excesses, and have not fulfilled those vows; hence they have been offended and have allowed you to fall into this snare. You must sue for their grace. If you obtain it, then my comradeship may be of some advantage to you, but otherwise not; for I would not dare to oppose the divine will.' Marie's moral may be seen as a wry comment on vows, both the wolf's (Are we really to think that oaths to saints would excuse his wickedness? And are these 'vows' indeed the reason he stumbles into the trap?) and the hedgehog's.

79.19: 'LBG' may have a pun not in the French: 'Bene facit qui benefacit' – He does well who confers a benefit. (Hervieux II, 640; Perry 687)

81.7: *d'un chesne* ADM; the others have *d'une rochier* (in the hole) of a rock.
81.52: *mauveis quor*, wicked heart AD. The others have *lur païs* (forsake) their country.

82.6: *jo l'otrei* AD. Most mss have *la letre vei*, I see the letter.
82.12: *il dit aignel* ADEIMNPY. Most of the other mss have *aignel, aignel*.

84.42: *nus*, us, ADHP. The other mss have *vus*, you.

85.18: *la peine*. There may be a pun intended between *la peine*, strenuous labour, and *le pein* (l 6), bread. Here 'bread' and 'loaf' are the translator's 'pain'ful approximation.
85.22: All but A add the following:
  Ne del bien ne del guerdun / Kil ad eu en sa maisun (D)
  No thought of wealth or recompense / Received while at his residence
85.23: *suvent*, often AD. The other mss have *e mesprent*, and did wrong.

86.4: *valeir*, value; that is, he would be valued more A. The other mss have *aler*, go; that is, he could go …
86.27: *la verité*, all mss except AD, which have *lëauté*, loyalty
86.28: *les fera*, lit: will (silence) them ADO. The others have *le*, will silence him, which seems the better reading.

87.9: *li preez*, I pray you AD; *mi alez*, go with me QS. The others have *i alez*, go there.

89.8: *verité*, truth ADV. The others have *l'uevre*, business.
89.18: *jugez*, judged, AD. The others have *encumbrez*, punished.

90.19: MS A indicates the beginning of the epimythium here.
90.24: *dire* ADNOPQW; *creire*, believe Y; the majority have *tenir*, hold; that is: Nor should you hold on to lies – more appropriate advice, it seems, for the kid.

92.3: *par tut*, everywhere AD. The others have *des chiens*, of the dogs

92.5: *de lui*, of him (whom you might meet) AD. the others have *del lou*, of the wolf.

92.18: *nus*, us *ad*. The others have *mei*, me.

92.34: *pent*, hanged ADY; *prent*, caught, in the other mss. The proverb is contemporary and supports *prent*: 'Fous ne crient devant qu'il prent' (Morawski, 788), though *pent* might be worth considering.

93.12: Mss other than ADFMNS add:

> Je ne te doi mes ensaignier / Car tu n'en as noient mestier. (Q)
> There's no more I must demonstrate / For now you have no need of it.

94.67: *preer*, pray AD. The others have *parler*, speak.

94.71–2: This last couplet is in AD only.

97.7: *Sepande* A, *seppente* D, *spande* N, *espande* H; *deesse* CFOPQW; *destinee(s)* MRSV. The Latin *Rom. Rob.* has Jupiter.

97.9: *tel criee*, thus created AD; *si atornei*, so adorned M. The others have *si honuré*, so honoured.

97.12: *la deuesse* in all mss except ORSV, which have *la destinee*

97.13: *Tu mesfez* AD; *tais*, hush MV. The others have *tais, fols!* hush, fool!

97.23: *comencer* A. The others have (D with correction) *cuveitier*, covet.

97.26: *Que lur turne*, which turns back on them, ADM; the others, *que lur honurs turne*, which turns their honours back.

98.15: *asemblent* AM, *ensemblent* D. The others have *emblent*, steal.

99.27: *esparnies*, hold back, AD. The others have *ublies*, forget.

99.47: *put* (pres. *poeir*, to be powerful) ADM. The others have *purfite*, useful, profitable.

100.4: Mss other than ADM add the following here:

Ne vouloit gueres demourer,	He'd no wish to stay long, and so
Quant arriere voit retourner,	When he felt it was time to go,
A dieu pria du revenir,	He prayed again to God that He
Qu'il nel lessast neent perir. (N)	Not let him perish on the way.

Warnke, arguing for the authenticity of these lines, notes (1) the possibility of scribal error, a jump from l 3 to the third additional line, as both begin with 'A deu preia …' and are followed in the next line with a verb ending *-ast*; (2) the consistency among mss in groups β and γ; and (3) the logic of praying for a

safe and speedy return (*die Fabeln* lv–lvi). However, a corresponding passage is not in 'LBG' (Hervieux II, 645–6; Perry 690); furthermore ll 15–16 seem to suggest an intended destination, not a return home.
100.16: *destina*, planned AD. The others have *desira*, desired.

101.20: Mss other than AD add the following:

Dont li respondi li vielz hom,	The old man answered him anon,
'Va la, ou pas ne te dout on.'	'Go where they don't fear anyone.'
'E se je la ne puis venir,	'And if I can't get there,' he said,
Quel part pourai terre tenir?' (Q)	'What country should I try instead?'

In 'LBG' (Hervieux II, 646; Perry 691) a young man asks his father where he should go after his death. The first two and the fourth responses correspond with Marie's three in A; his third response, 'Dwell in a land where you have nothing to do,' does not correspond with the additional lines above.
101.25: *enquert* ADI. The others have *parole*, speaks.

102.7: *cunfermeisun* AD. The others have *beneiçun*, benediction.
102.15: *muveir*, move AD; *avant venir*, advance M. The others have *jur veeir*, see daylight.
102.22: *de sun repeire* ADM. The others have *en altre terre*, to another land.

103.10: *mesure* AD; *une escuelle*, a bowl M. The others have *une grange*, a granary.
103.23: *aveir*, possessions AD; *maniere*, behaviour CFIOPQWY. Warnke adopts *manaie*, assistance, from HN.
103.26: *coveitent*, lust (v) AD; the majority have *avive*, alive. *Coveitent* is closer to Latin versions (*Rom.* III, 8 in Hervieux II, 496–7; Perotti's Appendix, 11, 'De mulierum libidine,' in Hervieux II, 70; and Perry 539) in which Venus, questioning Juno's chastity, compares the hen's scratching to the natural and never satisfied lust of women.

Epilogue 8: *E il fet que fol*, And he does but folly AD. The others have *cil uevre mal*, his work is bad.
Epilogue 16: *Alfrez* AD. The word seems to have been problematic for later scribes – did French copyists not know of King Alfred? – *Alrei* M, *Auurez* S, *Almes* H, *Amez* N, *Auree* Q, *Uures* R, *Mires* LV, *Henris* CFO.
Epilogue 19: *Si cum jeo poi plus proprement* AD; *si le trova premierement*, as I found it originally LRV. The others have *si cum jol truvai*, *proprement*, as I found it, accurately.

TABLE OF MANUSCRIPT CONCORDANCES

A	B	C	D	E	F	G	H	I	K	L	M	N	O	P	Q	R	S	T	V	W	Y	Z
Pr	Pr	Pr	Pr	Pr	Pr		Pr		Pr	Pr	Pr	Pr	Pr	Pr	Pr	Pr	Pr	Pr	Pr	Pr	Pr	Pr
1	1	1	1	1	1	–	1	–	1	1	1	1	1	1	1	1	1	1	1	1	1	1
2	2	2	2	2	2	–	2	–	2	2	2	2	2	2	2	2	2	2	2	2	2	2
3	3	3	3	3	3	–	3	–	–	3	3	3	3	3	3	3	3	3	3	3	3	3
4	4	4	4	4	4	–	4	–	4	4*	4	4	4	4	4	4	4	4	4	4	4	4
5	5	–	5	5	5	–	5	–	5	5*	5	5	5	5	5	5	5	5	5	5	5	5
6	6	–	–	6	6	–	6	–	6	6	6	6	6	6	6	6	6	6	6	6	6	6
7	7	7	7	7	7	–	7	–	7	7	7	7	7	7	7	7	7	7	7	7	7	7
8	8	8	8	8	8	–	8	–	8	8	8	8	8	8	8	8	8	8	8	8	8	8
9	9	9	9	9	9	–	9	–	9	9	9	9	9	9	9	9	9	9	9	9	9	9
10	10	10	10	10	10	–	10	–	–	10	10	10	10	10	10	10	10	10	10	10	10	10
11	11	–	11	11	11	–	11	–	–	11	11	11	11	11	11	11	11	11	11	11	11	11
12	12	12	12	12	12	–	12	–	–	12	12	12	12	12	12	12	12	12	12	12	12	12
13	13	13	13	13	13	–	13	–	–	13	13	13	13	13	13	13	13	13	13	13	13	13
14	14	14	14	14	14	–	14	–	–	14	14	14	14	14	14	14	14	14	14	14	14	14
15	15	15	15	15	15	–	15	–	–	15	15	15	15	15	15	15	–	15	15	15	15	15
16	16	16	16	16	16	–	16	–	–	16	16	16	16	16	16	16	–	16	16	16	16	16
17	17	17	17	17	17	–	17	–	–	17	17	17	17	17	17	17	–	17	17	17	17	17
18	18	18	18	18	18	–	18	–	–	18	18	18	18	18	18	18	–	18	18	18	18	18
19	19	19	19	19	19	19	19	–	–	19	19	19	19	19	19	19	–	19	19	19	–	19
20	20	20	20	20	20	20	20	–	–	20	20	20	20	20	20	20	–	20	20	20	20	20
21	21	21	21	21	21	21	21	–	–	21	21	21	21	21	21	21	–	21	21	21	21	21
22	22	22	22	22	22	22	22	–	–	22	22	22	22	22	22	22	–	22	22	22	–	22
23	23	23	23	23	23	23	23	–	–	23	23	23	23	23	23	23	–	23	23	23	23	23
24	24	24	24	24	24	24	24	–	24	24	24	24	24	24	24	24	–	24	24	24	–	–
25	25	25	25	25	25	25	25	–	25	25	25	25	25	25	25	25	–	25	25	25	25	–
26	–	26	26	26	26	–	26	–	26	26	26	26	26	26	26	26	–	26	26	26	–	–
27	27	27	27	27	27	27	27	–	27	27	27	27	–	27	27	27	–	27	27	27	–	–

*in later hand

TABLE OF MANUSCRIPT CONCORDANCES

A	B	C	D	E	F	G	H	I	K	L	M	N	O	P	Q	R	S	T	V	W	Y	Z
28	28	28	28	28	28	28	28	—	28	28	28	28	28	28	28	28	—	28	28	28	28	—
29	29	29	29	29	29	29	29	29	29	29	29	29	29	29	29	29	—	29	29	29	—	—
30	—	30	30	30	30	—	30	30	30	30	30	30	30	30	30	30	—	30	—	30	30	—
31	—	31	31	31	31	—	31	31	31	31	31	31	31	31	31	31	—	31	—	31	31	—
32	—	32	—	32	32	—	32	32	32	32	32	32	32	32	32	32	—	32	—	32	—	—
33	—	32	32	33	33	33	33	33	33	33	33	33	33	33	33	33	—	33	33	33	—	—
34	34	34	34	34	34	34	34	34	34	34	34	34	34	34	—	34	—	—	34	34	34	—
35	35	35	35	35	35	35	35	35	35	35	35	35	35	35	35	35	—	—	35	35	35	—
36	36	36	36	36	36	36	36	36	36	36	36	36	36	36	36	36	—	—	36	36	36	—
37	37	37	37	37	37	37	37	37	37	37	37	37	37	37	37	37	—	—	37	37	—	—
38	38	38	38	38	38	38	38	38	38	38	38	38	38	38	38	38	—	—	38	38	38	—
39	39	39	39	39	39	39	39	39	39	39	39	39	39	39	39	39	—	39	39	39	39	—
40	40	40	40	40	40	40	40	40	40	40	40	40	40	40	40	40	—	40	40	40	40	—
41	41	41	41	41	41	41	41	41	41	41	41	41	41	41	41	41	—	41	41	41	41	—
42	42	42	42	42	42	42	42	42	42	42	42	42	42	42	42	42	—	42	42	42	42	—
43	43	43	43	43	43	43	43	43	43	43	43	43	43	43	43	43	—	43	43	43	43	—
44	—	44	44	44	44	44	44	44	44	44	44	44	44	44	44	44	—	44	44	—	44	—
45	45	45	45	45	45	45	45	45	45	45	45	45	45	45	45	45	—	45	45	—	45	—
46	46	46	46	46	46	46	46	46	46	—	46	46	46	46	46	46	46	46	46	—	46	—
47	47	47	47	47	47	47	47	47	47	47	47	47	47	47	47	47	47	—	47	—	47	—
48	48	48	48	48	48	48	48	48	48	—	48	48	48	48	48	48	48	—	48	—	48	—
49	49	49	49	49	49	49	49	49	49	49	49	49	49	49	49	49	49	49	49	—	49	—
50	50	50	50	50	50	50	50	50	50	—	50	50	50	50	50	50	50	—	50	—	50	—
51	51	51	51	51	51	51	51	51	51	—	51	51	51	51	51	51	51	—	51	—	51	—
52	52	—	52	52	52	52	52	52	52	—	52	52	52	52	52	52	52	—	52	—	52	—
53	53	53	53	53	53	53	53	53	53	—	53	53	53	53	53	53	53	53	53	53	53	—

TABLE OF MANUSCRIPT CONCORDANCES

Z	Y	W	V	T	S	R	Q	P	O	N	M	L	K	I	H	G	F	E	D	C	B	A
–	54	54	54	54	54	54	54	54	54	54	54	–	54	54	54	54	54	54	54	54	54	54
–	55	55	–	55	55	55	55	55	55	55	55	–	55	55	55	55	55	55	55	55	55	55
–	56	56	56	56	56	56	56	56	56	56	56	–	56	56	56	56	56	56	56	56	56	56
–	57	57	57	57	57	57	57	57	57	57	57	–	57	57	57	–	57	57	57	57	57	57
–	58	58	58	58	58	58	58	58	58	58	58	58	–	–	58	58	58	58	58	58	58	58
–	–	–	59	59	59	59	59	59	59	59	59	59	59	59	59	59	59	59	59	59	59	59
–	60	–	–	60	60	60	60	60	60	60	60	60	60	60	60	60	60	60	60	60	60	60
–	61	–	61	61	61	61	61	61	61	61	61	61	61	61	61	–	61	61	61	61	61	61
–	–	62	62	62	62	62	62	62	62	62	62	62	62	62	62	–	62	62	62	62	62	62
–	–	63	63	63	63	63	63	63	63	63	63	63	63	–	63	–	63	–	63	63	–	63
–	64	64	64	64	64	64	64	64	64	64	64	64	64	64	64	–	64	–	64	64	64	64
–	65	65	65	65	65	65	65	65	65	65	65	65	65	65	65	–	65	65	65	65	65	65
–	–	66	–	–	66	66	–	66	66	66	66	–	66	–	66	–	66	–	–	66	–	66
–	–	67	67	67	67	67	67	67	67	67	67	–	67	–	67	–	67	67	67	67	67	67
–	68	68	68	68	68	68	68	68	68	68	68	–	68	–	68	–	68	68	68	68	68	68
–	69	69	69	69	69	69	69	69	69	69	69	–	69	69	69	–	69	69	69	69	69	69
–	–	70	70	70	70	70	70	70	70	70	70	–	70	70	70	–	70	70	70	70	–	70
–	71	71	71	71	71	71	71	71	71	71	71	–	71	71	71	–	71	–	71	71	–	71
–	72	72	72	72	72	72	72	72	72	72	72	–	72	72	72	–	72	–	72	72	–	72
–	–	73	73	73	73	73	73	73	73	73	73	–	73	73	73	–	73	–	73	73	–	73
–	–	74	74	74	74	74	74	74	74	74	74	–	74	74	74	–	74	–	74	74	–	74
–	–	75	75	75	75	75	75	75	75	75	75	–	75	75	75	–	75	–	75	75	–	75
–	76	76	76	–	76	76	76	76	76	76	76	–	76	–	76	–	76	–	76	76	–	76
–	–	77	77	–	77	77	77	77	77	77	77	–	77	77	77	–	77	–	77	77	–	77
–	–	78	78	–	78	78	78	78	78	78	78	–	78	–	78	–	78	–	78	78	–	78
–	79	79	79	–	79	79	79	79	79	79	79	–	79	79	79	–	79	–	79	–	–	79

TABLE OF MANUSCRIPT CONCORDANCES

A	B	C	D	E	F	G	H	I	K	L	M	N	O	P	Q	R	S	T	V	W	Y	Z
80	—	—	80	—	80	—	80	80	—	—	80	80	80	80	80	80	80	—	80	80	80	—
81	—	81	81	—	81	—	81	—	—	—	81	81	81	81	81	81	81	—	81	81	—	—
82	—	82	82	—	82	—	82	82	—	—	82	82	82	82	82	82	82	—	82	82	82	—
83	—	83	83	—	83	—	83	—	—	—	83	83	83	83	83	83	83	—	83	83	—	—
84	—	84	84	—	84	—	84	84	—	—	84	84	84	84	84	84	84	—	84	84	—	—
85	—	85	85	—	85	—	85	85	—	—	—	85	85	85	85	85	85	—	85	85	—	—
86	—	86	86	—	86	—	86	—	—	—	—	86	86	86	86	86	86	—	86	86	86	—
87	—	—	87	—	87	—	87	—	—	—	—	87	87	87	87	87	87	—	87	87	—	—
88	—	—	88	—	88	—	88	—	—	—	—	88	88	88	88	88	88	—	88	88	—	—
89	—	89	89	—	89	—	89	—	—	—	—	89	89	89	89	89	89	—	89	89	—	—
90	—	90	90	—	90	—	90	—	—	—	—	90	90	90	90	90	90	—	90	90	90	—
91	—	—	91	—	91	—	91	—	—	—	91	91	91	91	91	91	91	—	91	91	—	—
92	—	92	92	—	92	—	92	—	—	—	92	92	92	92	92	92	92	—	92	92	92	—
93	—	—	93	—	93	—	93	—	—	—	93	93	93	93	93	93	93	—	93	93	—	—
94	—	—	94	—	94	—	94	—	—	—	94	94	94	—	94	94	94	—	94	94	94	—
95	—	95	95	—	—	—	95	95	—	—	95	95	—	95	95	95	95	—	95	95	95	—
96	—	96	96	—	—	—	96	—	—	—	96	96	—	96	96	96	96	—	96	96	—	—
97	—	97	97	—	97	—	97	—	—	—	97	97	97	97	97	97	97	—	97	97	—	—
98	—	—	98	—	98	—	98	—	—	—	98	98	98	98	98	—	—	—	—	98	98	—
99	—	—	99	—	99	—	99	—	—	—	99	99	99	99	99	99	99	—	99	99	99	—
100	—	—	100	—	100	—	100	—	—	—	100	100	100	100	100	—	—	—	—	100	—	—
101	—	—	101	—	101	—	101	—	—	—	101	101	101	101	101	—	—	—	—	101	—	—
102	—	—	102	—	102	—	102	—	—	—	102	102	102	102	102	—	—	—	—	102	—	—
103	—	103	103	103	103	—	103	103	—	—	103	103	103	103	103	Ep1	Ep1	—	Ep1	103	103	—
Ep1	—	Ep1	Ep1	—	Ep1	—	Ep1	—	—	Ep1	Ep1	Ep1	Ep1	—	Ep1	Ep1	Ep1	—	Ep1	Ep1	—	—

TORONTO MEDIEVAL TEXTS AND TRANSLATIONS

General Editor: Brian Merrilees